c



a guide

First published in 1999
Virgin Publishing Ltd, London W6 9HT

# contents

Written by over 15 contributors in-the-know, this guide takes an inside track on Dublin. The focus is on having fun; where to hang out, shop, eat, relax, enjoy and spoil yourself. And there's a selection of the top cultural hot spots...

# arriving & departing

Dublin is well served by its international airport, two ferry ports, and by two mainline railway stations and a coach station that bring in travellers from elsewhere in Ireland. Distances between the access points and the city centre are small, and there is a choice of efficient transport links.

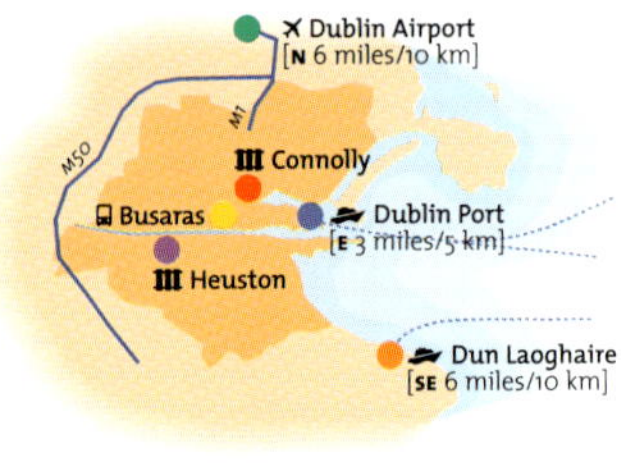


## by air

Dublin has only one airport with one terminal for flights to/from Britain, mainland Europe and North America. Domestic flights to/from Belfast, Cork, Donegal, Derry, Galway, Knock, Shannon, Sligo and Waterford also operate from the airport.

### transport options

**Airlink Express bus service**

30–35 min non-stop to/from the city centre. Route 747 to/from Busaras (central bus station) and Connolly station; route 748 to/from Heuston station via city centre (Eden Quay) and Busaras.

6.45am–11pm Mon–Sat, 7.30am–10.30pm Sun, every 20–30 min.

£3–3.50

Airlink: 873 4222

**buses 41, 41b & 41c**

45 min to/from the city centre (Eden Quay), stopping en route.

8am–11.30pm daily, every 20 min until 6pm, every 30–40 min until 11.30pm.

£1.10

**taxis**

20–40 min to/from the city centre.

24 hours.

£12–£15 (metered)

At busier times (Fri & Sun), you may have to wait longer.

If there are several of you; or you have lots of luggage, ask for a 'multi-seater' taxi which takes up to eight people. They cost the same as an ordinary taxi for up to four people, but for five and over there is an extra charge of 40p per head.

**Northside Express Taxis:** 832 7777

**Taxi Radiolink:** 850 0111

**useful numbers**

**Aer Rianta (Airport Authority):** 814 1111
www.dublin-airport.com
**Bank & Bureau de Change:** 844 5188
**Business Centre:** 844 5868
**Car Park:** 814 4328
**CIE (bus & rail info from the airport):** 844 4265
**Duty Free:** 814 4356
**Left Luggage & Porterage:** 814 4633
**Lost Property:** 814 4483
**Aer Lingus:** 705 6705
**Ryanair:** 1550 200 200 (premium rate)
**Forte Post House:** 808 0500
**Great Southern Hotel:** 844 6000

## by sea

There are two ferry points in Dublin: Dun Laoghaire (pronounced 'Dunleary') and Dublin Port, both linked to Holyhead in North Wales, and from there to the UK rail network.

### dun laoghaire

Stena Line operates in and out of Dun Laoghaire running its HSS (High Speed Service) for cars and foot passengers to/from Holyhead, a 90-min journey.

From Holyhead: 4.10am, 8.55am, 1.35pm and 6.25pm, plus 1.20am in high season. From Dun Laoghaire: 6.40am, 11.10am, 4.05pm and 9.45pm, plus 11.05pm in high season.

For foot passengers: £42 (low season) to £78 (high season) return between Dublin and London via Holyhead (including train travel). For a car (from Holyhead) and up to 5 adults: £174 (low season) to £498 (high season) return.

Call Stena Line for special offers.

Stena Line: 204 7777

### transport options

**DART**

25 min to/from Pearse, Connolly or Tara Street stations in the city centre.

6am–11.30pm daily, every 10–15 min.

£1.10

**buses 7, 7a & 46a**

40 min to/from Dun Laoghaire DART station or shopping centre and the city centre.

approx 7am–11pm Mon–Sat, every 10–15 min (less frequent Sun).

£1.10

**taxis**

20 min to/from the city centre (depending on traffic and destination).

24 hours.

£9–£10 (metered)

## dublin port

The crossing between Dublin Port and Holyhead takes three hours or more. Irish Ferries run a service for foot passengers and cars, while Stena Line run one for cars and freight only.

**Irish Ferries**

From Holyhead: 3.45am and 3.45pm. From Dublin Port: 9.45am and 9.45pm.

For foot passengers: £35 return. For a car and up to 5 adults: £198 (low season) to £418 (high season) return.
☎ 638 3333

**Stena Line**

From Holyhead: 3am and 3pm. From Dublin Port: 9am and 9.30pm.

For a car and up to five adults: £129 (low season) to £468 (high season) return.
☎ 204 7777

### transport options

**Special Dublin Bus**

10 min between Busaras (central bus station) and ferry terminal.

7am–11.10pm daily, every 30–40 min.

£1.50

**route 53**

10–13 min between the port gates and Beresford Place in the city centre.

7.30am–7.30pm daily, every 25–60 min. 80p

The bus stop is 10-min walk away from the boat.

**taxis**

5 min to/from the city centre.

24 hours; the rank is outside the terminal building.

£5 (metered)





# by rail

Iarnród Éireann, Ireland's national rail company, has an extensive network that operates from Dublin's two mainline stations. Heuston station is in the southwest – a 20-min walk or 10-min bus ride from the city centre – and Connolly station is close to the financial centre and Busaras (central bus station).

**entry points & main destinations**

**Belfast to/from Connolly,** 2 hr 10 min £17
**Cork to/from Heuston,** 2 hr 35 min £32
**Galway to/from Heuston,** 2 hr 35 min £15
**Kilkenny to/from Heuston,** 2 hr £11
**Killarney to/from Heuston,** 3 hr 40 min £33.50
**Limerick to/from Heuston,** 2 hr 5 min £27
**Rosslare Harbour to/from Connolly,** 3 hr £10.50
**Sligo to/from Connolly,** 3 hr 20 min £18
**Tralee to/from Heuston,** 4 hr 20 min £33.50
**Waterford to/from Heuston,** 2 hr 40 min £12
**Westport to/from Heuston,** 3 hr 45 min £15

**train essentials**

- Prices given are for an ordinary weekday return. Prices for train journeys are almost all the same for a single as a return. It is more expensive to travel on a Fri or Sun – the average increase is about £3; some destinations increase by £10.
- The Stationlink bus between Heuston and Connolly stations runs daily 7am–11pm, every 10–15 min (every 30 min after 7pm), a journey of 10–15 min. 60p.
- Iarnród Éireann offers a special KID+ intercity ticket for days out from Dublin for the family. It covers 2 adults and up to 4 kids under 16.
- An Explorer ticket allows travel around the Republic of Ireland for any 5 days out of 15. £67.
- Railtours Ireland with Iarnród Éireann run day trips to Wicklow [→32–33] and other destinations.

**useful numbers**

**Train info:** 836 6222 (Iarnród Éireann).
**Railtours Ireland:** 856 0045

**rail stations**

**Heuston**
Parkgate Street, D8
**Enquiries:** 703 2131
**Bureau de Change:** 661 4334
**Lost Property:** 703 2102

**Connolly**
Amiens Street, D1
**Enquiries:** 703 2538
**Bureau de Change:** 661 4334

more transport

# by coach

Bus Éireann runs a comprehensive service throughout the country, linking all the main towns and destination points. Dublin's main bus station is Busaras on Store Street across the road from the Custom House.

**entry points & main destinations**

**Belfast,** 3 hr £14
**Cork,** 4 hr 30 min £17
**Donegal,** 4 hr 30 min £13
**Derry,** 4 hr 30 min £14
**Galway,** 3 hr 30 min £10
**Kilkenny,** 2 hr £8
**Killarney,** 6 hr 30 min £19.50
**Knock,** 4 hr £12.50
**Limerick,** 3 hr 30 min £14
**Rosslare Harbour,** 3 hr £11
**Shannon,** 3 hr £14
**Sligo,** 4 hr £11
**Tralee,** 6 hr 30 min £19.50
**Waterford,** 2 hr 45 min £8
**Westport,** 5 hr £15.50

**coach essentials**

- Prices given are for a standard return ticket.
- There's no need to book ahead – pay at the bus station or on the bus itself.

**Busaras**
Store Street, D1.
Enquiries: 836 6111

# ↓ out & about

**Dublin is so compact, the most obvious, and enjoyable, way to see the city is to walk. Some of the sights, the beautiful coastal towns and the nearby countryside are, however, a bus or DART ride away.**

## general information

**travel passes & tickets**

The cheapest way to travel is with the Travel Wide ticket, giving unlimited bus travel for £3.30. If you are planning to go further afield, the Bus & Rail Short Hop gives unlimited bus and suburban rail/DART (Dublin Area Rapid Transport) travel for £4.50/day or £15.50/week. The Rambler ticket, for all travel on three consecutive days, is £5.50–£9 depending on the time of year. Daily family tickets (for two adults and up to four children) are good value, with unlimited bus travel at £5.50, and bus and DART for £6.50. You need a passport photo to get an ID card (for £2) for a weekly ticket. Travel passes are available from rail stations, and from many newsagents around the city. They can be used at any time of day, but not on Nitelink buses.

**disabled travellers**

Iarnród Éireann's produces a guide for mobility impaired customers, free from any station, with details of facilities and access for all stations. Disabled travellers should alert their station when travelling and every effort will be made to assist them. ☎ 703 2627

**kids**

On all forms of transport, fares for children under 16 are about half that of the adult fare; only one child under three per family can travel free.

## on the buses

The bus service in Dublin is comprehensive, but takes a little working out. Green double deckers, single deckers and the single-deck City Swifts make up the fleet. Dublin Bus have a desk at Dublin Tourism Centre [→121] offering a network guide with details of routes and a bus timetable. A number of sightseeing tours operate around the city [→45] and further afield [→32–33].

**using the buses**

- Buses stop only when they are hailed or if a passenger has pressed the bell.
- Bus stops vary in the amount of information on display. Some have a route map for buses the stop serves, others do not even show the numbers of buses that stop there.
- Buses are changing to an exact fare system called autofare. Ask the driver the fare for your destination then put the correct money (coins only) in the red box in front of the cabin.
- If you have a travel pass insert it in the validator machine to the right of the centre pole.
- Smoking is not permitted.

**bus essentials**

Day buses: 7am–11.30pm daily (around 9am Sun), every 10–15 min until 6pm, less frequently 6–11.30pm.

55p for 1–3 stages, 80p for 4–7 stages, £1 for 8–13 stages, £1.10 for over 13 stages. Weekly bus passes cost £11 within Citizone, £13 Travel Wide.

Buses are best avoided at peak times when they can be crowded and slow: 8–9.30am, 4.45–6.30pm Mon–Fri.

If you get lost, or lose your sense of direction 'An Lar' on the front of the bus means 'City Centre'.

Make sure you have plenty of change or a travel pass.

**Nitelink**

- Nitelink buses run on numerous routes to the suburbs. All buses operate from St Stephen's Green West on Thu, Fri and Sat nights at 12.30am, 1.30am, 2.30am & 3.30am. The fare is £2.50.

**☎ useful numbers**

Bus Éireann: 836 6111
Dublin Bus: 873 4222
Nitelink: 873 4222

## taking the DART

The DART (Dublin Area Rapid Transport) is the reasonably-priced rapid commuter rail line. It runs along the coast from Howth in the north, through the city and about 20 suburban stations, to Bray in the south (soon to be extended to Greystones). The city DART stations are Connolly, Pearse and Tara Street. The fact that it has only one line [→back cover], with few city-centre stations, means that it is only useful for some destinations, but it is reliable, rarely delayed and pleasant to use.

**using the DART**

- All trains stop at every station.
- You can buy a ticket at the station or use a travel pass.
- If you have a travel pass you can get on and off the train as you wish.
- No dogs, apart from guide dogs, are allowed.
- Smoking is not permitted on the DART
- Trains have automatic sliding doors – push the button beside the door for it to open at a station.

**DART essentials**

6am–11.30pm daily, every 10–15 min Mon–Fri (25 min Sat & Sun).

Minimum fare in the city centre is 80p. Maximum fare is £1.60 for a single between Howth and Bray.

It is best to avoid peak times: 7.30–10am, 4.30–7pm Mon–Fri.

**☎ useful numbers**

DART: 836 6222

**→back cover for transport map of city centre & DART route**

# taxis & hackneys

There is a serious shortage of taxis in Dublin. The situation is critical on Friday and Saturday nights when it is extremely difficult to get a taxi anywhere in the city. Taxis can be hailed on the street, and are found at ranks – but expect queues, especially when bars and clubs close. Hackney cabs (minicabs) must be ordered by phone.

### using taxis & hackneys

• All taxis are licensed and fares metered; hackneys are not metered and charge on mileage.

• There are a number of ranks around the city [→back cover]. The most useful are beside Connolly and Heuston stations, St Stephen's Green West, O'Connell Street, College Green, and outside Jury's Hotel in Ballsbridge.

• If you are lucky enough to see a vacant taxi – with its licence number and the word 'taxi' illuminated on its roof – you can hail it in the street.

• Taxis can also be ordered by phone.

• Smoking is permitted in some taxis.

• Hackney cabs are plain cars with a small licence plate at the back. They cannot legally be hailed in the street, but must be booked by telephone or directly at their offices.

• Tipping is optional.

• You can occasionally pick up a cycle rickshaw (usually for two passengers) in the city centre.

• Horse-drawn carriages go from the northwest corner of St Stephen's Green. They tend to be used for city tours rather than as taxis, but some may take you to your destination; most operate from 9 or 10am until approx 10pm.

### taxi & hackney essentials

24 hours (taxis & hackneys); it's advisable to book ahead for night journeys.

Taxis and hackneys cost 90p–£1 per mile.

### ☎ useful numbers

**Radio Link (taxi):** 850 0111
**National Radio Cars (taxi):** 677 2222
**Metro Cabs (hackney):** 668 3333
**Near Cabs (hackney):** 836 7411



# driving

Dublin is a small city with heavy traffic; so there's no need for a car here unless you are going on a few day trips.

### rules of the road

• Drive on the left.

• At roundabouts give priority to traffic on the right.

• Safety belts are compulsory for the driver and front- and rear-seat passengers.

• Children under 12 must travel in the back seats.

• Drink-drive laws are strict.

• Speed limits in urban areas are 30mph/48kmph unless otherwise indicated.

### at the wheel

Car hire is expensive – at least £150 per week for a small car, but check for off-season discounts or deals with airlines. You need a valid driving licence of at least two years' standing. Most firms only accept credit cards, which also serve as security; some need additional ID. Many have a minimum age of 23–25 and a maximum of 70–75.

### ☎ carhire numbers

**Argus:** 605 7701 (city centre); 844 4257 (airport)
**Avis:** 605 7501 (city centre); 605 7500 (airport)
**Budget:** 837 9611 (delivers to city centre); 844 5919 (airport)
**Hertz:** 660 2255 (city centre), 844 5466 (airport)
**Murrays Europcar:** 614 2800 (city centre); 844 4719 (airport)

### parking

• There are many car parks, but check the digital displays to see if spaces are available.

• Meters in the centre take 20p and 50p coins and cost £1 an hour. Newer meters take 10p coins and upwards. The maximum stay is often two hours.

• Pay-and-display parking areas allow 2 hours at £1 per hour. The machines take 10p coins and upwards.

• Disc parking offers scratch cards (available from local shops) costing £1 for an hour.

• Parking on double-yellow lines and in loading bays is prohibited at all times.

• Parking on single-yellow lines is often allowed in the evening and on Sundays, but check the parking notices on lampposts nearby.

• Clamping is operational in the city centre. It costs £65 to have the clamp released.

• If you park on a freeway or are causing an obstruction you will be towed away.

• If your car is clamped or towed telephone the Parking Shop: ☎ 602 2500

### ☎ useful numbers

**Automobile Association Rescue:** 677 9481

# cycling

Cycling is a good way to get around the city, but there are few designated cycle routes.

### bicycle hire

Typical rental costs are £7 to £10 per day or £30–£40 per week, plus a £40–£50 deposit or some ID/credit card details. Check that insurance is included. Bags, helmets and so on can also be rented. If you're cycling after dark it is illegal not to use adequate lights and reflectors. Some companies deliver bikes to your hotel for an extra charge. Bicycles can not be taken on buses, but can be transported on most trains (with the exception of the DART) for a small charge – check with Iarnród Éireann.

### ☎ bicycle hire contacts

**Belfield Bike Shop**, University College Dublin, D4: 260 0749
**Hollingsworth Cycles**, Templeogue Road, D6: 490 5094
**MacDonalds**, 38–39 Wexford Street, D2: 475 2586
**Track Cycles**, 8 Botanic Road, Glasnevin, D11: 850 0252

### bicycle tours

For organized bike tours around the city contact Dublin Bike Tours [→45]: ☎ 679 0899

# dublin's key zones

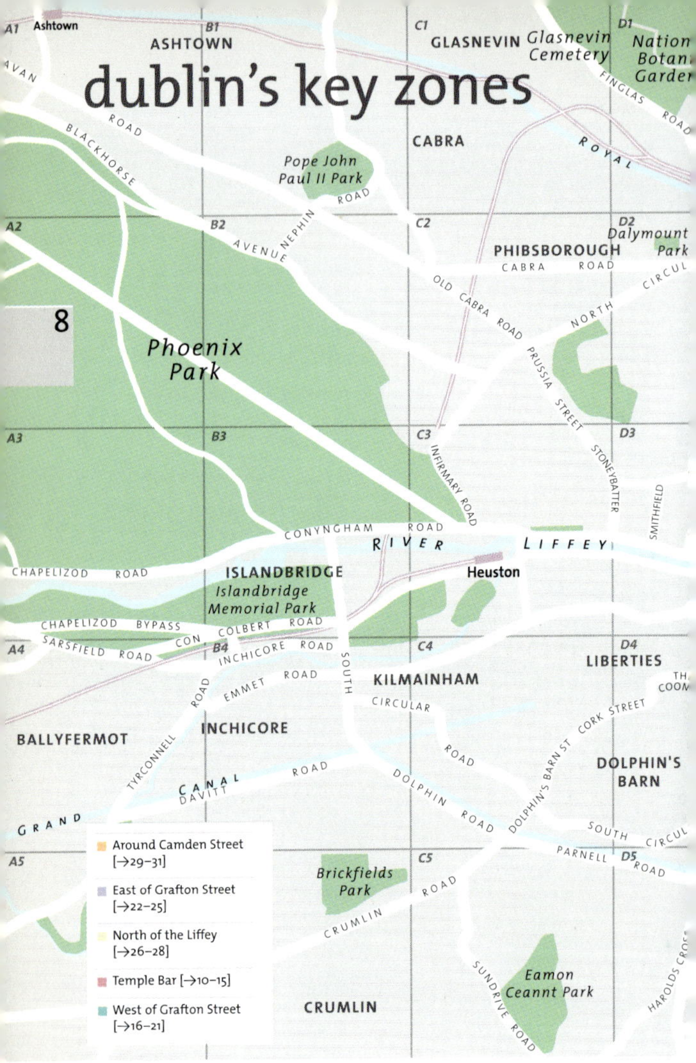


## directory

**Ballsbridge** ⁄F5: The beating heart of Dublin 4 – awash with lordly old houses, posh new flats and moneyed confidence.

**Dame Street** ⁄E3: Busy stretch, peppered with restaurants and bars leading into Temple Bar [→10-15].

**The Docks** ⁄G3: Currently a maze of cranes, Dublin's Docklands, heading for a new incarnation, are in the process of bidding adieu to wastelands of rusty debris.

**Donnybrook** ⁄F5: An upmarket suburb with rugby pubs and local football grounds.

**Financial Services District** ⁄E3: Hub of the 'Celtic Tiger'. Alive with suits surfing on the crests of high-flying commercial deals.

**Fitzwilliam Square** ⁄E4: Picture-perfect Georgian buildings which enchant by day and are, after dark, guarded by working ladies of the night.

**Glasnevin** ⁄D1: Well known for the star-filled cemetery [→55], leafy Botanic Gardens [→55] and the exceedingly unchanged Grave Diggers pub [→92].

**Grafton Street** ⁄E4: A pedestrianised Dublin institution celebrated in many a song and story. Its charm battles valiantly against the onslaught of chain stores.

**Grand Canal** ⁄D5: Great for serene walks along banks and over bridges [→55]. Only a stone's throw from the city centre.

**Henry Street** ⁄D3: Grafton Street's northside cousin, hopping with vocal roadside traders.

**Herbert Park** ⁄F5: Green stretch built in 1907 on the site of the Dublin International Exhibition. Crying out for strollers and joggers.

**Iveagh Gardens** ⁄E4: Concealed city oasis in which James Joyce and Flann O'Brien have trod.

**Kildare Street** ⁄E4: Spot the politicians, bookworms and neophyte archaeologists heading towards Leinster House [→47], the National Library or the Natural History Museum [→53].

**Kilmainham** ⁄B4: Noteworthy for the jail [→53] which fenced in Nationalist rebels and the Irish Museum of Modern Art [→56].

**Lansdowne Road** ⁄F4: Home of Irish rugby, Lansdowne Road Stadium buzzes with tribal fervour during internationals when nearby pubs and Jury's Hotel are thronged.

**Liberties** D4: Once replete with spirited, atmospheric slums, but fast becoming a trendy place to lay your hat. Francis Street is known for pricey antiques [→74].

**Merrion Square** E4: Elegant Georgian houses and the National Gallery [→57] gather around the square in which Oscar Wilde reclines loftily upon a rock.

**O'Connell Bridge** E3: Almost equal in width and length. Good views over the River Liffey.

**O'Connell Street** E3: A touchy subject for many Dubliners who see the burger joints as thorns in the side of what could be the city's pride and joy.

**Parnell Square** D2: Georgian expanse with myriad eminent establishments: the Gate Theatre [→52], Dublin Writers Museum [→50] and Hugh Lane Gallery [→56]. Pause for thought in the Garden of Remembrance.

**Phoenix Park** A2: Largest city park in Europe with a spread of sports grounds and historical sights. Home of the Zoo and Áras an Uachtaráin [→55].

**Quays** D3–F3: They stretch along the Liffey which is spanned by 14 bridges. Hard to find a Dubliner who can name each quay.

**Rathmines & Ranelagh** D5 & E5: Come October, students flock to these residential areas looking for a suitable gaff to rest their Milton-filled heads.

**Ringsend** F4: A mixture of new developments and corporation houses which exude something of a downbeat Legolandish feel.

**Royal Canal** C1: The Grand's northside rival. Since 86 some of the banks have been revamped.

**Smithfield** D3: Famous for the vibrant horse and fruit markets and narrow Victorian streets all set for a 21st century makeover.

**St Stephen's Green** E4: Bustling, lush park at the bottom of Grafton Street.

**South Great George's Street** D4: Full of lively night-time haunts with casual restaurants and pubs aplenty for post-prandial bevvies.

**Temple Bar** D3: Previously a swathe of grimy, derelict buildings, this now somewhat contrived 'Cultural Quarter' will dazzle or disappoint depending on expectations [→10–15].

# temple of temptation



Sashay through Temple Bar for a taste of new Dublin at its vibrant best. What was once a derelict and rundown collection of houses and cobblestoned streets has been transformed into the metropolitan darling of Dublin, oozing style, class and not a small amount of culture. Bars, pubs and clubs, now make the area swing at times like an out-of-control pendulum.

Just ten years ago, the area was a haven for artists and creative types looking for cheap spaces and studios to rent. It quickly caught on as the city's cultural quarter and now, thanks to lashings of EC money, has been luvvied up, almost beyond recognition. Affordable rates may be a thing of the past, but the area's buzz has certainly intensified with the arrival of hip youngsters who reside in swanky modern apartments, and breathe continuous life and soul into the area.

With the invasion of visitors (and the less-than-welcome descent of raucous stag and hen parties), the area is fast gaining a reputation as the Ibiza of the north. But Temple Bar is about enjoying life at a variety of paces, from the Saturday market to the lively art scene and the contagious club culture. If life in the fast lane gets too much, sip a cappuccino or relax with a pint in one of the more low-key bars and cafés which vie for attention in this southbank Mecca.

## day

Numerous style-conscious and quirky outlets line Temple Bar's lanes. On Saturday mornings the food market [→77] is the best place in town to buy exceptionally fresh organic produce.

Good browsing territory for art buffs includes the Gallery of Photography [→57]; Temple Bar Gallery [→57] and Arthouse [→56]. For more cultural kicks Dublin Castle [→48]; Trinity College [→49]; Christ Church Cathedral [→48]; and Dublin's Viking Adventure [→53] are all just a short walk away.

## night

An overwhelming variety of pubs, bars, cafés and restaurants dominate the agenda. When the sun goes down, choose your genre and take your pick.

☆ Big on entertainment, hot spots includes the Irish Film Centre [→103] and the Temple Bar Music Centre [→99]. In the summertime, free late-night movies are shown on Fridays in Meeting House Square. Also at weekends, the nearby Olympia provides some of the bigger theatrical attractions early on [→105], changing into a throbbing music venue [→101–102] after midnight (comedians and tribute bands a speciality).

Buses can be picked up from Dame Street or from termini on Aston Quay and Fleet Street.

Taxi ranks are located at Aston Quay and College Green.

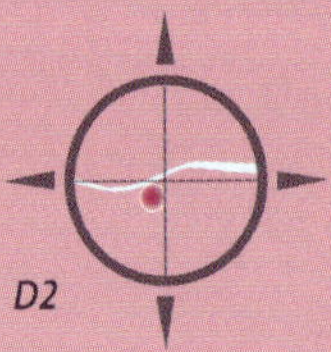

D2

# shopping

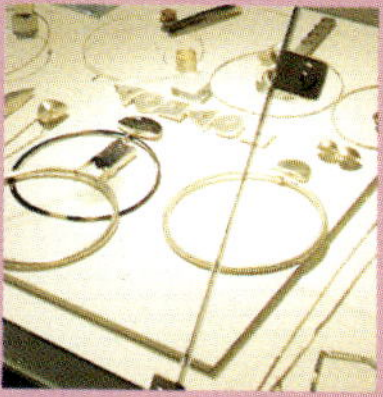

## *fashion*

Where else in the city would you find a West Coast skateboard, silver lurex hot pants and a pair of Cutler & Gross yellow-tinted shades?

Streetwear fans should pick their way through the crew of attitude-ridden skateboard kids doing their *thang* outside the Central Bank to hit **The Real McCoy** for affordable slick shiny combats or a range of Manga T-shirts. And if you're in the mood for more of the same (and who doesn't need a new bowling shirt or a blue plastic handbag?), head next door to **Helter Skelter**. Hardcore skaters need look no further than **Skate City** where you can acquire all the kit that matters. Check out the latest skate video, a well-sourced range of skateboards and skates, flick through the rails of home-grown skate gear, or hang out with the chilled owner. For more eclectic urban style, try ***SéSí**, where it would be easy to revamp your wardrobe after a session of thumbing through the tightly-packed rails of second-hand fur coats and edgy Irish-designed clubbing gear. Top it off with colourful henna tattoos, glitter tights and original Mary Quant makeup. For the shoes, step into the post-apocalyptic interior of ***DV8**, which is simply awash with all styles and prices, from strappy high heels to retro trainers and synthetic boots for your vegan sister. The highlight is watching the sales assistants whizz down an aluminum slide from the upstairs storeroom.

Enter **Christopher** at your peril – the clubbing gear is nearly as loud and frantic as the dance music blaring from their sound system. Chiffon babydoll dresses, latex catsuits or lycra dancing numbers make this a popular port of call for glamour girls. More outrageous one-off designs can be found in the revamped ***Peekaboo** ↘. If their reasonably-priced silver, cone-shaped bra tops or psychedelic-patterned dresses don't set extroverts alight, personal commissions are welcome. For a well-cool blast from the past, have a scout around in **Flip** or **Sharpsville** for a second-hand pinstripe suit, an American retro leather jacket, or the perfect, brash Hawaiian shirt.

This is the fashion promised land for the dedicated clubber and urban style guru......

## *jewellery & accessories*

Temple Bar has more than its fair share of jewellery outlets, offering everything from glow-in-the-dark resin rings to studs for body piercings and traditional Irish brooches. For those with an eye set firmly on designer accessories, the ***DesignYard** ✓ showcases Irish and European contemporary jewellery using materials as diverse as silver, gold, precious stones, rubber, plastic and even recycled toothbrush holders. More affordable, quirky silver pieces for both sexes can be found in **Taboo** – if the novelty furry sheep rucksacks don't catch your eye first. Don't miss the spacious eyewear store, ***Eyecon**, for a range of modern specs to suit all wallets.

If your personal image is reflected more in your writing implements, visit **Pen Corner** for old-fashioned ink pens, chic writing paper and the latest designs in wrapping paper and greeting cards.

## *interiors*

Antique Irish linen, kaleido-scope-coloured strip lighting and contemporary Irish furniture – Temple Bar delivers the lot.

For the ultimate in chic, check out ***Haus** ▲, in the ground floor of Dublin's first eco-friendly building, (complete with solar-panel heating), which sells modern furniture and Philippe Starck accessories. Alternatively, pick up a design souvenir from the ***Crafts Council of Ireland** (at DesignYard) or browse through their visual database of all Irish furniture makers for a special commission. A quick and easy design fix can be had in ***Urbana**, an interiors warehouse with 14 stall-like shops spread over two floors. Highly imaginative window displays succeed in packing in the punters.

## *books & music*

Sci-fi-lovers can pick up new and secondhand books and comics in the **Flying Pig** and take a peek at their gallery of constantly updated work by young Irish cartoonists. The long, frustrating search for that original *X-Men* edition often ends in ***Forbidden Planet**, which houses two floors packed with comics, magazines, videos, memorabilia, postcards and posters.

Film buffs shuffle for space in the small but well-stocked **Cinemania**, where exclusive movie-stills photography, books and postcards play second fiddle to the loud but friendly best-film-ever debate between the owner and his regular customers. If your film tastes run to the specialist level, the **Irish Film Centre** (IFC) is the place to browse, with an impressive stock of early Irish and European film books. Art fans can pick up books and an ever-changing range of original prints from Irish and International artists in the **Gallery of Photography** [→57].

Slip into ***Comet** and mingle with the city's best DJs as they rifle through the week's quirky finds or newest imports. For a one-stop full-on Irish spin, ***Claddagh** will soothe the troubled brow of the U2 fan as well as offering sheet music for every instrument from the tin whistle to the bodhran. **Virgin Megastore** is the obvious stopping-off point for the latest release, newest book, mag, vid or computer game.

## *food*

***Temple Bar Market** is a one-stop gourmet triumph. All the action takes place every Saturday when some two dozen stall holders flaunt their produce to those in search of a tasty snack or the makings of a swanky dinner party. A variety of treats include wild Irish smoked salmon and mussels, homemade breads, pastas and marinades, olives and sundried tomatos, Irish farmhouse cheeses and crumble-in-your-mouth potato cakes and patisseries. Squeeze onto one of the square's many wooden benches to enjoy your goodies.

On the other six days of the week, the **Crow's Nest Deli** should satiate hunger pangs with freshly baked breads and a good selection of exotic sausages.

# eating & drinking

## *restaurants*

When Temple Bar started to 'happen' a few years back, it was hailed as Dublin's cultural quarter. In the early days, it is fair to say that it had about as much culture as a pot of pasteurized yoghurt, but now things are rather different. It's here you will find two of the city's most compelling restaurants, The Clarence's acclaimed Tea Room and the Mermaid Café. ***The Tea Room** [→87] is an oasis of epicurian delights in a stylish setting. The chef uses fresh Irish produce in the most ambitious ways and everything from pre-dinner breads to divine desserts look almost too good to devour. The nearby ***Mermaid Café** [→84] is a restaurant famed for its daily menu of tasty,

healthy and innovative concoctions served in discreet designer style.

Alongside these two remarkable retreats are dozens of relatively cheap and often cheerful spots to mop up the intake of alchohol. **La Med** is a cosy restaurant heavy on Mediterranean accents and wooden furniture. In direct contrast is big and bustling **Trastevere** which also serves Cal-Ital dishes. Diners in this glass window encased venue either relish in being a voyeur or cringe at being in a goldfish bowl.

**Elephant & Castle** ↗ is so popular there is nearly always a queue. The good news is that turnover is fast and they serve up some of the best burgers, omelettes, chicken wings and salads in town – it's not cheap, but worth a visit, especially for Sunday brunch [→84]. For a more novel, anytime, anyplace burger joint with heaps of Harley-Davidson memorabilia try **Thunder Road Café**. You will be in hog heaven, if a juicy burger, pitchers of beer and, very, very loud music are your scene. Dancing on the table with other diners by the end of the night is also fairly commonplace.

For something a little more trad **Gallagher's Boxty House** serves up boxty, a filling potato-based affair with a range of add-ons. How traditional this kind of Oirish food may be is a matter of conjecture, but as it currently appears on many cosmopolitan menus overseas, this is the place to have your first experience.

Ethnic food is sparse in this part of town but ***Monty's of Kathmandu** [→86] has a good lunch menu, and in the evenings the Nepalese chefs truly let their hair down. The resulting regional dishes can be quite sublime and not terribly expensive. Heading further southeast in a culinary sense, ***Chameleon** [→85] offers trad Indonesian *rijstafel* in a cosy, funky environment, beloved of media types. This is a place where your eyes will always be bigger than your stomach... For those with an appetite to rival Homer Simpson, the **Mongolian Barbecue** is an eat-as-much-as-you-want establishment where quantity compensates for a lack of more subtle qualities.

The traditional rectitude of Italian peasant food is set to stay in Temple Bar. Both ***Botticelli** [→89] – big, busy, noisy – and ***Ar Vicoletto** [→89] – small, slightly kitsch but cosy – dish up the likes of gnocchi with wild mushrooms or *salsicce e fagioli* at very keen prices. In both places, food is fresh, hearty and tasty. If a good night out dining *al italiano* is calculated by metres of pasta to the punt, the nearby **Da Pino** scores highly. It's been around longer than most and has survived the test of time. For real Italian atmosphere, try ***Il Baccaro** [→90]. Less about food than wine, this basement dive gets its authenticity from all the young Italians who pack out the cavernous venue and hoover up liberal quantities of hooch from Piedmont with an occasional nibble of *sardo* or *bresaola*. Lots of fun, but it helps if you're Italian.

**Milano** is a cool, clean and uncluttered pizzeria where a quick bite and a glass of wine is enjoyable and relatively cheap. Cool, clean and uncluttered is a fairly new concept in Dublin restaurants and ***Eden** ↘ [→83] was one of the first examples of the this. What could be just a fashionable eating house, with loads of glass and light, is brought supernova by the stunningly assured and simple cooking of Eleanor Walsh. Nearby ***Dish** [→83] doesn't manage such simplicity and the globally-influenced food can be a bit hit and miss. It is worth the gamble, however, as when on form this fashionable low-key restaurant has plenty of ambience, a funky crowd and cool music. More formal and packed with charm, ***Bruno's** [→83] is a relatively big restaurant, where everything seems to roll on castors. A window seat provides a safe ringside street view, while the menu offers an eclectic combination of Euro-Irish dishes accented by French flourishes and served with great finesse. For fully-fledged French ***Les Frères Jacques** [→87] has a cosy, enticing setting, impeccable standards and food with that certain *je ne sais quoi*....

Temple Bar naturally lends itself to a lazy café culture with considerable panache.

## *cafés*

Spend an hour or so lounging in the boho ***Joy of Coffee** [→91] and you'll probably learn more about what's happening in Dublin than any amount of earnest culture-vulturing could unearth. Across the winding way, you can send email postcards home and sip good coffee in the **Arthouse** café while various malcontents play Doom around you. A rumbling tummy will bring you, like many locals, to **Café Irie's** funky environs in search of big sandwiches to be scoffed to a soundtrack of top tunes. The amiable vibes in ***Café Gertrude** [→91] and, more importantly, their fine lunchtime menu with excellent salads and tasty gourmet sandwiches are another reason to linger.

## *pubs & bars*

In the space of a decade, virtually every brick and stick in the area has been replaced since its bohemian days, so those searching for the authentic pub experience should look elsewhere. That said, nowhere embodies Dublin's celebrated carnival spirit better than Temple Bar.

Trendy self-absorption and gay banter are much in evidence in Parliament Street's Front Lounge and Turk's Head. The ***Front Lounge** features a broad expanse of retro hotel-lobby chic embellished with original artworks, soothing piped Bacharach and deep plush seating. The mood of laid-back decadence makes it a favourite with suave continentals, winsome waifs, gay bachelors and designer scruffs. The ***Turk's Head** offers a more upbeat alternative for snappy dressers; with elegant decor, slightly conservative music and a good in-house nightclub. The third point of Parliament Street's hipper-than-thou triangle is ***Thomas Read**, a big, bustling hostelry, where the huge windows entice novice poseurs to come and study the moves of old hands.

The social whirl at **Danger Doyle's** moves at a different tempo. Unabashedly young, loud and brash, the weekend party spirit is fuelled by a heady cocktail of raging hormones, bare midriffs, fake tans and sweet slushy drinks. The same crowd graduate to the ***Foggy Dew**, an attractive split-level pub blasting chart music to ward off the middle-aged.

In its heyday, the **Palace** was the hub of literary Dublin. Images of famous regulars abound, and the scene has been preserved intact. The upside is a marvellous old-style front bar and the Guinness which Dubliners hold in high regard; the downside a run-down back lounge. The ***Porterhouse** also serves pints to cherish. Provisioned with a range of lagers, ales and stouts brewed on the premises, this airy but busy pub has live music and a cheery Cal-Ital restaurant. The **Temple Bar**, revamped with mock-traditional interior, makes an alluring setting for an off-peak pint.

With perhaps the greatest concentration of pubs on earth, Temple Bar is where Europe comes to party.

An unruly clamour at the **Octagon Bar** seems unthinkable at the U2-owned Clarence, the most reserved and stylish spot around. Posh pints for music pilgrims and the loads-a-money men. Swank setting; comfy chairs; stiff prices.

No pub has embraced the tourist invasion as enthusiastically as the **Oliver St John Gogarty**. A busy complex with several bars, a seafood restaurant and sundry diddly-aye bands. Just across the cobblestones, the **Auld Dubliner** prospers without really trying and the slightly restrained air offers better prospects of holding a conversation.

## *art houses*

Many of Dublin's art houses and cultural centres are clustered together in the heart of Temple Bar. The **Irish Film Centre** [→103], with its bar, café and movie screenings, is a key meeting place for the trendy and articulate. ***Arthouse** [→56] across the road is a truly multi-media centre which trains people in all areas of hi-tech communication, and also exhibits some exciting art projects. Out the door and you face the ***Temple Bar Music Centre** [→99] which plays host to everything from live rock, hip hop jams, offbeat club nights, stand-up comedy and even the occasional fashion show. There's an efficient bar and a cute café area which adheres to the overall postmodern image of the place. For kids, the architecturally brilliant **Ark** [→58] hosts children's creative courses and workshops.

## *clubs*

U2 spotters queue for Bono's hip, exclusive and expensive underground club ***The Kitchen** [→98]. Those denied entry can take refuge at the subterranean **Klub Zazu** which offers a staple diet of commercial dance and old classics, and always seems to have a drink promotion to get you in the mood.

Populist and popular, ***Club M** [→98] has been a Dublin insitution since the days before discos became clubs. It flaunts Temple Bar's biggest dance floor and flashiest lightshow. A trendy-free zone, which is tacky, but hilarious. And the lucky ones get to use the jacuzzi in the VIP area! Mixing live acts with classic disco anthems, **Bad Bob's Backstage Bar** is open late and always stuffed to the rafters.

**The Ark** B3
11a Eustace Street
670 7788

**Arthouse** B3
Curved Street
605 6800

**Ar Vicoletto** B3
5 Crow Street
670 8662 £–££

**Auld Dubliner** C2
17 Anglesea Street
677 0527

**Il Baccaro** B3
Meeting House Square
671 4597 £–££

**Bad Bob's Backstage Bar** A2
35–37 Essex Street East
677 5482

**Botticelli** B2
3 Temple Bar
672 7289 ££

**Bruno's** B2
30 Essex Street East
670 6767 ££

**Café Gertrude** C2
3 Bedford Row
677 9043 £

**Café Irie's** B2
11 Fownes Street Lower £

**Chameleon** B2
1 Fownes Street Lower
671 0362 £££

**Christopher** C2
12 Crown Alley
679 8891

**Cinemania** B3
7 Eustace Street
670 3665

**Claddagh** B2
2 Cecilia Street
677 0262

**Club M** C3
Blooms Hotel,
6 Anglesea Street
671 5485

**Comet** C3
5 Cope Street
671 8592

**Crafts Council of Ireland** B2
12 Essex Street East
679 5371

**Crow's Nest Deli** B3
10 Crow Street
671 0444

**Da Pino** A3
38–40 Parliament Street
671 9308 £–££

**Danger Doyle's** B2
24 Eustace Street
670 7655

**DesignYard** B2
12 Essex Street East
677 8453

**Dish** B3
2 Crow Street
671 1248 ££

**DV8** C2
4 Crown Alley
679 8472

**Eden** B2
Meeting House Square
670 5372 ££

**Elephant & Castle** C2
18 Temple Bar
679 3121 ££

**Eyecon** B3
11 Fownes Street Upper
670 9183

**Flip** B3
4 Fownes Street Upper
671 4299

**Flying Pig** B3
17 Crow Street
679 5099

**Foggy Dew** B3
1 Fownes Street Upper
677 9328

**Forbidden Planet** C1
5–6 Crampton Quay
671 0688

**Les Frères Jacques** A3
74 Dame Street
679 4555 £££

**Front Lounge** A3
33 Parliament Street
670 4112

**Gallagher's Boxty House** C2
20–21 Temple Bar
677 2762 £–££

**Gallery of Photograpy** B3
Meeting House Square
671 4654

**Haus** B3
3–4 Crow Street
679 5155

**Helter Skelter** B3
4a Fownes Street Upper
671 4299

**Irish Film Centre** B3
6 Eustace Street
679 5744

**Joy of Coffee** B2
25 Essex Street East
679 2244 £

**The Kitchen** A2
The Clarence, Wellington Quay
677 6635

**Klub Zazu** B2
23–24 Eustace Street
670 7655

**La Med** B2
22 Essex Street East
670 7358 ££

**Mermaid Café** A3
69–70 Dame Street
670 8236 ££

**Milano** B2
19 Essex Street East
670 3384 £

**Mongolian Barbecue** C3
7 Anglesea Street
670 4154 £–££

**Monty's of Kathmandu** B3
28 Eustace Street
670 4911 ££

**Octagon Bar** A2
The Clarence, Wellington Quay
670 9000

**Oliver St John Gogarty** C2
18–21 Anglesea Street
671 1822

**Palace** D2
21 Fleet Street
677 9290

**Peekaboo** B3
7 Crow Street
670 3253

**Pen Corner** C3
12 College Green
679 3641

**Porterhouse** A3
16–18 Parliament Street
679 8847

**The Real McCoy** B3
3 Fownes Street Upper
671 4299

**SéSí** C2
13 Temple Bar Square
679 0523

**Sharpsville** B3
3a Fownes Street Upper
671 4299

**Skate City** C3
14 Crown Alley
679 9900

**Taboo** B3
13 Fownes Street Upper
671 6871

**The Tea Room** A2
The Clarence, Wellington Quay
670 7766 £££

**Temple Bar** B2
48 Temple Bar
677 3807

**Temple Bar Market** B2
Meeting House Square
671 5717

**Temple Bar Music Centre** B3
Curved Street
670 9202

**Thomas Read** A3
1 Parliament Street
670 7220

**Thunder Road Café** C2
50–57 Fleet Street
679 4057 ££

**Trastevere** B2
1 Temple Bar Square
670 8343 £–££

**Turk's Head** A3
27–30 Parliament St
679 2567

**Urbana** B2
43–44 Temple Bar
670 3083

**Virgin Megastore** D1
14–18 Aston Quay
677 7361

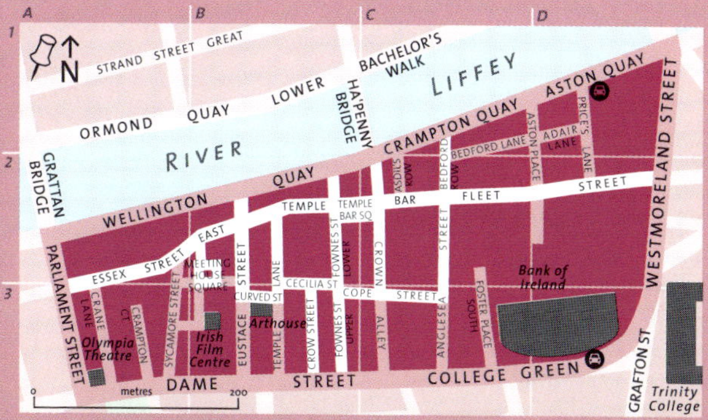

# the wild west

This area may not have many cultural assets, but it certainly makes up for it with other diversions. When it comes to finding self-indulgent ways to spend both time and money, look no further. Colonizing these backwaters, to the west of the mighty Grafton Street, are cool café-bars, which are as European as the labels filling the new designer shops. This zone is a magnet for those in search of some retail therapy, first-class dining, a night on the razz, or just a spot of people-watching. And there's just the right amount of café action to keep the caffeine levels up – a crucial consideration for the part of Dublin that truly never stops.

The beauty of this westerly spot is that the mix is just right. The old order can still get on with what matters, while the new kids tart up the block and begin to do things their way. And when it comes to preening and posing, and ducking and diving, there's no competition because it's what the inhabitants are best at.

## day

Shopping nirvana, with outlets selling a tempting array of goodies.

Dublin Castle [→48], Trinity College [→49] and the Douglas Hyde Gallery [→56] are nearby. Marsh's Library [→54], Christ Church Cathedral [→48] and St Patrick's Cathedral [→47] are a short walk away. Alternatively stop off for a cultural coffee at Bewley's Oriental Café [→51].

## night

From the bustle of the chic new café-bars to the palatial restaurants, the area booms when the sun goes down.

☆ Theatrical entertainment comes in the form of the Gaiety and Andrew's Lane theatres [→105].

Buses run along South Great George's Street, Dame Street and from the terminus at St Stephen's Green West.

Taxi ranks are located on Balfe Street, St Stephen's Green West and College Green. Pony Cabs have an office on South Great George's Street (☎ 661 2233).

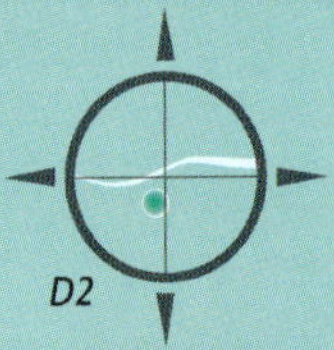

D2

# shopping

## *fashion & accessories*

Grafton Street is chocka with chainstores, but its many offshoots yield hidden treasures. The jewel in the crown is ***Brown Thomas**. Purveyor of chic and up-market fashion, accessories, homeware and cosmetics, this opulent department store is a style lover's dream come true. The designer threads at ***Whistles** and the ***Design Centre** – which flies the flag for innovative Irish fashion – are also worth burning a hole in your pocket for. It's always the quiet ones you have to watch and ***Costume** is no exception. No frills, no fuss, just exclusive and quirky labels are sold in this great-looking shop, aimed at the upper end of the market. Conservative glamour, meanwhile, is the well-established mantra of ***Richard Alan**.

The area has streetwear stores galore. Check out the stock at ***Tribe** if you can squeeze past the droves of skateboard kids, DJs and wannabe home-boys discussing low-slung waistbands. Thumping jungle music leads the way around ***Urban** where Mecca-wearing kids thumb the rails for the newest Wu Tang shirt. Guerrilla girls do it for themselves in the first of ***Sabotage**'s two outlets, while the boys shuffle into silver parkas in adjoining **Jungle**, before heading for Sabotage's second shop for a spin on the playstation and rummage around the Psycho Cowboy rack. All wooden floor and gilt mirrors, ***Cuba**'s interior looks gorgeous enough to live in and if your wardrobe runs to Evisu and rare street labels, you're home. It is fair to say that nearly every Irish teen owns a ***Hobo** T-shirt and no wonder. The home-grown answer to international street style, Hobo's empire is growing faster than its reputation for zany window displays. If, however, you cannot live without reassuringly familiar cult labels, beat a hasty retreat to ***Genius** or ***Raidar** where a fresh spin on niche street brands will sort every homeboy out.

Getting-a-head comes effortlessly with a bumper choice of sassy headgear from the ***The Hat Studio**. And when your feet start craving attention, do as the Spice Girls do and shove them into a wedge heel in ***Buffalo**. For a different high, check out the extraordinary goodies in **Miss Fantasia**, essentially a funky sex shop, but also a mecca for extrovert clubbers and those in search of the alternative. Alternative is exactly what you'll find in **Asha**, which never fails to surprise. Ignore the teenagers buying post-modern hash pipes and check out their truly eye-brow-raising PVC and leather fashion. More conventionally, the **Leather Studio** offers a choice of fashionable and affordable leather items you'd actually wear outside the home. If your tastes are more boudoir, look no further than ***Susan Hunter** whose tiny shop offers a select range of lingerie including the divine La Perla collection. More affordable bed and casual wear comes in the form of **Out of the Blue** whose Betty Ford Clinic T-shirt has become legendary.

It's here that Dubs come in search of everything from the ideal present to a drop-dead-gorgeous outfit.

## *vintage clothing*

The George Street Arcade is the next best thing to a flea market. The epicentre of Dublin's vintage-clothing trade, secondhand fur coats mingle with Chinese silk jackets and an eclectic mix of clubgear. Sooner or later you'll end up in the arcade's most impressive store, **Jenny Vander**, which is also the oldest antique clothing shop in the country. When you've finished plundering the womenswear, take a peek upstairs at **Rufus the Cat** for the boys. Top rummagers have included Bob Geldof, Yasmin Le Bon and Michael Keating. Slip across the road to Castle Market for equally cool pickings in **Harlequin** ◄ which pulls out all the stops to stock a fab collection of quality clothes and accessories. Everything but the kitchen sink is on offer in **Wild Child** where weird novelty playing cards are displayed alongside clothes rails bulging with outrageous gear from the 50's, 60's and 70's. For an even more surreal experience, head for **A Store is Born** where the rails are stripped clean each Saturday by delighted fashionettes.

## *jewellery*

Join the star client trail and head for ***John Farrington** where Adam Clayton of U2 spent 40 grand on an engagement ring for Naomi Campbell. Grand gestures can also be made in ***Hervé Coulon** or ***Weir & Sons**, a swish elegant store dating back to 1869 which will satisfy every taste. Still on the pricey side but definitely more quirky is ***Rhinestones**, where art deco and Victorian glass pieces are the order of the day. Anyone who has flicked through *Vogue* in the last five years will be familiar with ***Vivien Walsh**, whose cutting-edge designs are displayed in her elegant emporium. If minimal and very modern is more your cup of tea, look no further than the silver treasure-trove that is ***Angles**. Worth queueing up for a browse (the shop is packed with just five people inside), don't miss out on the highly individual contemporary pieces from Irish and international designers. Brimming with choice, **Equinox** is home to a wide-ranging collection of art deco silver and unusual but affordable glassware.



more shopping | restaurants | cafés

## *interiors*

Settle down on a cowhide ottoman (complete with ears and tail), switch on a set of fairy lights set in plastic tulips and make yourself comfortable at ***Foko** ▲. Equally fun home accessories can be found in ***Pad**, a tiny shop bursting at the seams with cards, candles, lights and other goodies. If your tastes are more traditional, take a look in **Costelloe & Costelloe**, a popular port of call for easy interior design ideas.

The second floor in Powerscourt Townhouse provides rich pickings for antique collectors. **The Silver Shop** will end your search for unusual silver pieces, while ***Delphi Antiques** next door has a selection of art deco jewellery making it near impossible to leave empty-handed. ***J W Weldon**'s two outlets sell silver antique pieces unlike anything else in the city.

## *books & music*

Forget the larger bestseller or top 20 outlets – small and individual book and music stores are where it's at. Finding no need to dress up, **Road Records** is the place to catch excited music heads clutching lucky finds to their Carharrt hoodies. Nearby, **Smile Records**' well-worn boxes of vinyl can unearth rare editions as well as serving that obsession for Barry Manilow ... Like a favourite chair, **Tower Records** is difficult to leave once you get comfy. Noisy, untidy and usually crowded, this music store has it all, and some. The friendly staff never mind whether your musical tastes are mainstream or obscure. **Subcity** looks after all your comic needs and the laid-back staff will, if you want, debate the superiority of *Star Trek* versus *Space 1999*.

## *food*

Grab a table outside ***Cooke's Food Hall** and sample the famous breads saturated with fabulous Italian olive oils. The ***Big Cheese Company** tempts every palate with a generous range of cheeses and a choice of American cookies and Canadian maple syrup. For chocolate lovers, the huge display at **Butler's Chocolates** makes for agonizing decision-making. Other foodies will be lured by the smells wafting from **Guy Stuart Foods** which sells olives, sun-dried tomatoes, olive oils and pestos. To complete the picnic, choose a slice of exotic salami from ***Magills**' selective deli.

## *make-up*

***Make-Up Forever**'s brightly coloured windows may look imposing from the outside but a calm oasis awaits within. Friendly staff hand over secrets of the trade with a full make-over, and help make sense of their sometimes scarily bright make-up products – the electric orange eye shadow for example. Prepare to be dazzled in the newly opened **Blueiru** as you skip from the Kiehls counter to the new Nars nail polishes while keeping one eye out for a Jade Jagger necklace and the fabulously smelling candles up front.

# eating & drinking

## *restaurants*

A revolution in Dublin dining came in the late 80's when chef Johnny Cooke returned from California bringing Cal-Ital food to a disbelieving city. ***Cooke's Café** [→90] may be a little rubbed at the edges these days but is still a great and buzzy place to eat. It is frequented by the occasional ageing rock star and lots of people with winter tans and chunky gold jewellery. Upstairs at the ***Rhino Room** [→84], the open chargrill locks in juicy flavours and scents the air with the most tantalizing whiff of thyme and seared meat. It's equally good for a coffee and a self-indulgent slice of chocolate cake.

Nearby, diversity is the order of the day with establishments such as the ***Good World** [→85], Ireland's capital of dim sum, where the food compensates for the somewhat chilly, inscrutable service, and **The Bistro**, where pizza, pasta and exceptional chicken wings can be had for a fraction of the price charged in trendier places. Add to that the bourgeois charm of **Muscat**, with its sharply executed dinner party classics and a very decent wine list, and you have five restaurants satisfying all one's cravings.

***Mao** [→83] may be terribly cool but style does not win out over substance – both are of the highest order. The food is a fusion of Oriental flavours and there are splendid stir fries, Malaysian curries, feisty reworkings of things like spring rolls, plenty of Asian beers and untypically delicious desserts. Equally trendy, and good value, ***Wagamama** [→86] functions with great clinical efficiency, and delivers vast bowls of noodles in double-quick time, and remarkably cheaply.

***Restaurant Peacock Alley** ↗ [→87] is one of Dublin's most fashionable restaurants, while **Christopher's**, also in the Fitzwilliam Hotel, delivers similar style food in much less formal surroundings (and offers better value). Both restaurants are under the baton of Conrad Gallagher, Ireland's most convivial answer to Marco Pierre White. The antithesis is the **Trocadero** where much the same kind of people go, but not for the food. The Troc is for late-night eating, and provides material for mopping up prodigious quantities of alcohol. Resolutely old-fashioned, it's a great fave with media/fashion folk and the gay community.

***QV2** [→90] is a lovely dining room, ideally suited to lingering late into the night. Overhauled a few years ago, it has been remodelled into a cosy but spacious restaurant which combines modern European cuisine with Irish sparkle. Cheaper and more eclectic, **Tosca** serves shank of lamb, black-pudding salad and excellent bread with an affordable wine list. Buzzing with atmosphere, it's a fun place to binge without breaking the bank. And if you want to know what Bono will look like in ten years' time, watch out for his brother, Norman Hewson, the hands-on owner.

Vegetarian restaurants are thin on the ground, but if pigging out – literally – isn't your idea of dining, **Juice** serves great juices, nectars, salads, bakes and decent organic wine in a café setting. Veggie food at the heartier end of the spectrum is dished up at **Blazing Salads**, a busy self-service joint – have no fear of missing your daily fibre target here. ***Zafraan** [→86] takes vegetarian food very seriously. This very attractive, very modern Indian restaurant is as far away from the Balti house as you can get. ***Shalimar** [→86], on the same street, is another excellent Indian with plenty of veggie options to choose from.

Loud, cramped, smoky and noisy, the ***Steps of Rome** [→89] may deter many would-be diners, but there's nowhere better for a slice of pizza, a glass of Barbera d'Asti, a sliver of gateau and a chaser of espresso – so good you might imagine yourself in Milan. **Trentuno** is bigger, quieter and not quite so much fun, but it manages to provide trattoria staples at reasonable prices and it's all cool, clean and uncluttered – just like its core clientele.

The regulars at **Odessa**, part of the burgeoning Ri-Ra [→99] complex, are generally young, frequently clubbers, and occasionally fashion designers, models and actors. The food is worryingly Tex-Mex but quite palatable. Nobody comes here to rave about textures and flavours – it's a place in which to drink loads of wine and be terribly laid-back and cool. The weekend brunches are packed affairs so advance booking is darn near essential.

With restaurants on every street corner, this is the ideal location to test-drive your taste buds...

## *cafés*

You could spend all day in the mighty ***Bewley's Oriental Café** [→51] and still not have experienced all there is to see, hear, eat and drink. A veritable institution and landmark, it's good and reliable at any hour of the day, pulling a huge cross-section of punters. If you prefer to mingle with a more choosy clientele, check the lobby of the **Westbury Hotel** where old dears and shiny suits hold court.

The best sarnies in town are to be found in ***Simon's Place** [→91], a godsend for the hungry during the day thanks to the owner's expertise and the low prices. And for some of the best views, head straight to ***The Dome** [→91] which overlooks St Stephen's Green. For the incorrigible caffeine addict, ***Kaffe Moka** [→91] ➤ runs till the early hours with a sometimes decent food menu but an always brilliant coffee selection. You can enjoy a pretty good cuppa in **Gloria-Jeans**, the nearest thing Dublin has to Starbucks, while in **Costa**, they have the full range of options available, from a latté to a double espresso. **Metro** is quiet and subtle – ideal for enjoying a good lunch before hitting the streets for more action. Indeed, if you're on a serious shopping trip, abandon the racks in Brown Thomas and trip downstairs (or up to the second floor) to savour ***Brown's**, the department store's chic eating and drinking corner.

## *pubs, bars & clubs*

The area west of Grafton Street has some of the capital's oldest and finest hostelries, and it remains the promenade of choice for Dublin's preening classes. Deservedly cherished by natives and visitors, the ***International Bar** stands firm against the tide of frenzied refurbishment. Best experienced when the evening sunlight filters through the stained-glass windows, this lived-in bar boasts a friendly boho crowd, great Guinness and an upstairs comedy cellar (ho ho). When it comes to good pints, stained glass and a bohemian buzz, ***The Long Hall** is equally well-endowed. In addition, this alluring, old-skool boozer harbours a magnificent long bar and some wonderfully eccentric decor.

The picturesque front bar of ***O'Neill's** harks back to bygone times, but venture further in and you'll uncover a warren of modern alcoves swarming with execs, students and weary tourists. ***The Stag's Head** is another magnet with a reputation for premium Guinness and superb pub grub. Lavishly remodelled in oak to look old and grand, it attracts a lively studenty crowd. College pedigrees are also commonplace amongst the patrons of ***Thing Mote**. Unlike some of its pale, interesting and pierced clientele, the pub itself isn't much to look at.

**Grogan's** is blessed with the greatest asset any property can have – location. Buskers, businessmen, artists and road-sweepers seek refuge here from encroaching theme-pub mania. **Neary's** chief attraction also lies in its staunch refusal to move with the times. The two, street-level lounges have a down-at-heel elegance, and close proximity to the Gaiety Theatre ensures a steady traffic of luvvies and a nightly after-show rush.

The rustic Victorian interior of ***McDaid's** simply oozes character. Literary pilgrims come to cast an eye over Brendan Behan's old lurching ground, but the place also attracts a chic young set. Also drawing big crowds of weekend funsters is the ***Hairy Lemon**. A split-level monkey-puzzle of dinky alcoves and mini-stairways, it's a rare triumph in the quest for designer atmosphere.

There's nothing intimate about ***Hogan's**, a big, bustling barn of a place dominated by a huge, oval bar. Its best attribute is the easy-going mixed crowd and the weekend late licence when DJs play some ace tunes. Nearby, the sounds at ***The Globe** ▲ are also picked with care, befitting one of Dublin's undisputed temples of cool. The most striking aspect of this wood-effect café-bar is the clientele. While the beautiful people of the city's clubland hang out at The Globe, their slightly younger, less cocksure counterparts swig sugary brews at the loud and proud-of-it ***Drumm's Emporium**. Expect no subtlety either at ***The George**, a raucous gay bar on a Wild West theme where karaoke isn't a dirty word.

For music buffs, this area has all kinds of everything. Compact and cool, ***Ri-Ra** [→99] is rated by many as Dublin's premier club. The ***Gaiety Theatre** [→98], meanwhile, hosts Latin and soul nights augmented by classic movie screenings, while ***Da Club** offers comedy [→104], live music [→101] and a convivial air.

## *directory* D2

**A Store is Born** C2
34 Clarendon Street
679 5866

**Angles** C2
10 Westbury Mall
679 1964

**Asha** C3
212 St Stephen's Green Centre
478 1396

**Bewley's Oriental Café** C2
78 Grafton Street
677 6761 £–££

**Big Cheese Company** B1
14–15 St Andrew's Lane
671 1399

**The Bistro** B2
4 Castle Market
671 5430 ££

**Blazing Salads** C2
21c Powerscourt Townhouse
671 9552 £

**Blueiru** B2
7 William Street South

**Brown's** C2
Grafton Street
679 5666 £

**Brown Thomas** C2
Grafton Street
605 6666

**Buffalo** B1
16 Exchequer Street
671 2492

**Butler's Chocolates** C1
24 Wicklow Street
671 0591

**Christopher's** C3
109 St Stephen's Green West
478 7040 £££

**Cooke's Café** B2
14 William St South
679 0536 £££

**Cooke's Food Hall** B2
15 Castle Market
679 9923

**Costa** C2
15 Westbury Mall
679 7886 £

**Costelloe & Costelloe** C3
14a Chatham Street
671 4209

**Costume** B2
10 Castle Market
679 5200

**Cuba** B1
13 Trinity Street
672 7489

**Da Club** B3
2 Johnson's Place
670 3137

**Delphi Antiques** C2
Powerscourt Townhouse
679 0331

**Design Centre** C2
Powerscourt Townhouse
679 5718

**The Dome** C3
St Stephen's Green Centre
478 1287 £

**Drumm's Emporium** B1
1–5 Exchequer Street
679 1776

**Equinox** C2
Powerscourt Townhouse
670 5400

**Foko** B2
66–67 South Gt George's Street
475 5344

**Gaiety Theatre** C3
King Street South
677 2956

**Genius** C2
6a Clarendon Street
679 7851

**The George** B1
89 South Gt George's Street
478 2983

**The Globe** B1
11 South Gt George's St
671 1220

**Gloria-Jeans** C2
Powerscourt Townhouse
679 7772 £

**Good World** B2
18 South Gt George's St
677 5373 ££

**Grogan's** B2
15 William Street South
677 9320

**Guy Stuart Foods** B2
George's Street Arcade

**Hairy Lemon** B3
41 Stephen Street Lwr
671 8949

**Harlequin** B2
13 Castle Market
671 0202

**The Hat Studio** C2
33 Clarendon Street
679 7988

**Hervé Coulon** C2
9 Westbury Mall
670 8212

**Hobo** C1
6–9 Trinity Street
670 4869

**Hogan's** B2
35 South Gt George's St
677 5904

**International Bar** C1
23 Wicklow Street
677 9250

**Jenny Vander** B2
20 George's St Arcade
677 0406

**John Farrington** B2
32 Drury Street
679 1899

**Juice** B2
9 South Gt George's St
475 7856 £££

**Jungle** B2
George's Street Arcade

**J W Weldon's** C2
55 Clarendon Street
677 1638

**Kaffe Moka** B2
39 William St South
679 8475 £

**Leather Studio** C2
2 Westbury Mall
679 9044

**The Long Hall** A2
51 South Gt George's St
475 1590

**Magills** C3
14 Clarendon Street
671 3830

**Make-Up Forever** C2
38 Clarendon Street
679 9043

**Mao** B3
2–3 Chatham Row
670 4899 £–££

**McDaid's** C3
3 Harry Street
679 4395

**Metro** B2
43 William St South
679 4515 £

**Miss Fantasia** C3
25 William St South
671 3734

**Muscat** C2
64 William St South
679 7699 £££

**Neary's** C3
1 Chatham Street
677 8596

**Odessa** B1
13 Dame Court
670 7634 ££

**O'Neill's** C1
2 Suffolk Street
679 3671

**Out of the Blue** C2
12 Westbury Mall
671 6795

**Pad** B3
20 Stephen St Lower
478 1080

**QV2** C1
14–15 St Andrew's St
677 3363 ££

**Raidar** C3
106 St Stephen's Green Centre
478 3221

**Restaurant Peacock Alley** C3
109 St Stephen's Green West
478 7015 £££

**Rhinestones** C1
18 St Andrew's Street
679 0759

**Rhino Room** B2
14a William St South
670 5260 ££–£££

**Richard Alan** C2
58 Grafton Street
677 5149

**Ri-Ra** B1
1 Exchequer Street
677 4835

**Road Records** B2
16b Fade Street
671 7340

**Rufus the Cat** B2
20 George's St Arcade
677 0406

**Sabotage** B1
14 Exchequer Street
670 4789

**Shalimar** B2
17 South Gt George's St
671 0738 ££

**The Silver Shop** C2
Powerscourt Townhouse
679 4147

**Simon's Place** B2
George's Street Arcade
679 4698 £

**Smile Records** A2
59 South Gt George's Street
478 2005

**The Stag's Head** B1
1 Dame Court
679 3701

**Steps of Rome** C3
Chatham Street
670 5630 £

**Subcity** B1
2 Exchequer Street
677 1902

**Susan Hunter** C2
13 Westbury Mall
679 1271

**Thing Mote** C1
15 Suffolk Street
677 8030

**Tosca** C1
20 Suffolk Street
679 6744 ££

**Tower Records** C2
16 Wicklow Street
671 3250

**Trentuno** C2
31 Wicklow Street
677 4190 £–££

**Tribe** C3
209 St Stephen's Green Centre
475 0311

**Trocadero** C1
3 St Andrew's Street
677 5545 ££

**Urban** B2
30 Drury Street
670 4757

**Vivien Walsh** A3
24 Stephen St Lower
475 5031

**Wagamama** B3
King Street South
478 2152 £

**Weir & Sons** C2
96 Grafton Street
677 9678

**Westbury Hotel** C3
Clarendon Street
679 1122 ££–£££

**Whistles** C3
18 Balfe Street
670 5520

**Wild Child** A2
61 South Gt George's St
475 5099

**Zafraan** A2
41 South Gt George's St
677 0999 ££

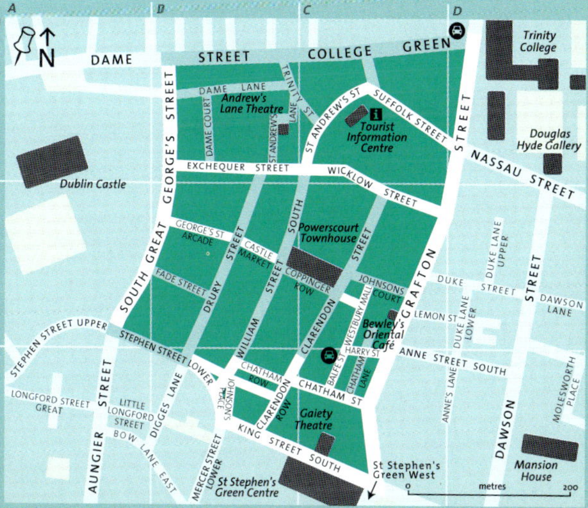

# eastern promise





Strolling east from the buzz of Grafton Street brings the business heart of the capital into focus – streets are chocka with the bustle of offices and the snarl of motorbike couriers. The elegant Georgian squares and streets are also a reminder of times when commerce was a far more sedate affair, and working from home had a whole different meaning.

For those with time on their hands, this area is as much about parklife as it is about snazzy Georgian pads. St Stephen's Green, Trinity College's elegant playing fields and the oasis of Merrion Square provide plenty of spots to catch the summer rays. Meanwhile the cluster of museums, art galleries, shops, bars and cafés hum with people. Afternoon drinkers loll into the night becoming part of the throng who turn the pubs and gourmet restaurants into thriving hubs of bonhomie.

## day

This area is home to exclusive upmarket fashion and interiors outlets, and some of the city's finest book stores.

A clutch of museums and sights includes: Trinity College [→49]; the National Museum of Ireland [→48]; the Natural History Museum [→53], the Heraldic Museum [→52] and Leinster House, home to the Irish Parliament [→46]. The area is also rich in art galleries – of note are the National Gallery; Douglas Hyde Gallery; RHA Gallagher Gallery; Ib Jorgensen Fine Art Gallery and the Kerlin Gallery [→56].

For more laid-back pursuits head for St Stephen's Green [→55], Merrion Square or the playing fields of Trinity College.

## night

Bar hopping will introduce the thirsty to new- and old-skools of Dublin publore while the gourmet will be challenged by the diversity of restaurants.

☆ After the bars close, there are a couple of clubs, but structured entertainment is thin on the ground.

Buses for this area operate along Kildare Street, Dawson Street and Merrion Square.

Taxi ranks are locataed on Dawson Street, College Green and St Stephen's Green West and North.

The DART operates from nearby Pearse station to the coastal towns [→34–37].

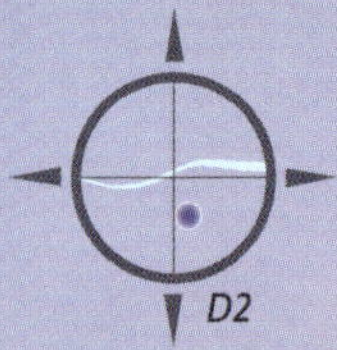


# shopping

### *fashion & accessories*

Serious wallet-emptying territory comes in the form of ***Alias Tom**, whose cutting-edge men's fashion means you may be queueing for the changing rooms with the likes of Boyzone and Aidan Quinn. True label lovers go mad in ***BT2**. The beat of thumping soundtracks means its exclusive stock of unisex sportswear (think Tommy Hilfiger, Prada Sport and Calvin Klein jeans) often plays second fiddle to the posing by Dublin's teen population. Meanwhile ***O'Connors** keeps it simple with piles of denim and affordable streetwear. Keeping an eye fixed on European and international labels, ***Michael Barrie** lures the guys with its huge choice of suits and casual wear. For a store with impeccable service, stop by the 50-year-old ***FX Kelly**, which sells sophisticated tailoring and casual gear. For another generous helping of old-fashioned service and conservative understated dressing, make a beeline for **Kennedy & McSharry** or **Kevin Howlin**. But if Italian style is your aim, ***Massimo** stock a well-cool selection of smart separates. More relaxed in approach ***Monaghans**' fine cashmere sweaters fill the shelves along with sportswear labels. For shirts, head for the internationally-renowned ***Thomas Pink** ↗ where luxurious silk ties nestle alongside a rainbow of shirts. If you still cannot find the perfect shirt, ***The Custom Store**'s made-to-measure service will produce your own creation.

For women whose tastes are more classy lady than Sporty Spice, ***Pia Bang** offers smart French and Danish tailoring at keen prices. More cutting edge is ***Platform**, tiny but brilliantly stocked with some unusual Belgian designs. European labels fill the rails in ***Airwave**, a casualwear mecca for men and women. And for something slinky try ***Fogal**, a well-priced lingerie shop, whose window displays never fail to raise an eyebrow. Or drop in to ***Cocoon**, home to even more drop-dead-gorgeous lingerie with equally hedonistic prices. For the essential shades, ***Optica** namechecks all the usual labels as well as a few gems fashion victims won't yet have set eyes on.

The ***Kilkenny Shop** and **Blarney Woollen Mills** both offer a good overview of Irish style. Choose between a ruffled John Rocha dress, a Magee three-piece tweed suit or some homeware at the former, or from contemporary Fishermen out of Ireland knitwear to a trad oak walking-stick at the latter. Another Irish lifestyle shop is the **Dalkey Design Company** which sells an unusual range of knitwear, jewellery and linen. Trad Irish jewellery designs reign in the ***National Museum Shop**.

### *books*

Whether you're a first-edition collector, a comic book connoisseur, a design-bible fiend or a murder-mystery addict, the bookshops here will offer hours of blissful browsing. Bargain-hunters stock up at ***Greene's**; Irish literature fans at ***Hodges Figgis**; and detective-story lovers at ***Murder Ink**. For bestsellers, go to ***Waterstone's**; for special editions from leading Irish writers, ***Cathach Books** is the place.

### *interiors*

This area is awash with outlets catering to the current obsession of home-styling. Antique-lovers will find it hard to prise themselves away from the irresistible treasures in ***Anthony Antiques**, but should leave time for ***H Danker**, an affordable antique silver store. Ceramics collectors will find a second home in ***Louis Mulcahy**'s studio while the ***The Natural Interior** brings shoppers back to (grass) roots with its stylish natural floor-covering and fabrics. Once inside the cool glass portals of ***Minima**, on the other hand, you'll easily succumb to the modern look with lashings of designer chrome, glass and leather. Easier on the wallet, **Habitat** is an unmissable port of call for bright and fun home accessories.



# eating & drinking

more restaurants | pubs, bars & clubs | directory & map

### *restaurants*

This part of town is probably the most eclectic in terms of eating out. You can go from the formal but gastronomically dizzying peaks of ***Restaurant Patrick Guilbaud** [→87], with its two Michelin stars, to the friendly pasta-and-a-glass of wine ***Unicorn** [→89] within a few hundred metres. The former, considered by many to be Dublin's best restaurant, turns out consistently brilliant dishes while the Unicorn has earned a reputation on its infectious atmosphere.

Very much a product of Conrad Gallagher's new-age kitchen, ***Lloyd's Brasserie** ✓[→82] is the young turk's basement restaurant and piano bar which dishes up beautiful fresh things to Dublin's beautiful young things round the clock. Winning in the cool stakes is ***Jacob's Ladder** [→83], which sustains its reputation as one of the city's trendiest dining spots. Situated overlooking Trinity College's sports fields, it caused a stir on opening with an inventive, radical approach to food from a very driven chef. Another sheer delight is ***L'Ecrivain** [→87] which tempts demanding foodies

(who don't take themselves too seriously), with the best in contemporary hiberno-nosh. The menu isn't all that comes with an Irish accent – walls are covered in local art and the genteel dining room takes its inspiration from traditional Georgian parlours.

The **Shelbourne Hotel** used to be a byword for beige food at astronomical prices, but all has changed utterly. It's still pricey, but the food, particularly seafood, is first class. The view of St Stephen's Green is a dream, and this is the best place to power-breakfast in Dublin. For a more contemporary approach, also in the hotel, ***The Side Door** [→82] has everything from designer-fish-and-chips to Mediterranean risotto. Staff are young and the decor is job-lot Alessi.

**Ayumi-Ya Japanese Steakhouse** offers healthy portions, attentive service, an extensive menu for lovers of raw and cooked food, and an authentic atmosphere. Also thriving on good, unpretentious grub, a laid-back feel and unexacting prices is ***La Cave** [→82].

A small elderly French bistro with attitude that stays open late when it gains in popularity and lessens in sobriety. Alternatively, staple French classics in a more sedate atmosphere are *plat du jour* in the moderately-priced **La Mère Zou**.

If you're after the sassiest selection of must-eat pizzas in town, along with a bit of a buzz, decent wine and infamous cheesecake then the ***Gotham Café** [→82] scores highly. A hip, speedy and good-value pit stop with plenty of imagination. The *Rolling Stone* magazine covers all over the walls and makes for effective and economic interior design. Atavistic appetites craving something a little more juicy will be drawn to **FXB**. The meat is as good as it gets, expertly hung and perfectly sizzled. Chips and onions are spot on, and what more could you want but a bottle of something big and red? It may not be haute cuisine, but many would say it's better. Hearty, chunky, traditional home-style food is the order of the day at ***The Pembroke** [→88], a confident, clubby restaurant oozing coziness.

## *cafés*

***Café Java** [→91] by name and, by gum, it's Java to the gills. A brilliant stop-off, it gets full at lunchtime, so catch the morning slot for great breakfasts (or the afternoon lull for top coffee). The ***Shelbourne Hotel** [→91] is the place for historic teas – lashings of tea or coffee, big plates of dainty sandwiches and loads of fancy sweet nibbles – treat yourself and join the ladies-who-lunch and are still peckish at 3.30pm. Alternatively, graze on grub while gazing over Grafton Street from the swanky **BT2** café, or **Hodges Figgis** café – ideal if you're in need of some coffee to help the book-buying decision. The two cafés in the **Kilkenny Shop** may be old-skool but if this means big, wholesome, tasty, homemade portions, who's complaining?

## *pubs, bars & clubs*

***Kehoe's** gets packed at night with the cream of the city's arty intelligentsia, real and imagined. The beautifully-preserved main bar is an authentic slice of 50's Dublin. ***Toner's** fetching Victorian interior is arguably an even greater national treasure. Lined with ancient bric-a-brac, it recalls a sepia-tinted age when all pubs were seductively dim and cluttered. While few Dubliners are bowled over by ***O'Donoghue's** authenticity, it passes nicely for The Real Thing for its droves of visitors. The lane at the back brazens it out as a beer garden during the summer: the Guinness is good and the party spirit is stoked by musicians filling the shoes of the legendary Dubliners folk group.

With Ireland's Parliament, (the Dáil), located on Kildare Street this area is the spiritual heartland of the upwardly mobile – and many of the pubs cater accordingly. ***Doheny & Nesbitt** has long been a hotbed of high-powered wheeler-dealering and scandal-mongering, but for a more memorable experience, try the ***Dawson Lounge**, a pub so petite and discreet it's hardly there at all. It serves good Guinness and doubles as a sauna at peak times. Those craving wide open spaces need look no further than ***Café en Seine**,✔ a continental-style bar notable for the cacophony of warbling mobile phones. The myriad mirrors no doubt contribute to its popularity with a youngish self-regarding set. Conspicuous consumption is also very much *plat du jour* at ***The Pembroke**. Extensively refurbished, it gleefully flaunts its new trappings – glass ceiling, ornamental spreading vine, imposing bar edifice. However, **The Bailey**'s recent facelift has left it looking like a set from the kitsch 60's space flick *Barbarella*. The decor will strike some as a tasteless joke, but the wall-to-wall beautiful people aren't deterred. Beauties are conspicuously absent from neighbouring **The Duke**, an anti-fashion pub with a down-to-earth clientele.

Dublin's frilliest nightclub is the aptly-named ***Lillie's Bordello** [→98], haunt of international megastars and the Svengalis behind them. Admission to the inner sanctum, The Library, is guarded like Fort Knox to all but visiting starlets, but if you're sober and dressed up, getting in to the rest of the club shouldn't pose a problem. Big and bustling,

*Renard's [→99] offers a great line in late jazz, and a popular club in the basement. Upstairs is more salubrious and stays open late. Hipsters hang out at the **Altar** where the music is superb and entrance is free (except Sat). Meanwhile ***Republica** [→99], with its fish tanks and minimal steel bars, aims for a trendy crowd and gets the young guns out on-the-town.

# directory D2

**Airwave** A1
36 Grafton Street
679 8374

**Alias Tom** A1
Duke Hse, Duke Lane
671 5443

**Altar** C3
22 Ely Place

**Anthony Antiques** B1
7–9 Molesworth St
677 7222

**Ayumi-Ya Japanese Steakhouse** C3
132 Baggot Street Lwr
662 0233 ££

**The Dailey** A1
2 Duke Street

**Blarney Woollen Mills** B1
21–23 Nassau Street
671 0068

**BT2** A1
28–29 Grafton Street
605 6666 £

**Café en Seine** B1
40 Dawson Street
677 4369

**Café Java** A1
5 Anne Street South
670 7239 £

**Cathach Books** B1
10 Duke Street
671 8676

**La Cave** B1
28 Anne Street South
679 4409 ££

**Cocoon** A1
26 Royal Hibernian Way
679 5916

**The Custom Store** A1
20 Royal Hibernian Way
677 4086

**Dalkey Design Company** A1
21 Anne Street South
672 8015

**Dawson Lounge** B2
25 Dawson Street
677 5909

**Doheny & Nesbitt** C3
5 Baggot Street Lwr
676 2945

**The Duke** B1
9 Duke Street
679 9553

**L'Ecrivain** C3
112 Baggot Street Lwr
661 1919 £££

**Fogal** A1
19 Creation Arcade
677 4525

**FXB** C3
1a Pembroke Street Lwr
676 4606 ££

**FX Kelly** A2
48 Grafton Street
677 8211

**Gotham Café** A1
8 Anne Street South
679 5266 £–££

**Greene's** C1
16 Clare Street
676 2554

**Habitat** A2
7 St Stephen's Gr N
677 1433

**H Danker** A1
10 Anne Street South
677 4009

**Hodges Figgis** B1
57 Dawson Street
677 4754 £

**Jacob's Ladder** B1
4–5 Nassau Street
670 3865 ££–£££

**Kehoe's** A1
9 Anne Street South
677 8312

**Kennedy & McSharry** B1
39 Nassau Street
677 8770

**Kevin Howlin** B1
31 Nassau Street
677 0257

**Kilkenny Shop** B1
5–6 Nassau Street
677 7066 £–££

**Lillie's Bordello** A1
Adam Court, Grafton St
679 9204

**Lloyd's Brasserie** C2
20 Merrion St Upper
662 7240 ££–£££

**Louis Mulcahy** B1
51c Dawson Street
670 9311

**Massimo** A1
1 Creation Arcade
670 5227

**La Mère Zou** B2
22 St Stephen's Gr N
661 6669 ££

**Michael Barrie** A1
20 Duke Street
671 5265

**Minima** B2
35–38 St Stephen's Green North
662 7894

**Monaghans** A1
2 Royal Hibernian Way
679 4451

**Murder Ink** B1
15 Dawson Street
677 7570

**National Museum Shop** B2
Kildare Street
677 7444

**The Natural Interior** B1
46 Dawson Street
677 1666

**O'Connors** A1
23 Grafton Street
677 1763

**O'Donoghue's** C3
15 Merrion Row
676 2807

**Optica** A1
1 Royal Hibernian Way
677 4705

**The Pembroke** C3
31 Pembroke St Lower
662 2534 ££

**Pia Bang** A2
46 Grafton Street
671 5065

**Platform** A1
8 Duke Lane
677 7380

**Renard's** B1
35 Frederick St South
677 5876

**Republica** B1
Earl of Kildare Hotel
Kildare Street
679 4388

**Restaurant Patrick Guilbaud** C2
Merrion Hotel
21 Merrion St Upper
676 4192 £££

**Shelbourne Hotel** B2
27 St Stephen's Gr N
676 6471 ££–£££

**The Side Door** B2
Shelbourne Hotel,
27 St Stephen's Gr N
676 6471 ££

**Thomas Pink** A2
29 Dawson Street
670 3647

**Toner's** C3
139 Baggot Street Lwr
676 3090

**Unicorn** C3
12b Merrion Court,
Merrion Row
662 4757 ££

**Waterstone's** B1
7 Dawson Street
679 1415

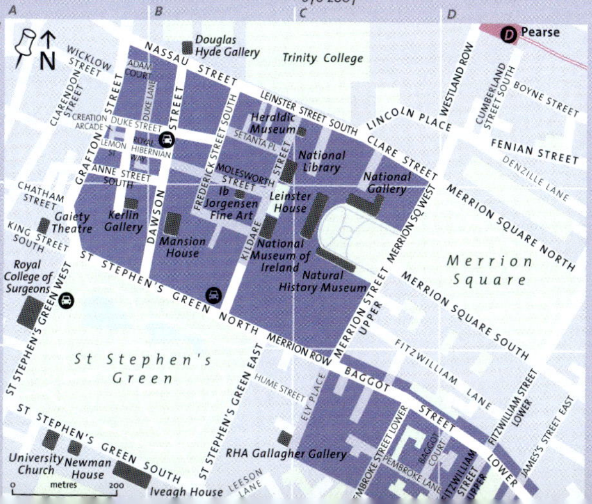

# magnetic north

North of the murky Liffey is a place where the pretensions and sophistication inherent in Dublin's southside seem a long way away. O'Connell Street, the city's main drag, may have more neon than Las Vegas, and may also at times resemble a convention of burger salesmen, but this area is undergoing a sea of change. The regeneration, which is spreading from the Financial Services District in the east to Smithfields in the west, is luring southsiders across the Liffey for a slice of the action. And, with the millennium looming, the area will see the construction of a towering steel spike (popularly nicknamed the Stiletto in the Ghetto) which will dominate Dublin's skyline, beaming light over the city.

And yet, the streets continue to chime with the old. The market, chaotic shops, old-world pubs and the GPO [→47] are all indelibly part of the fabric of the area. North of the river, they don't believe in throwing out the old to make room for the new because there's room and time for both.

## day

Moore Street Market [→77], high-street chain stores and a pile of bargain-basement shops are packed with shoppers from 10am.

More leisurely pursuits include the Hugh Lane Municipal Gallery of Modern Art [→56], Dublin Writers Museum [→50], James Joyce Centre [→50] or the Old Jameson Distillery [→51].

## night

Burger joints galore with a sprinkling of good restaurants and cafés. A mix of charming old pubs, Early Houses and late-night bars ensure nightlife in this area is on the up.

☆ The city's largest theatres, the Gate and Abbey, are firmly rooted on northern soil, along with the Peacock [→105]. New blockbuster films are shown at The Savoy and Virgin Multiplex [→104].

Bus termini and pick up points are dotted all over the area [→back cover].

There are three taxi ranks on or just off O'Connell, one on Eden Quay and one on Capel Street.

D1

# shopping

Shopping in this grittier part of town offers a truly authentic Dublin experience. ***Moore Street Market** ✔ is alive with fruit & veg sellers, cheeky 'real designer' stallholders, and pram-wielding peddlers flogging ciggies and bumper bars of chocolate. Some of the vendors have pitched their stalls here for over four generations. Seamlessly adding to the cacophony of market sounds are the thumping tunes of the area's discount music stores. Of note are ***Freebird Records** for the biggest stock of CDs at knockdown prices, and ***Abbey Discs** for bumper-to-bumper nirvana and the best house/techno tracks in the city. Worth a trawl is ***Eason's** bookshop, a well-known landmark chock full of gems from obscure Italian fashion mags to tubes of glitter glue. Next up is **Chapters**, piled high from floor to ceiling with a huge range of secondhand books.

Capel Street is home to two of the city's best-known sex shops. Upfront and in your face, the goodies in both branches of **Utopia** leave little to the imagination. On the same street, but somewhat different, ***Louis Copeland** is a distinguished menswear emporium. It carries the largest selection of suits in the country and has been going strong for nearly a century. Mainstream shopping for the masses – no polished floors or discreet service here – comes in the way of the Jervis Shopping Centre. Housing 40 or so shops including a clutch of British chains, this complex lures the city's spenders. Many head straight for **Debenhams**, the British department store which has so successfully allied designer flair with high-street appeal and prices. Nearby ***Arnott**, Ireland's oldest department store, is now set to compete. Once renowned for its steady, middle-of-the-road reputation, it has leapt fearlessly into the future with a sleek new extension and a complete overhaul of stock.

**Lime & Lemongrass**, housed in a converted abbey, manufacture on site and sell a range of sauces, oils and marinades as well as delicious pestos, pastas and cheeses. Eyecatching treats for the home come in the form of ***Solo**, an unusual, one-off furniture shop offering interesting modern ethnic pieces from Asia and New Zealand.



# eating & drinking

## *restaurants & cafés*

O'Connell Street may be a shrine to fast food, where McDonald's marks the high tide of culinary ambitions, but there are some scattered outbreaks of excellence. ***101 Talbot** [→82] is a sheer joy if you like chunky, uncomplicated, but mildly funky food served in functional surroundings. ***Chapter One** [→88], in the Dublin Writers Museum [→50], has pretensions to grandeur, and while the food is good in a modern classic way, the overall feel is slightly twee. This is a haunt of businessmen, lured by posh food (and valet parking) in an unlikely part of town. In stark contrast is the ***Bangkok Café** [→85], a rather dingy little joint serving feisty Thai classics at knockdown prices. Go early and pray to get a table. It's an unlikely fashionable nosh spot for media types and off-duty chefs. For ethnic spice in sleek John Rocha-designed surroundings, the new **Morrison Hotel** [→113] promises Asian fusion in the more formal Halo restaurant and oriental cuisine in Lobo, which has a clubby late-night bar.

Lunch at the **Winding Stair** [→91] may not stretch to much beyond soup and sandwiches, but it's all prepared with spanking fresh ingredients and plenty of tender loving care. Its main business is a second-hand bookshop, making it ideal for a bohemian literary lunch. Another spot for a leisurely lunch, or coffee, is the **Cobalt Café**, a calm oasis with subtle decor, a mellow ambience, roaring fires and a neighbourly atmosphere.

Department stores like **Clery's** have grown wise to the lure of the coffee-bean, and their rooftop cafés (including an art deco tea room) provide excellent city-wide views to match the expansive range of beverages. History oozes from the walls of the **Gresham Hotel** [→114] which seems to appeal to caffeine-quaffers who clutter the lounge with their shopping bags. **Café Aroma** and **Bewley's** offer other havens for harassed shoppers needing a refuel. Aroma has good soups and sandwiches, while Bewley's does everything from its trademark cherry log to the perennial French fry. For a truly authentic Italian café, ***Panem** [→91] is unbeatable. Strong coffee, fine sandwiches and irresistible chocolate biscuit cake mark this one as a favourite.

## *pubs & bars*

The cluster of streets around the north quays were traditionally given a wide berth by glamour-seekers, but a frenzy of redevelopment is fast changing all that.

Three hip northside hangouts with dramatic spaces, late licences and DJ's lure revellers in droves. No Dublin dive matches ***Zanzibar** ▲ in terms of sheer opulence and exoticism. Overlooked by lofty mezzanine balconies, the main floor resembles a bustling Arabian bazaar, hemmed in by twisting columns, drooping palms and giant urns. More modest in scale, neighbouring ***Pravda** retails tongue-in-cheek Soviet nostalgia, exotic beers and a variety of vodkas. Meanwhile, if slick Scandinavian

more pubs & bars | directory & map

is more your scene, look no further than ***Life**.

The friendly crowd at ***Keating's** spans several generations, though at weekends the young northside-set tend to take over. Dominated by an ornate winding staircase, this is a music pub where new money hasn't yet taken hold. The old clientele hang on with rather more determination at the **Bachelor Inn**. This sleepy stronghold of middle-aged males eager for conversation represents a remnant of a disappearing Dublin. The pulse-rate speeds up at the **Oval Bar**, a compact wooden pub, immensely popular with all sorts. Even more compact is ***Out on the Liffey**, a cramped and unpretentious no-frills gay bar, unlikely to find favour with glamour queens. ***Conway's** is an old-fashioned friendly local which has been serving Dubliners for 250 years. This is pub perfection itself, and an epidemic of overhanging beer-guts bears testament to the quality of Guinness.

There are several Early Houses in the vicinity, open at 7am on weekdays to service workers at the local fish and fruit markets. Low-key and dimly lit, the first hour witnesses a reverential hush as the (mostly male) drinkers slowly ease their way in to the day. The ***Chancery Inn** is at its best as dawn lights up its long hall, while the **Boar's Head** is a surreal slice of 40's rural Ireland. Resembling a rickety farmhouse parlour, **Hughes** is popular with bin men and barristers alike. Arguably the busiest Early House is ***Slattery's**, which draws a crowd of ordinary Dubliners by day, live music fans by night and a loyal gay gathering every Monday.

## *directory* D1

**Abbey Discs** C3
21 Liffey Street Lower
873 3733

**Arnott** C2
12 Henry Street
805 0400

**Bachelor Inn** C3
31 Bachelor's Walk
873 1238

**Bangkok Café** C1
106 Parnell Street
878 6618 £

**Bewley's** B2
40 Mary Street
677 6761 £–££

**Boar's Head** B3
149 Capel Street
873 2294

**Café Aroma** C2
GPO Arcade, Henry St
873 3072 £

**Chancery Inn** A3
1 Inns Quay
677 0420

**Chapters** C3
108 Abbey St Middle
872 3297

**Chapter One** C1
18 Parnell Sq North
873 2266 £££

**Clery's** C2
18 O'Connell St Lower
878 6000 £

**Cobalt Café** C1
16 North Great George's Street
873 0313 ££

**Conway's** C2
70 Parnell Street
873 2687

**Debenhams** B3
Jervis Shopping Centre
878 1222

**Eason's** C2
40 O'Connell St Lower
873 3811

**Freebird Records** C3
1 Eden Quay
873 1250

**Gresham Hotel** C2
O'Connell St Upper
874 6881 ££

**Hughes** A3
19 Chancery Street
872 6540

**Keating's** B3
9–10 Jervis Street
872 4031

**Life** D2
Irish Life Mall, Abbey Street Lower
872 4031

**Lime & Lemongrass** B3
2–3 Mary's Abbey
872 2965

**Louis Copeland** B3
39 Capel Street
872 1600

**Morrison Hotel** B3
Ormond Quay Lower
878 2999 ££

**101 Talbot** D2
101 Talbot Street
874 5011 £–££

**Out on the Liffey** B3
27 Ormond Quay Upper
872 2480

**Oval Bar** C3
78 Abbey St Middle
872 1259

**Panem** B3
20 Ormond Quay Lwr
873 3293 £

**Pravda** C3
2–3 Liffey Street Lwr
874 0090

**Slattery's** B3
129 Capel Street
872 7971

**Solo** B2
135 Capel Street
872 1052

**Utopia** B3
164 Capel Street
872 9045

**Winding Stair** B3
40 Ormond Quay Lwr
873 3292 £

**Zanzibar** B3
37 Ormond Quay Lwr
878 7212

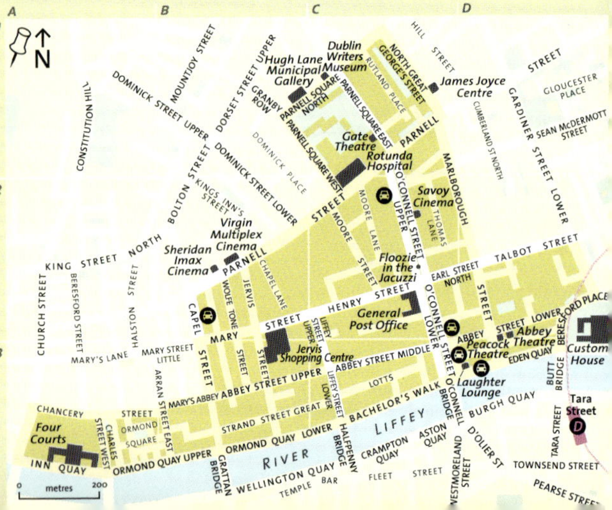

# sound of the south



With the early-morning fruit and veg market, the idiosyncratic shops and the cream of the city's live music venues and clubs in situ, Camden and Wexford streets reverberate with activity all day long and well into the night...

This vibrant and rumbustious area has become a potent fusion of old skool and upwardly mobile Dublin. Alongside the numerous traditional establishments are a new wave of trendy young businesses, such as Whelan's and the PoD,▲ which create a truly cosmopolitan environment.

Houses, which were once pretty working class, are now worth a cool quarter of a million, and are filled with affluent young sorts who live alongside auld Dubs. The repopulation, and the consequent contradictions of the goings-on, have brought a new energy to the area, but the raffish, if somewhat down-at-heel, charm remains firmly intact.

## day

Not a shoppers' haven, but some unusual, quirky stores and a fruit and veg market make it worth a browse.

St Stephen's Green [→55] and the Grand Canal [→55] offer some peace and quiet close by. Shaw's Birthplace [→50] is in the area and the Irish Jewish Museum [→52] nearby.

## night

Early evening revolves around buzzy bars, live music venues, and a few good local and upmarket restaurants.

☆ This is Dublin's late-night zone and there is no such thing as a quiet night here. Late clubs, music venues and eateries guarantee a full-on bustle into the small hours.

Bus Nos: 16, 16a, 19, 19a, 83, 121, 122 & 155 operate along Camden Street to and from the city centre.

There is no taxi rank, but taxis can usually be found on the street before midnight. Alternatively book one from Camden Cabs ☎ 475 4000.

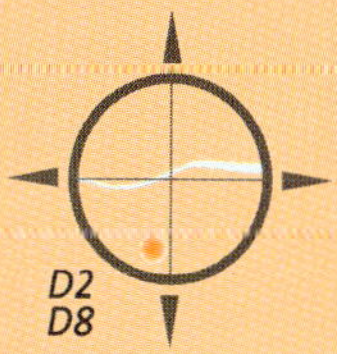


# shopping

more shopping | restaurants | bars | clubs | map & directory

Home to a diverse population of merchants, Camden Street offers some treasures to be unearthed beyond the ubiquitous butchers and the pound shops. A clutch of charity shops at the top end of Camden Street give way to more specialist outlets such as **Daintree** which lures stationery-lovers with funky paper from every corner of the globe. Nearby, one of the city's new-skool florists, **Tiger Lily**, sells a different bunch of carnations to the norm, and is the next best thing to a Monet watercolour.

The tiny **Robinsons Trading Store** is a veritable Aladdin's cave full of household bric-a-brac, including gold and stucco cherubs, beehive glasses, candles and plates. For antiques, **Renaissance** ▲ is also worth a look, though the stock tends to be functional rather than collectable. Nearby, master potter Marianne Klopp can be seen in action at **Camden**

**Crafts**, a showcase for her appealing blue and green, glazed creations.

Hunger attracts many Dubliners to the **Bretzel**, where the Sunday morning queue for fresh bagels, sweet treats and rye bread can snake all the way down the street. Fruit and veg requirements can be taken care of by the army of stallholders who hold court on Camden Street, hawking dirt-cheap produce and wordly views on the day's weather.

**Supper's Ready** is a wee deli with a classy take-away menu and top-class service. For wine or beer to accompany your repast, head for **Carvill's** off-licence, where the choice can be intoxicating in itself.

The conversion of the railway building into a hopping night-time zone epitomizes new-meets-old Dublin.

# eating & drinking

## *restaurants & cafés*

While this is not one of the city's grand gourmet centres, there are still a few must-eats in the sea of greasy chippers, especially if you're prepared to go a little further. Indeed, if there is money jangling in your pocket, give your belly a treat and head to ***Thorntons**, where Kevin Thornton serves up magical food in a beautiful canal-side setting. The dishes (lip-smacking international with a very Irish twist) can do no wrong as the satisfied purrs of happy eaters bear testament. Up the block lies **Locks**,✓ an old-fashioned dining room with a posh clientele tucking into large plates of no-nonsense nosh and relishing the upmarket ambience.

Back at street level, **Bucci** is the cosy Italian eatery every neighbourhood needs. Comfortable rather than cutting-edge, its healthy servings of unpretentious pastas and pizzas hit the spot. Equally unpretentious, but more dazzling in terms of cuisine is ***Kapriol**, one of Dublin's oldest Italianos. Cosy, wooden booths make for secluded dining while the tome of a menu makes choosing a lengthy process – an equally ambitious wine list makes for equally lengthy decision-making.

Chilli cravings can be kept at bay by the creations of ***Saagar** [→86]; or at **Pad Thai**, one of the few Thai gaffs in town, where trendy decor and fine food attract a succession of smart, sussed and hip diners. **One Pico**, meanwhile, is where Eamon O'Reilly holds court, and his take on modern Irish cooking attracts people who know their grub and, more importantly, enjoy what he does with simple, plain ingredients.

During the day, the **Pig & Heifer** has the best sandwiches in the area. Huge walnut or rye bread doorsteps are just the beginning – little wonder there are queues here every lunchtime. If you are looking for a burger and milkshake, the chrome attractions of **Eddie Rockets** Yankee-style diner may take your fancy.

## *bars & pubs*

Drinking your way around is a grand way to get to know the locality. On a balmy summer evening head for the best garden in town at ***Dicey Reilly's**. Otherwise a top place to start or wind down (to 1.30am Thu & Fri), is the ***Bleeding Horse**; a pub with enough nooks and crannies for as many secret meetings or liaisons as you could wish for. **Cassidy's** and **Flannery's** are more traditional haunts. The former's claim to fame is as the pub where Bill Clinton had a pint when he visited in 95, while Flannery's is where hard-core drinkers take advantage of the late weekend licence.

Two examples of the super-pub class are within easy stumbling distance. The ***Chocolate Bar** (part of the PoD complex) looks as if it has been airlifted from Barcelona. A brill cocktail menu, comfy seats and a

surreal men's loo are just some of the attractions. ***Odeon**, a newcomer, located in the old train station ticket hall, is packed with happy after-workers, pre-club darlings and those keen to see and more importantly be seen.

## *music venues & clubs*

If it's singing and dancing you're after, you've come to the right place. Whelan's and the Mean Fiddler sit cheek-by-jowl, yet offer two quite different takes on live music. ***Whelan's**, recently snapped up for a cool 4.5 million, is a beautiful, atmospheric wooden oasis – the perfect setting for a most eclectic playlist. Indie, world music, folk, jazz, classical and the Cajun Kings – you name it, they've booked it. The ***Mean Fiddler** may resemble the lounge of a Sealink ferry, but it has a formidable reputation of past headliners such as Mercury Rev and Iggy Pop and many, many more. Both venues also operate late-night clubs, but the true clubbing mecca is at the other end of the street. The ***PoD**, one of the planet's finest night spots, is housed in a former train station and has changed the face of clubbing, setting standards in everything from sound and lighting to comfort and music policies. Upstairs, **Red Box**, a brilliantly adaptable space, hosts large-scale club events (international superstars Carl Cox, Darren Emerson and Cream are regular visitors) and major live gigs. If this superclub action gives you a hankering for more intimate surroundings, then there's always **Velvet**, a basement club with a burgeoning reputation for quality music and cutting-edge DJs.

## *directory* D2 & D8

**Bleeding Horse** *D3*
25 Camden St Upper
475 2705

**Bretzel** *C4*
1a Lennox Street
475 2724

**Bucci** *C2*
7 Camden St Lower
475 1020

**Camden Crafts** *C2*
23 Camden St Lower
478 0118

**Carvill's** *C2*
39 Camden St Lower
475 1791

**Cassidy's** *C2*
42 Camden St Lower
475 1429

**Chocolate Bar** *D2*
Old Railway Station, Hatch Street Upper
478 0225

**Daintree** *C2*
62b Pleasants Place
475 4641

**Dicey Reilly's** *D1*
Harcourt Hotel, 21 Harcourt Street
478 4066

**Eddie Rockets** *C1*
17 Wexford Street
875 2077

**Flannery's** *C2*
6 Camden St Lower
478 2238

**Kapriol** *C2*
45 Camden St Lower
475 1235 £££

**Locks** *A4*
1 Windsor Terrace
454 3391 £££

**Mean Fiddler** *C1*
26 Wexford Street
475 8555

**Odeon** *D2*
Old Railway Station, Harcourt Street
478 2088

**One Pico** *C2*
1 Camden St Upper
478 0307 £££

**Pad-Thai** *D4*
30 Richmond St South
475 5551 ££

**Pig & Heifer** *C2*
2 Charlotte Street
478 3182 £

**PoD** *D2*
Old Railway Station, Harcourt Street
478 0225

**Red Box** *D2*
Old Railway Station, Harcourt Street
478 0116

**Renaissance** *C2*
41 Camden St Lower
475 2461

**Robinsons Trading Store** *C1*
15a Wexford Street
475 2152

**Saagar** *D1*
16 Harcourt Street
475 5012 £–££

**Supper's Ready** *C2*
5 Pleasants Street
475 4556

**Thorntons** *B4*
1 Portobello Road
454 9067 £££

**Tiger Lily** *C2*
1 Grantham Street
475 8564

**Velvet** *D2*
Harcourt Hotel, 60 Harcourt Street
478 3677

**Whelan's** *C1*
25 Wexford Street
478 0766

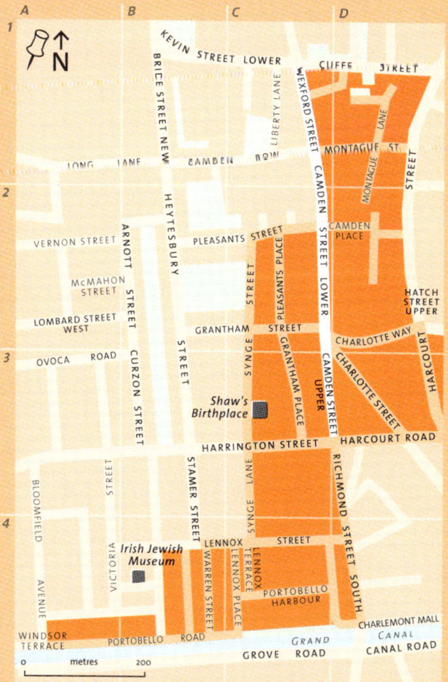

# around dublin

## transport options

**DART** ☎ 836 6222 £1.50–£2.50 return
Connolly, Tara Street and Pearse stations to all stops on the DART route as far as Howth in north and Bray in south. *10–25 min daily.*

**Iarnród Éireann** ☎ 836 6222 £2.50–£10.50 return
Connolly station to Drogheda (via Malahide); Connolly station to Rosslare Harbour (via Dun Laoghaire, Bray, Wicklow, Rathdrum, Arklow & Wexford) *phone for details.*

**44 (Dublin Bus)** ☎ 873 4222 £1.10–£2.50 return
Hawkins St to Enniskerry *8am–11pm hourly Mon–Sat (10am Sun).*

**St Kevin's Bus Service** ☎ 281 8119 £10 return
St Stephen's Green to Glendalough (via Bray, Kilmacanogue, Roundwood & Laragh) *11.30am departure daily.*

**Bus Éireann** ☎ 836 6111 £3.20–£9 return
Busaras to Arklow (No. 133 via Ashford, Wicklow & Rathdrum); Busaras to Cavan (via Dunshaughlin, Navan & Kells); Busaras to Granard (via Trim & Athboy); Busaras to Monaghan (via Slane) *phone for details.*

## sightseeing tours

**Bus Éireann** ☎ 836 6111 £14–£17
Full day tours from Busaras to Glendalough & Wicklow (Jan–Mar: Wed, Sat & Sun; Apr–Sep: daily); Glenroe, Avoca *(Ballykissangel)* & Wicklow Mountains (Jun–Sep: Sat); Newgrange & Boyne Valley (Feb–Apr & Oct–Nov: Thu & Sat; May–Sep: Mon–Thu, Sat & Sun); Russborough House & Powerscourt (Jun–Sep: Tue).

**Dublin Bus** ☎ 873 4222 £12
Half day South Coast tour from 59 O'Connell Street Upper to Blackrock, Dun Laoghaire, Killiney, Bray, Avoca Handweavers and Wicklow Mountains (daily).

**Gray Line Tours** ☎ 605 7705 £15.50–£27
Full and half day tours from Dublin Tourism Centre to Glendalough (Tue, Thu–Sun); Newgrange (Mon–Tue, Thu & Sat); Newgrange & Glendalough (Tue, Thu & Sat); Newgrange & Malahide (Mon); Powerscourt & Enniskerry (Mar–Oct: Wed).

**Mary Gibbons** ☎ 283 9973 £16
Half day tours from Dublin Tourism Centre to Newgrange (Mon, Wed & Fri); Wicklow Mountains (Tue, Thu, Sat & Sun).

**Railtours Ireland** ☎ 856 0045 £19
Combined train & bus half day tours from Connolly Station to Arklow, Avoca *(Ballykissangel)*, Bray, Rathdrum & Wicklow (Mon–Sat).

## directory

| | | |
|---|---|---|
| **Ashford** D5 | 🍴 ⚑ | |
| **Athboy** A2 | 🍴 | |
| **Avoca** C6 | 🛍 🍴 🍺 | |
| **Avondale Estate** C5 | 👁 | →38 |
| **Bettystown** C1 | ⚑ | |
| **Blackrock** C3 | 🛍 🍴 🍺 | →35 |
| **Bray** D4 | 🛍 🍴 ⚑ | →37 |
| **Brittas Bay** D6 | 🍺 | |
| **Blessington** B4 | 🍴 ⚑ | |
| **Blessington Lakes** B4 | 🍴 | |
| **Clontarf** C3 | | →35 |
| **Dalkey** D4 | 🛍 🍴 🍺 | →37 |
| **Donore** B1 | 🍺 | |
| **Drogheda** C1 | 🍺 | |
| **Duleek** B1 | 🔑 | |
| **Dun Laoghaire** D3 | 🛍 🍴 🍺 ⚑ | →36 |
| **Dunlavin** B5 | 🍴 🔑 | |
| **Enniskerry** C4 | 🛍 🍴 ⚑ 🔑 | |
| **Fairview** C3 | | →35 |
| **Glendalough** C5 | 👁 🛍 🍺 ⚑ | →38 |
| **Glenmalure** C5 | 🛍 | |
| **Howth** D3 | 🍴 🍺 | →34 |
| **Kells** A1 | 🛍 🍴 ⚑ | |
| **Killiney** D4 | | →37 |
| **Kilmacanogue** D4 | 🛍 ⚑ | |
| **Knowth** B1 | 👁 | →42 |
| **Laragh** C5 | 🍺 | |
| **Malahide** C3 | 👁 🛍 🍺 ⚑ | →34 |
| **Mornington** C1 | ⚑ | |
| **Mount Usher Gardens** D5 | 👁 | →38 |
| **Newgrange** B1 | 👁 | →42 |
| **Newtown Mount Kennedy** D5 | ⚑ | |
| **Navan** B1 | 🍴 ⚑ | |
| **Powerscourt House & Gardens** C4 | 👁 | →39 |
| **Proudstown** B1 | ⚑ | |
| **Rathnew** D5 | 🍴 🔑 | |
| **Ratoath** B2 | ⚑ | |
| **Roundwood** C5 | 🛍 🍴 🍺 | |
| **Russborough House** B4 | 👁 | →39 |
| **Sandycove** D3 | 👁 🛍 🍴 🍺 | →36 |
| **Sandymount** C3 | 👁 🛍 🍴 🍺 | →35 |
| **Shillelagh** B6 | ⚑ | |
| **Slane** B1 | 🛍 🍴 🍺 🔑 | |
| **Trim** A2 | 🛍 | |
| **Wicklow** D5 | 🍴 🍺 ⚑ | |

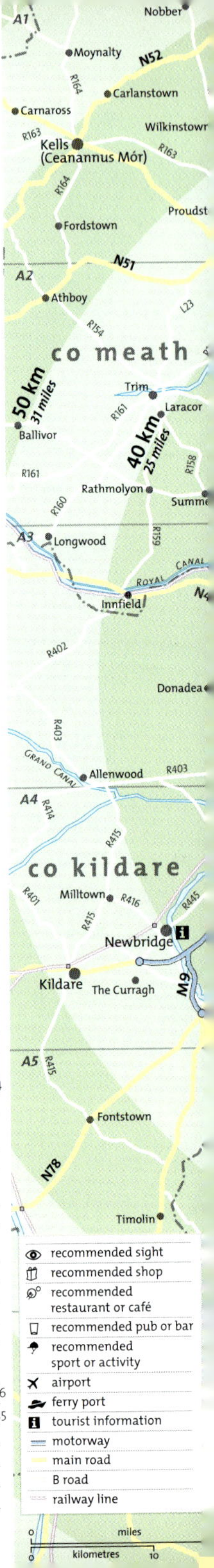

N
C1
D1
co louth
Clogherhead
Collon
Ballymakenny
N2
Drogheda
Valley
Boyne
Mornington
Slane
Newgrange
Knowth
River Boyne
Brú na Bóinne Visitors' Centre
Donore
Bettystown
Laytown
Julianstown
Duleek
IRISH SEA
C2
D2
Stamullin
Balrath
Ardcath
Balbriggan
Bellinter
Clonalvy
Naul
Balrothery
Skerries
N3
Garristown
N1
Lusk
Rush
Ballyboghil
Dunshaughlin
Ratoath
Ashbourne
Lambay Island
co dublin
Donabate
Swords
Malahide
Mullagh
20 km
12 miles
C3
D3
Dublin Airport
Portmarnock
Clonee
Dunboyne
M50
M1
Balgriffin
Baldoyle
Kilcock
Mulhuddart
Kilmore
Howth
Ballymun
Clonsilla
Corduff
Sutton
Lion's Head
Maynooth
Royal Canal
Whitehall
Dollymount Strand
Leixlip
Clontarf
M4
Lucan
Cabra
Fairview
N4
dublin
Dublin Bay
Clondalkin
Sandymount
Celbridge
Grand Canal
Walkinstown
Blackrock
River Liffey
Newcastle
Dun Laoghaire
Tallaght
Sandycove
Rathcoole
Saggart
N81
Dundrum
Stillorgan
C4
D4
Dalkey
Oldbawn
Sandford
Killiney
N7
co dublin
N11
Brittas
Killiney Bay
Kilteel
M11
Naas
Bray
Kilbride
Enniskerry
Kilmacanogue
Blessington
Powerscourt House & Gardens
Russborough House
Poulaphouca Reservoir
Greystones
wicklow mountains
Delgany
Ballymore Eustace
Blessington Lakes
Mullaghcleevaun 850m
Newtown Mount Kennedy
C5
D5
Hollywood
Wicklow Mountains National Park
N162
Newcastle
Roundwood
N81
Glenmacnass
Tonelagee 819m
Mount Usher Gardens
Ashford
Glendalough
Laragh
Rathnew
Glenmalure
Wicklow
Stratford
Lugnaquilla Mountain 926m
Glenealy
Wicklow Head
co wicklow
Rathdrum
Avondale Estate
Aghavannagh
C6
D6
Kiltegan
N11
Brittas Bay
Hacketstown
Aughrim
Avoca
Mizen Head
Clonmore
Woodenbridge
Arklow
Tinahely
co wexford
Shillelagh
Inch

# darting around

From Howth in the north to Bray in the south, Dublin's coastal satellites are chill-out areas for city dwellers and hideaways for the natives. DART [→6] there and back to catch spectacular views, recharge your batteries and experience another side to capital living. All along this gorgeous coastline, which ranges from Mediterranean-like stretches in the south to more rugged cliffs on the northside, lie some homely towns and villages. They're more than just pretty seaside stops – Howth and Dun Laoghaire are thriving settlements with largish populations and numerous attractions. Others like Dalkey are truly village-like where every well-heeled inhabitant knows what every other well-heeled inhabitant does – and to whom.

## *malahide*

*C3*

*suburban train (from Pearse station) to Malahide 32a, 42*

In this charming residential hub, which sometimes thinks it's still a village, there's **Malahide Castle** and the cute **Fry Model Railway Museum** [→54] to offer keen sightseers. The castle is quite spectacular – the oldest part of the building is the 12th-century tower, but there are also traces of various enhancements carried out by different owners through the centuries. Art buffs will relish the castle's large collection of portraits and Irish furniture; while the Fry Model Railway Museum is a must for anyone who wanted a toy train-set for Christmas but never got one. A cornucopia of delights, the museum details the Irish rail landscape down to the very last sleeper.

For a more nautical flavour, call at **Fingall Windsurfing** who'll provide tips on when to catch the next breaker and the equipment hire to do it. If your taste is more sartorial, head for the large mirrors and racks of top-ranking fashion at **Diffusion**. Meanwhile, wine connoisseurs and gourmets can indulge in a choice of over 300 wines, tasty grub or cool kitchen equipment in the **Dublin Wine Company**. And to kill that thirst which has inevitably built up, head to ***Gibney's**, one of the finest pubs on any side of the city, attracting locals and blow-ins alike; or **The Yacht**, where city slickers and ladies who lunch enjoy a glass or two.

**Diffusion**
47 Clontarf Road
☎ 833 1592

**Dublin Wine Company**
Main Street
☎ 845 6770 £–££

**Fingall Windsurfing**
Upper Strand
☎ 845 1979

**Gibney's**
New Street
☎ 845 0242

**Malahide Castle & Fry Model Railway Museum**
Malahide Castle Demesne
☎ 846 3779

**The Yacht**
73 Clontarf Road
☎ 833 8364 ££

## *howth*

*D3*

*to Howth 31, 31b*

A visit to Howth is not complete without a hike along the cliff path up Howth Head. The views ✔ from the summit are top-drawer, and make it worth the trek. To the east of the hilltop lies Ireland's Eye, a rocky island which sea birds (including puffins), rather than the monks of old, now call home. For some refuelling at the top, the ***Summit Inn** is a friendly place for a swift pint. Once safely back at sea-level, savour the best catches of the day from the busy harbour by booking a posh pew at **The King Sitric** – fishy delights in comfortable, cosy surroundings. Or, if it's still daylight, why not dine alfresco on fish and chips and watch the comings and goings of the marina? Watching over the activities are the ruins of Howth Castle which date from Norman times.

**The King Sitric**
East Pier
☎ 832 5235 £££

**Summit Inn**
Thormanby Road
☎ 832 4615

## fairview & clontarf

C3

*to Clontarf Road* *20a, 20b, 130 (to Fairview), 130 (to Clontarf)*

North of the city centre, Fairview is the first indication you've left the heart of the city behind. Opposite the large expanse of **Fairview Park** are a long strip of local shops. Just beyond Fairview is Clontarf, a mainly residential suburb with superb sea-views all along the Clontarf Road. Summer Sundays see this stretch chock-a-block with rollerbladers and cyclists who are heading to and from Howth. If that sounds too energetic, join the dippers at **Clontarf Baths**, a popular bathing spot half way along the Clontarf Road.

**Clontarf Baths**
Clontarf Road

**Fairview Park**
Fairview Strand

## sandymount

C3

*to Sandymount* *3*

Sandymount is the most village-like of all the coastal stops near the capital. Around the small, picturesque green, sample a quick hair-of-the-dog in the convivial **O'Reilly's** pub before buying a top-notch sarnie across the way in **Brownes Deli**. Then lazily saunter down to the 2-km-long strand of beach, munching as you go. A pair of sculptures marks the spot where Gertie Mac-Dowell, a passer-by, flashed her knickers to Leopold Bloom in Joyce's *Ulysses*.

It is possible to abandon the DART at this stage and walk south, following the sweeping line of the bay, past Strand Road and on to the next lively oasis, Blackrock. Alternatively, head back inland and explore what the still-regal spread of Ballsbridge has to offer. There's no shortage of great eating places here, with a coterie of high-class restaurants such as ***Roly's Bistro** [→88] and **Fitzers**, as well as many grand, impressive mansions such as the **Royal Dublin Society (RDS)**. One of the more fascinating and lesser known of the city's museums is the **National Print Museum** in the nearby Beggars Bush complex. Its collection of all sorts of printing presses and early computer prototypes beats looking at another roomful of old bones. It is also home to a brilliant café.

**Brownes Deli**
18 Sandymount Green
☎ 269 7316

**Fitzers**
RDS, Ballsbridge
☎ 667 1301 ££

**National Print Museum**
Garrisons Chapel, Beggars Bush, Haddington Road
☎ 660 3770

**O'Reilly's**
5 Seafort Avenue
☎ 668 3675

**Royal Dublin Society**
Ballsbridge
☎ 668 0866

**Roly's Bistro**
7 Ballsbridge Terrace
☎ 668 2611 ££

more coastal towns

## blackrock

C3

*to Blackrock* *7, 7a, 8, 45*

Blackrock's centre, slightly hidden off the main road, is something of a shoppers' paradise with a brace of shopping malls as well as scores more individual outlets. Aside from the bustling ***Blackrock Market** (weekends only), which is home to everything from junk to jewels, there are also a couple of upmarket outlets jostling for custom. **Khan** and **Dashiki** flog designer labels and exclusive lingerie respectively to monied ladies in extra-large cars. The price-tags are a sure indicator that this is the well-off side of town. Cool Italian and Swedish furniture and home accessories can be found at ***Enclosure**, while top-of-the-range Oriental and Turkish rugs are the speciality of ***Peter Linden**. For a bit more of a buzz, head to the very loud **Wicked Wolf** pub and join the young crowd for an all-day breakfast (and a pint); or check out the excellent branch of ***Aymui-Ya** [→85] for full-on Japanese food or a packed *bento* box to take away. And then there's the best espresso in the town to savour in ***Café Java** [→91].

**Aymui-Ya**
Newpark Centre
Newtownpark Avenue
☎ 283 1767 ££–£££

more directory [→36]

**Blackrock Market**
19a Main Street
☎ 283 3522

**Dashiki**
8 Rock Hill
☎ 283 4505

**Enclosure**
8 Main Street
☎ 283 6310

**Café Java**
Main Street
☎ 278 1571 £

**Khan**
1 Rock Hill
☎ 278 1646

**Peter Linden**
George's Avenue
☎ 288 5875

**Wicked Wolf**
2 Main Street
☎ 283 6424 £

posh cakes and Earl Grey, or to **Teddy's Ice Cream Parlour** for yummy ice-cream. If that's not substantial enough, the spruce **Brasserie Na Mara** ➚ has clever, smartly mod cooking; or the excellent **Purty Kitchen,** a short stroll away, serves some of the best seafood dishes in the county from lunchtime until late.

The town is also home to some classy shops. ***Crate & Barrel** is full of great modern classic furniture, while **SWALK** has all the cards, pencils and notebooks you could ever need.

## *dun laoghaire*

*D3*

*Ⓓ to Dun Laoghaire 🚌 7, 7a, 8, 46a*

The ever bustling harbour of Dun Laoghaire (pronounced Dun Leary) has been refurbished in recent years and the space-age ferry depot and mini marina of yachts are certainly an improvement on the grimy days of old when most England-bound emigrants were happy to say farewell before taking the boat to Holyhead. The piers that circle the harbour are chocka at weekends, with strollers inhaling the bracing sea air. This may not placate the more adventurous, so the **Dublin Bay Sea Thrill** [→60] is ideal – 40 minutes on a high-speed boat. When tiredness sets in, head to the old-world tea-rooms of the **Royal Marine Hotel** for

**Brasserie Na Mara**
1 Harbour Road
☎ 280 6767 £–££

**Crate & Barrel**
56–57 George Street Upper
☎ 280 5965

**Dublin Bay Sea Thrill**
Carlisle Terminal, East Wall
☎ 260 0949

**Purty Kitchen**
Old Dunleary Road
☎ 284 3576 £–££

**Royal Marine Hotel**
Marine Road
☎ 280 1911 £–££

**SWALK**
Unit 213b, DunLaoghaire Shopping Centre
☎ 280 3709

**Teddy's Ice Cream Parlour**
1a Windsor Terrace
☎ 284 5128

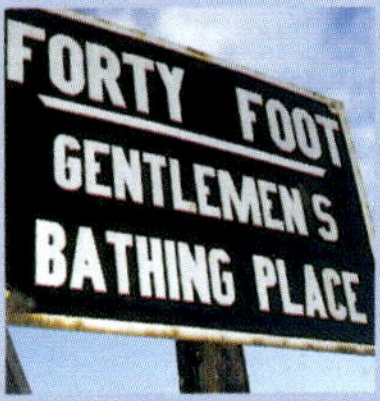


## *sandycove*

*D3*

*Ⓓ to Sandycove 🚌 7, 7a, 8, 46a*

A short walk away from Dun Laoghaire is Sandycove and the Forty Foot, ✔ an infamous bathing pool that used to be a male-only nude dipping spot. These days everyone is welcome to splash in, and it has become a popular spot for Christmas day swims. Overlooking the water sports is the **James Joyce Museum** [→50], in the Martello tower which James Joyce called home for a week.

Sandycove's real find is the excellent **Stage Two**, a secondhand fashion emporium stocking snazzy designer labels alongside more common names. Treats for the house come in the form of ***Reverie**, an intriguing interiors shop with new and old furniture and gifts from France. Indulge further with treats for the body at **Bliss**, an ultra-modern flounce-free beauty parlour specializing in massage. Those with the munchies are in luck if ***Caviston's** [→84] deli is open – select from all manner of gourmet delights or, in fine weather, sit outside and choose from their tantalizing seafood menu.

**Bliss**
30 Sandycove Road
☎ 280 8345

**Caviston's**
59 Glasthule Road
☎ 280 9120 £–££

**James Joyce Tower**
Joyce Tower
☎ 280 9265

**Reverie**
19 Sandycove Road
☎ 284 4123

**Stage Two**
67a Glasthule Road
☎ 280 8117

## *dalkey & killiney*

D4

*to Dalkey or Killiney* · *8 to Dalkey*

Dalkey and Killiney are Dublin's exclusive addresses, full of houses with lusty sea-views and expensive price tags. Dalkey is a friendly, charming village marked by two impressive harbours, a legacy from its days as a fishing centre. Today, it is home to far more genteel pursuits. Indeed, you could quite happily while away time quaffing beverages and exchanging tall tales with the locals in ***Queens** before filling up on fine pasta or pizza from **La Romana** in the same building. Or, sample some of the concoctions at the **Thai House**, which many believe to be the best Thai restaurant in the region. For a modern take, the new **Monkberry's** has had rave reviews and serves up delicious, beautifully-presented food in impressive, contemporary surroundings.

Continue the splurge and revamp your wardrobe with some of Ireland's top designer knitwear from **Design Knitwear Direct** or the **Dalkey Design Company** – also home to sumptuous handmade bags, French antiques and other adornments befitting a posh country home.

A short trip by DART or a bracing walk away is Killiney. Along the way are staggering views across Dublin Bay which are almost Mediterranean in aspect. No wonder, then, that houses on Sorrento Terrace ✔ and Vico Road are home to celebs like Bono, Lisa Stansfield, film director Neil Jordan, racing-driver Damon Hill and nouveau-riche computer whizzkids.

**Dalkey Design Company**
20 Railway Road
☎ 285 6827

**Design Knitwear Direct**
4 Coliemore Road
☎ 285 7759 (appointment only)

**Monkberry's**
22 Castle Street
☎ 284 7185 ££

**Queens & La Romana**
12 Castle Street
☎ 285 4569 £–££

**Thai House**
21 Railway Road
☎ 284 7304 ££



## *bray*

D4

*to Bray* · *45, 84*

Once a refined Victorian seaside resort, Bray is now overrun during summer with day-trippers from the big smoke. Bray marks your arrival in County Wicklow [→38–41] and makes a useful starting point for the Wicklow Mountains or towns like Enniskerry, Glendalough or Roundwood. In the town itself, there's an abundance of attractions which harken back to more innocent times, and that's before you reach the candy-floss outlets, day-glo funfairs and loud amusement arcades ✔ which crowd the seafront. Every generation will find some salty R&R here and the kids will love it [→58].

Traditional seaside entertainment – fresh walks, gaudy hurdy-gurdy's, sandy beaches, cosy tea shops, and more...... Bray will lift your spirits.

If furnishing fabrics are your bag, choose from the gorgeous selection at **Material World**. There are also two highly-regarded restaurants, both worth the trip south alone. For vegetarians, **Escape** ↗ is a godsend, providing smart dishes in surroundings which don't exactly reek of lentils and sandals. The ***Tree Of Idleness** [→83] is home to some outstanding Greek-Cypriot cooking in old-fashioned but hugely comfortable surroundings. It is no wonder that it has a long, loyal list of regulars.

**Escape**
1 Brennans Terrace
☎ 286 6755

**Material World**
2 Church Terrace
☎ 286 6668

**Tree Of Idleness**
Seafront, Bray
☎ 286 3498 ££

# the wicklow way

Perfect terrain for those who live to lace their hiking boots, hug the wheel, swing a golf club or down a few pints in postcard-pretty villages, County Wicklow's untamed mountain range conceals many eclectic gems. Beach bums needn't fret either – the peaks can easily be abandoned for the sandy stretch of Brittas Bay.

## sightseeing

### *avondale estate* C5

Straight out of a classic 19th-century novel, the life of Charles Stewart Parnell – filled with clandestine love, fiery idealism and brutal betrayal – accounts as much for the enduring fascination with Avondale, Parnell's birthplace, as the estate's lush surrounds. In 1890, Parnell, the erstwhile 'Uncrowned King of Ireland,' was annihilated by the press, the hierarchy and the nation he had tried to save. Parnell's sensational downfall was entwined in a sex scandal when it was revealed he had been having a long-term relationship with Kitty O'Shea, the wife of Captain John O'Shea.

Avondale was inherited by Parnell as a whippersnapper of 13. Designed by James Wyatt, who was all for symmetry and balance, the house was built in 1779 and harbours hidden surprises like fake doors and concealed staircases. Replete with smoking caps and nifty treasures linked to the bearded parliamentarian, Avondale today is an unusual amalgam of old-world and modern touches. Known as the 'cradle of Irish forestry', the extensive grounds are full of rare tree species and silvicultural gems. Birds tweet to their heart's content along the many walking trails.

Rathdrum ☎ 0404 46111
£3 (free to grounds).
◑ house: *11am–6pm daily (5pm in winter), last admission one hour before closing.* ◑ grounds: *24-hours daily.*
❑ ♿ ground floor only

### *mount usher gardens* D5

Even those who have never spared a thought for a seed or a hoe will be instantly bewitched by these bucolic Elysian fields – the multi-coloured fruits of over 130 years of dynamic digging, planting and pruning. A global hotchpotch, the lawns, meadows and light woodlands are home to over 5000 blooms, shrubs, ferns and trees, snatched from five continents and spirited away to the wilds of Ashford.

Originally planted by the green-and-nimble-fingered Walpole brothers in the late 1800's, the gardens are intersected by the gurgling river Vartry, which is spanned by four miniature suspension bridges. Verdant surprises hiding behind every bush will have horticultural enthusiasts in seventh heaven.

Ashford ☎ 0404 40116
£3 (free to grounds). ◑ *mid-Mar–Oct: 10.30am–6pm daily.*
❑ ♿ limited

### *glendalough* C5

Dotted around this lush and enchanting 'valley of two lakes' are clusters of remains from the holy heyday of an ancient monastery. which was founded by St Kevin in the 6th century. Among the ruins are deserted churches and many sanctified spots, including the cell and bed of St Kevin, which overlook the Upper Lake. It was from this bed that the pioneering, pious Kevin is reputed to have thrown a determined young – and naked – admirer into the lake. She drowned but Kevin clung tenaciously to his endangered virginity and apparently lived to a grand old age. The Upper Lake is tranquil and a stunning setting for a saunter along one of the scores of self-guided trails.

A visitors' centre contextualizes the sacred settlements and gives the official low-down on the saint and the fate of his idyllic hang out.

Glendalough
☎ 0404 45325 (Visitors' Centre ☎ 0404 45352)
w www.heritageireland.ie
free (£2 to Visitors' Centre)
◑ *mid-Mar–mid-Oct: 9.30am–6pm daily (Jun–Aug: 9am–6.30 daily); mid-Oct–mid-Mar: 9.30am–5pm daily.*
❑ ♿

## *powerscourt house & gardens* ► C4

Gazing from the upper terrace of Powerscourt Gardens, it is easy to imagine you've landed in the middle of a Merchant-Ivory production. Home to the titled Wingfields for over 300 years, the Powerscourt estate was bought, in 1961, by the Slazenger family. A blaze in 1974 ravaged the 18th-century house, but a vigorous process of rejuvenation is well underway. A small section of the formidable mansion is open, housing enticing shops and a café, run by Avoca Handweavers.

Brimming with outdoor treats, this artfully constructed Eden – 20 hectares of splendour – may well leave you lamenting the state of your own back yard. The grounds are utterly alluring, inviting explorers to roam around the imperial trees and resplendent blooms while the Sugar Loaf mountain casts a sceptical, weathered eye on all shenanigans. Marble and bronze statues line the descent to the Triton fountain and lake. A thoroughly Japanese patch, lordly gates, terraces, grottoes, ponds and a pepper pot tower await. Italianate magnificence is balanced by a touch of Stephen King gothic – the authentic pet cemetery which shelters the remains of Tiny, Teddy, Princess and other prized animals.

Five kilometres from the gardens, a celebrated cascade wows the masses. Surrounded by wildlife, and with a nature trail at its base, the Powerscourt waterfall, at over 120 m, is the highest in Ireland.

Enniskerry ☎ 204 6000
**w** www.powerscourt.ie
a shuttle bus operates from Enniskerry. £5 house & gardens; £3.50 gardens only; £1.50 house only (prices are less in winter) £2 waterfalls ◑ house & gardens: *9.30am–5.30pm daily (winter times may vary).*
◑ waterfalls: *9.30am–7pm daily (winter: 10.30am–dusk daily).* ❑ ♿ to house and perimeter of the gardens.

## *russborough house* B4

An out-and-out Palladian classic by the great and prolific Richard Castle who died before this opulent early 18th-century edifice was completed. Since the 50's, the house has been renowned for housing Sir Alfred Beit's art collection – an impressive stash of paintings dominated by Dutch, Flemish and Spanish masterpieces. The interior of the mansion prompts jaws to drop in awe at the intricate rococo ceilings and the grand staircase which basks in ebullient plasterwork – said to represent the 'ravings of a maniac'.

Blessington ☎ 045 865 239
£3 ◑ *Jun–Aug: 10.30am–5.30pm daily; Apr–May & Sep–Oct: 10.30am–5.30pm Sun.*
❑ ♿

# shopping

A craft-collector's paradise, Wicklow wills you to spend the readies on tantalizing handmade articles. At the Old Mill in Avoca Village, ***Avoca Handweavers**, established in 1723, still continues to painstakingly fashion technicolour dream cloths for their nationwide and North American stores. Seeing the masters at work certainly heightens the appreciation of every twist in the fibre. The **Glendalough Woollen Mills** is a similar, though much smaller and less renowned, enterprise which also allows visitors to observe the process of creation. Wicklow's other branches of ***Avoca Handweavers** at Kilmacanogue, situated in a spacious 19th-century arboretum, and Powerscourt House are exceedingly well-stocked with impressive domestic-ware, sartorial gems and choice munchies. For more first-hand trading, you can pop into the studio shops of potters like **Geoffrey Healy** or **Belinda Brayshaw**, ✔ (both of whom supply Avoca Handweavers) and buy straight from source. Other aesthetic crafty bits 'n' bobs can be found at the **Roundwood Store** or the **Enniskerry Trading Company**.

**Avoca Handweavers** C6/D4
Old Avoca Mill, Avoca
☎ 0402 35105
◑ *9am–6pm daily (winter: 9.30am–5.30pm daily).* all

Kilmacanogue, Bray
◑ *9.30am–5.30pm Mon–Fri, 9.30am–6pm Sat & Sun.*
V/MC

**Belinda Brayshaw** C5
Glenmalure
☎ 0404 46839
◑ *9.30am–5.30pm Mon–Fri, 2–6pm Sat & Sun (winter: 9.30am–5.30pm Mon–Fri).*
V/MC

**Enniskerry Trading Company** C4
The Square, Enniskerry
☎ 286 6275 ◑ *10.30am–6pm daily.* AE/MC/V

**Geoffrey Healy** D4
The Rocky Valley, Kilmacanogue ☎ 282 9270
◑ *9am–6pm Mon–Fri, 10am–6pm Sat, 12–6pm Sun (winter: 9am–6pm Mon–Fri).* MC/V

**Glendalough Woollen Mills** C5
Glendalough
☎ 0404 45156
◑ *9.30am–5.30pm daily.*
AE/MC/V

**The Roundwood Store** C5
Roundwood
☎ 281 8454
◑ *11am–5pm Tue–Sun (winter: 11am–5pm Fri–Sun.* V

# eating & drinking

## restaurants & cafés

Wicklow is awash with fine eateries, mostly offering hearty home-style country creations from the pick of the wonderfully fresh local produce. Unashamedly floral, local, seasonal and organic in outlook is the small, and popular **Old Rectory**. Located in a lovingly renovated, pinker than pink, Victorian house, it is well-known for the 'floral cuisine' of co-owner and chef, Linda Saunders. The daily-changing menu at **Tinakilly Country House** regularly creates paeans to modern Irish cooking. Everything from banana bread to the chutneys is homemade. Another culinary refuge for city-weary Dubliners and Wicklow-based celebs is the **Roundwood Inn**, renowned for its superb Irish and European cuisine. The bar also serves food, including healthy portions of Irish stews and seafood.

Other havens of gourmet fodder include **Rathsallagh House** – a comfy old farmhouse set in 500 acres of peaceful parkland, and the restaurant at **Tulfarris House** which is snuggled between the mountains and the impressive Blessington Lakes. **Chester Beatty Inn**, a pub-cum-restaurant, is a popular choice for a reasonably-priced modern feast.

For tea you will be spoilt for choice. **Hunter's Hotel** is as famous for its leisurely afternoon tea on the lawn as its top-quality no-nonsense restaurant nosh. When hunger pangs demand a bite-break, the **Terrace Café** in Powerscourt House and the tea rooms at **Russborough House** or **Mount Usher Gardens** make for wise choices enhanced by splendiferous scenery. Both **Avoca Handweavers** ▲ stores have a café, well stocked with yummy chow.

**Avoca Handweavers** C6
Avoca Mill, Avoca Village & Kilmacanogue, Bray
☎ 0402 35105 ☎ 286 7466
◑ *9.30am–5.30pm Mon–Fri, 9.30am–6pm Sat & Sun.*
MC/V £–££

**Chester Beatty Inn** D5
Main Road, Ashford
☎ 0404 40206
◑ *12.30–2.30pm Mon–Fri, 6–9pm daily.* AE/MC/V ££

**Hunter's Hotel** D5
Newrath Bridge, Rathnew
☎ 0404 40106
◑ *8.30–10am & 1pm–2.30pm Mon–Sat, 12.45–2.30pm Sun, 7.30–8.45pm daily.* all £££

**Mount Usher Gardens** D5
Ashford ☎ 0404 40116
◑ *mid-Mar–Nov: 10.30am–6pm daily.* none £

**Old Rectory** D5
Wicklow ☎ 0404 67048
◑ *Mar–Dec: dinner served at 8pm daily (reservation essential).* all ££–£££

**Rathsallagh House** B5
Dunlavin ☎ 045 403 112
◑ *7–9pm Mon–Sat.* all ££–£££

**Roundwood Inn** C5
Roundwood ☎ 281 8107
◑ *12–9.30pm daily. (reservation essential).* AE/MC/V ££–£££

**Russborough House** B4
Blessington ☎ 045 865239
◑ *Jun–Aug: 10.30am–5.30pm daily; Apr–May & Sep–Oct: 10.30am–5.30pm Sun & bank hols.* MC/V £

**Terrace Café** C4
Powerscourt House, Enniskerry ☎ 204 6066
◑ *9am–6pm daily.*
AE/MC/V £

**Tinakilly Country House** D5
Rathnew ☎ 0404 69274
◑ *10am–9pm daily (reservation essential)*
all ££–£££

**Tulfarris House** B4
Blessington Lakes
☎ 045 867 555
◑ *12.30–8.30pm (bar food) 7.30–9.30pm (set menu).*
all £ (bar), £££ (dinner)

## pubs & bars

On leaving Dublin for Wicklow, you generally bid farewell to self-consciously trendy and pseudo-traditional city pubs. Sometimes these are replaced by thronging touristy taverns or local haunts which can exude something of a downbeat, shabby charm. The **Glendalough Tavern** and Avoca's **The Meetings** are well peopled due to their proximity to popular sights. The latter wears its Thomas Moore connection with visible pride and hosts outdoor trad sessions. Actors from *Ballykissangel* regularly hobnob in and around **Fitzgerald's** of Avoca – the pub and valley in which the series is shot. **Lynham's Laragh Inn** is a good pre- or post-Glendalough bet for a pint of the dark stuff. From the heights of the black and white **Coach House** you can imbibe away in the beer garden or veg among the antiques inside. In Wicklow town, the buzzing **Phil Healy's** and the **Bakery Wine Bar**, perfect for vino and tapas, are routinely filled with those in the know. Popular with the sandy-toed Brittas Bay set is the flagstone-floored **McDaniels**.

**Bakery Wine Bar** D5
Wicklow ☎ 0404 620 101
◑ *10am–late daily (winter: 10am–5pm).*

**Coach House** C5
Roundwood
☎ 281 8157
◑ *12–11pm daily.*

**Fitzgerald's** C6
Avoca ☎ 0402 35108/35310
◑ *10am–11pm daily.*

**Glendalough Tavern** C5
Glendalough ☎ 0404 45135
◑ *12–11pm daily.*

**Lynham's Laragh Inn** C5
Laragh ☎ 0404 45345
◑ *11am–11pm daily.*

**McDaniels** D6
Brittas Bay ☎ 0404 47285
◑ *11am–11pm daily.*

**Phil Healy's** D5
Wicklow ☎ 0404 67380
◑ *12.30–11pm daily.*

**The Meetings** C6
Avoca ☎ 0402 35226
◑ *10.30am–11pm Mon–Sat, 12–11pm Sun.*

# activities & sports

Wicklow is a magnet for walkers and avid ramblers. Covering a whopping 130 km, the Wicklow Way is Ireland's first marked long-distance walking route. You can pick up the trail from a suitable spot such as Glencree (8 km west of Enniskerry) or embark on many others walks. Contact **Wicklow County Tourism** for an Ordnance Survey map and more information. Exploring the locale on two wheels is also a popular option for the fit, and suitably sturdy bicycles can be hired from **Wicklow Hire Services**.

For those seeking an equestrian fix, Wicklow has an endless supply of daring and docile creatures to whisk you over rugged ground and soft Irish bogs. **Brennanstown Riding School** adjoins the wonderfully wooded Killruddery Estate and has excellent facilities. The **Devil's Glen Equestrian Centre**, only an hour from Dublin, offers cross-country courses designed to unleash your demonic side, while the **Laragh Trekking Centre** in the heart of Glendalough will have you galloping near the saintly confines of St Kevin's spiritual home.

Generally underused during the week, magnificent golf courses are spread high and low across Wicklow's hills and vales, and green fees aren't half bad by international standards. Designed by dynamic duo Tom Craddock and Pat Ruddy, **Druids Glen**, home of the Irish Open and **Powerscourt Golf Club**, in the grounds of the regal estate, are truly sumptuous options. **Old Conna** is a venerable alternative with good views of the coastline and mountains while the 9-hole course at **Bray Golf Club** is a cherished fave.

To really get the adrenalin going, you can always paddle a canoe, master a windsurfer, sail a boat or embark on any number of other activities from abseiling to clay pigeon shooting at either the **Blessington** or the **National Adventure Centre**. Alternatively bomb around the countryside on Honda and Yamaha quad bikes from the **Wicklow Hills Quad Trekking** or, for an even greater high, the **Paragliding/Hang-gliding Centre** [→63] should come up with the goods.

**Blessington Adventure Centre** *B4*
Burgage, Blessington
☎ 045 865092 from £3/hr (tennis) to £12 (pony trekking) MC/V

**Bray Golf Club** *D4*
Ravenswell Rd, Bray ☎ 286 2484 £17/day MC/V

**Brennanstown Riding School** *D4*
Hollybrook, Kilmacanogue, Bray ☎ 286 3778 £15/hour none

**Devil's Glen Riding School** *D5*
Ashford ☎ 0404 40013 £15/hour AE/MC/V

**Druids Glen Golf & Country Club** *D5*
Newtown Mount Kennedy ☎ 287 3600 £55–80/day all

**Laragh Trekking Centre** *C5*
Glenmacnass, Glendalough ☎ 0404 45282 £30/half day, £60/day none

**National Adventure Centre – Tiglin** *D5*
Ashford ☎ 0404 40169 £99/weekend (inc board & activities) MC/V

**Old Conna Golf Club** *D4*
Ferndale Road, Bray ☎ 282 6055 £27.50/round V

**Paragliding/Hang-gliding Centre** *D4*
Kilmacanogue, Bray ☎ 830 3884 £120/2 day course MC/V

**Powerscourt Golf Club** *C4*
Enniskerry ☎ 204 6033 £50–60/day AE/MC/V

**Wicklow County Tourism** *D5*
St Manntan's House, Kilmantin Hill, Wicklow ☎ 0404 66058

**Wicklow Hills Quad Trekking** *B6*
Cronelea, Shillelagh ☎ 055 29260 *Apr–Oct.* £20 pp (groups of 2–6) none

**Wicklow Hire Services** *D5*
Wicklow ☎ 0404 68149 £6/day MC/V

# hotels

Lusty sea views, elegant period surroundings, lovely gardens and fab four-poster beds (where the likes of Rod Stewart and Julia Roberts have kipped), make **Tinakilly Country House** a prime location for romancing couples. Another Rathnew hide-away which makes another perfect base for exploring Wicklow's wonders is **Hunter's Hotel** – a quirky 18th-century former coaching inn with open fires, a cozy ambience and beautiful gardens. Keen golfers will be at home at **Rathsallagh House**, which has its own golf course on the estate, as well as tennis courts and an indoor pool. The award-winning breakfasts are worth struggling out of bed for.

On a smaller scale, **Enniscree Lodge** is a wonderfully remote, very intimate, charming place where guests are likely to be more tempted to linger in front of the blazing fire, than venture out into the untamed grounds or the beautiful Glencree Valley which the hotel overlooks.

High-quality cuisine makes it even easier to abandon those hiking boots and simply stay put.

**Enniscree Lodge** *C4*
Glencree Road, Enniskerry ☎ 286 3542 F 286 6037 10 £40 pp

**Hunter's Hotel** *D5*
Rathnew ☎ 0404 40106 F 0404 40338 16 £57.50 pp

**Rathsallagh House** *B5*
Dunlavin ☎ 045 403112 F 045 403343 17 £75 pp

**Tinakilly Country House** *D5*
Rathnew ☎ 0404 69274 F 0404 67806 29 from £85 pp

# bountiful boyne





Loaded with durable legacies, the Boyne Valley in County Meath embraces flabbergasting panoramas and scores of potent Christian and pre-Christian remains. Besides the ancient hills, ruined abbeys, antique crosses and numerous passage tombs to marvel over, there are many less worthy pursuits in which to indulge. Meath's alluring craft shops give cocksure Dublin stores a run for their money, while a handful of excellent pubs and restaurants satisfy other cravings. The energetic can step up a gear with a canter, a brisk hike or even a spot of golf.

## sightseeing

### *newgrange & knowth*

*B1*

Few facts exist about the meaning of the sophisticated stone-age creation of Newgrange. The passage grave was constructed around 3000 BC and is estimated to have taken about 70 years to complete. It is built from tons of glistening quartz, granite and burly stones – some engraved with spirals and similarly intriguing shapes.

Annually, on December 21st, a few lucky ones hope to experience a Neolithic pre-Christmas rush. On the dawn of the winter solstice, as well as for two days before and after, a creeping trail of sunlight penetrates the weather-tight chamber. If there's no sun tho', there's no show.

Newgrange and neighbouring attraction Knowth – also a passage grave – are overrun with visitors and entry is not guaranteed. Both sites can only be accessed through the Brú na Bóinne Visitors' Centre. Causing a predictable hoo-ha when it was built, the centre, ostensibly in profound architectural touch with the magnitude of its surrounds, offers a carnival of reconstructed and multimedia treats.

In order to guarantee access (especially in peak season) it is advisable to take an organized tour [→32] from Dublin. Otherwise you could end up gazing wistfully across the fields at the mystical, elusive mass, as you're forced to make do with a Disney-esque second best.

Last admission 45 min before closing. Last tour of monuments 1 hr 30 min before closing.

Brú Na Bóinne Visitors' Centre, 8 km east of Slane.
☎ 041 24488
£2 Visitors' Centre only; £3 Centre & Newgrange; £2 Centre & Knowth; £5 Centre, Newgrange & Knowth *May–Sep: 9am–6.30/7pm daily; Oct–Apr: 9.30am–5/5.30pm daily.*
to Visitors' Centre only

## shopping

For glorious handmade goodies – glass, ceramics, leather, jewellery, textiles, candles etc – try **Meath County Crafts** in the Trim Visitors' Centre. **Mary McDonnell's** in Slane showcases the work of local fellow craftspeople, along with her own unique cushions, quilts and wall hangings. **The Courtyard**, also in Slane, is a one-stop shop for unusual Irish and international crafts – many of which are one of a kind.

**The Courtyard** *A1*
Cookstown House, Kells
☎ 046 40346
*Mar–Dec: 10am–6pm Tue–Sat.* MC/V

**Mary McDonnell's Craft Studio** *B1*
Newgrange Mall, Slane
☎ 041 24722
*10am–6pm Tue–Sat, 2–6pm Sun.* MC/V

**Meath County Crafts** *A2*
Visitors' Centre, Mill Street, Trim
☎ 046 37227
*10am–12.30pm & 1.30–5pm Mon–Fri, 12–5pm Sun.* MC/V

# eating & drinking

When history makes you hungry, **The Ground Floor** in Kells and sister restaurant **The Loft** in Navan will ply you with tasty evening meals in the midst of funky artwork and twinkling candlelight. Two other evening affairs which offer a medley of dishes are **Hudson's Bistro**, a cosy Cal-Ital-style restaurant, and the **Old Darnley Lodge** which is just as adept at rustling up a veggie surprise as a steak supreme. For homemade lunches or afternoon teas **Boyles Tea Rooms** and **The Courtyard** specialize in delectable morsels.

**Daly's**, which has an extensive pub and à la carte menu, is the nearest place to have a tipple or nibble when visiting Newgrange (apart from the reasonable café in the Visitors' Centre).

**The Poet's Rest** and **Live & Let Live** are popular taverns for drinking sessions in the attractive village of Slane, while **Carbury's** is a quirky, authentic option on the banks of the Boyne in Drogheda. Trad music sessions (Thursday evening and Sunday lunch) add to its popularity.

**Boyles Tea Rooms** *B1*
Main Street, Slane
☎ 041 24195
◑ *11am–11pm Mon, Wed–Sat, 12.30–11pm Sun.* ▤ MC/V £

**Carbury's** *C1*
North Strand, Drogheda
☎ 041 37409
◑ *7–11.30pm Mon–Sat, 12.30–11.30pm Sun.*

**The Courtyard** *B1*
Trimgate Street, Navan
☎ 046 23569 ◑ *10.30am–4.30pm daily.* ▤ MC/V £–££

**Daly's** *B1*
Dunore
☎ 041 23252 ◑ *11am–11pm daily.* ▤ MC/V £–££

**The Ground Floor** *A1*
Bective Square, Kells
☎ 046 49688
◑ *6–11pm Mon–Thu, 6pm–midnight Fri & Sat, 5–10pm Sun.* ▤ MC/V ££–£££

**Hudson's Bistro** *B1*
30 Railway St, Navan
☎ 046 29231 ◑ *5.30pm–10.30pm Tue–Fri, 5.30–9.30pm Sun.* ▤ AE/MC ££

**Live & Let Live** *B1*
Main Street, Slane
☎ 041 24158
◑ *4.30–11pm Mon–Sat, 12.15–11pm Sun.*

**The Loft** *B1*
26 Trimgate Street, Navan
☎ 046 71755
◑ *6–11pm Mon–Thu, 6pm–midnight Fri & Sat, 5–10pm Sun.* ▤ MC/V ££

**Old Darnley Lodge** *A2*
Main Street, Athboy
☎ 046 32348
◑ *7.30–9.30pm Mon–Sat, 12.30–9.30pm Sun.* ▤ all ££

**The Poet's Rest** *B1*
Chapel Street, Slane
☎ 041 24579
◑ *12pm–midnight daily.*



# activities & sports

Golfers can weather the challenges of the renowned, traditional links course at **Laytown & Bettystown**, said to have a tough par of 71, where pro Des Smyth began his career. Or raise a club to long-gone kings at **Royal Tara** – a scenic tree-lined parkland course. For those yearning to jump into the saddle, **Borallion Riding Centre**, in a peacefully pastoral setting (within walking distance of Navan), is a safe bet as is **Kells Equestrian Centre** which stands proudly on 60 hectares of land. **Paul Berrill Cycles** will happily supply the robust with bicycles to pedal through the highlands and lowlands of the Valley of the Kings.

Feeling more subdued? Saunter along the path stretching 8 km from Navan to Slane on the banks of the River Boyne. Season permitting, cast a line into the trout and spring salmon-laden waters of the River Blackwater. **Navan & District Angling** will fix you up with a day pass. Alternatively, succumb to the rush of the races at **Navan** or **Fairyhouse**.

**Borallion Riding Centre** *B1*
Balreask, Trim Road, Navan
☎ 046 73688 ▦ £10–£15/hr
▤ none

**Fairyhouse Racecourse** *B2*
Ratoath ☎ 825 6167
▦ £8–£20 ▤ none

**Kells Equestrian Centre** *A1*
Normanstown, Carlanstown, Kells ☎ 046 46638
▦ £12/hr ▤ none

**Laytown & Bettystown Golf Club** *C1*
Bettystown ☎ 041 27170
▦ £23–£28/day ▤ MC/V

**Navan & District Angling** *B1*
Trimgate Street, Navan
☎ 046 21130 ▦ £10–£20/day

**Navan Racecourse** *B1*
Proudstown
☎ 046 21350 ▦ £7–£8
▤ V (accepted once inside)

**Paul Berrill Cycles** *C1*
Tower Cross, Mornington
☎ 041 27088 ▦ £6/day

**Royal Tara Golf Club** *B1*
Bellinter, Navan ☎ 046 25508
▦ £18–£22/day ▤ none

# hotels

Two enticing sleeping spots are situated a short drive from Newgrange and Knowth. **Annesbrook** is a lovely 18th-century historic house set in four hectares of gardens and woodland. Eminent past visitors include George IV and Thackeray. Also family-run, the **Conyngham Arms** is a charming mid-19th-century inn in Slane, a quaint and tiny village which nevertheless has seven pubs to choose from.

**Annesbrook** *B1*
Duleek
☎ 041 23293 F 041 23024
◆ 5 ▦ £35pp

**Conyngham Arms** *B1*
Slane
☎ 041 24155 F 041 24205
◆ *16* ▦ £80 double

# dublin's sights, museums & galleries

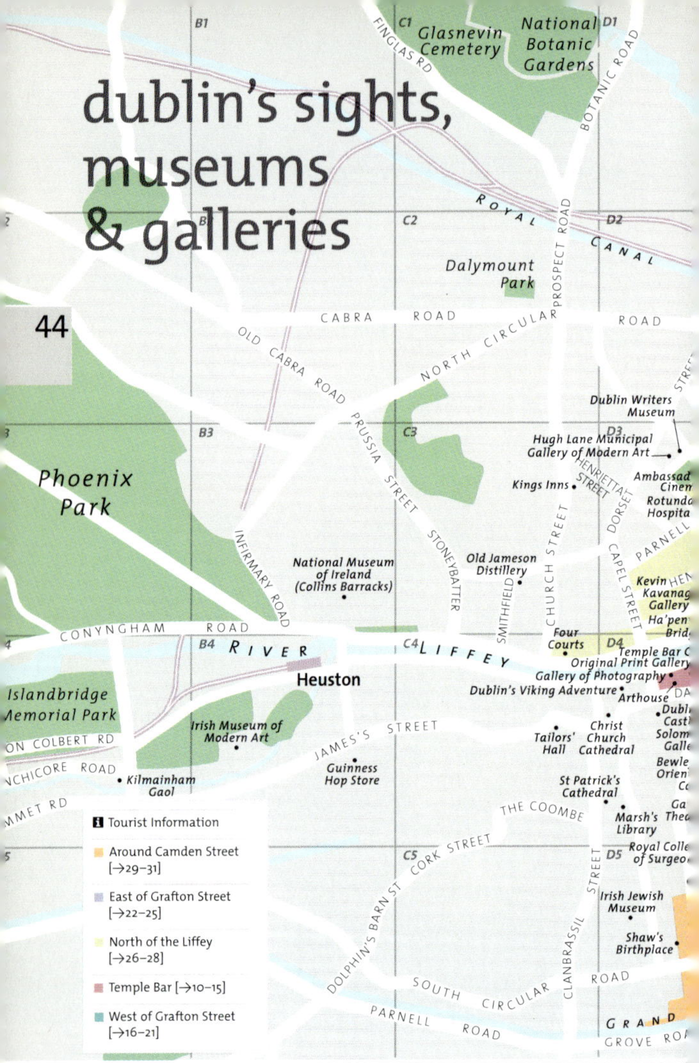




## directory

Shaw's Birthplace D5 [→50]
Solomon Gallery D4 [→57]
Tailors' Hall C4 [→47 & 52]
Temple Bar Gallery D4 [→57]
Trinity College D4 [→49]
Windmill Lane E4 [→47]

## tours

### bus tours

Dublin Bus offers two historical city tours. Book direct with the bus company ☎ 873 4222, your hotel or Dublin Tourism Centre [→121]. Tours leave from Dublin Bus HQ: 59 O'Connell St Upper.

**Grand Dublin Tour** is an open-top sightseeing tour that goes via Trinity College, Guinness Hop Store, St Patrick's Cathedral, Christ Church Cathedral and Phoenix Park. £10 departs 10.15am & 2.15pm daily; duration 2 hr 45 min.

**Dublin City – Hop on-Hop off** One ticket gives you the freedom to hop on and off at 12 stops throughout the day. Buses run at 10–30 min intervals between Dublin Bus HQ, Dublin Writers Museum, Trinity College, National Gallery, St Stephen's Green, Dublin Tourism Centre, Dublin Castle, **St Patrick's Cathedral**, Guinness Hop Store, National Museum of Ireland and the Old Jameson Distillery. £7 between 9.30am–4.30pm daily.

### horse & cart tours

Canny folk with a horse and cart [→62] will take you on a romantic city tour from St Stephen's Green (summer only).
vary duration approx 30 min–1 hr.

### bicycle tours

**Dublin Bike Tours** operates small leisurely group trips from the front gate of Christ Church Cathedral – there are refreshment stops en route. Book in advance.
☎ 679 0899 £12
Apr–Oct: departs 10am & 2pm Mon–Fri & Sun; 6am, 10am & 2pm Sat; duration 3 hr.

### walking tours

**Audio Tours Ireland** offers a walking tour with map and audio guide, which talks you through from **Ha'penny Bridge** to **Merrion Square**, via sights such as **Trinity College** and **Dublin Castle**. Collect from Aston Hotel, 7–9 Aston Quay, D2
☎ 670 5266
£6 duration 2 hr.

# culture vultures

Be charmed by Georgian buildings and quirky street statues, or dive indoors to marvel at the cultural life and venerable seats of learning.

## ↓ landmarks

**Bank of Ireland & House of Lords**
2 College Green | D2
Wisdom, Justice and Liberty stand guard over this purpose-built parliament (1729), most of which became a bank in 1803. Huge colonnades and curving walls make the bank one of College Green's main attractions.

**Christ Church Cathedral** | Christ Church Pl | D2
The 12th-century crypt and Romanesque doorway of Christ Church [→48] now witness the daily whizzing of cars under the cathedral's enclosed bridge. In the 1870's, there were extensive restorations thanks to a donation from a generous local whiskey distiller.

**Custom House** | Custom House Quay | D1
Über-Georgian architect James Gandon's river-front marvel (1791) was damaged by a five-day fire in the 1921–22 civil war. Records were obliterated, the dome melted, stonework cracked but a patched-up Custom House, dotted with sculptures and coats-of-arms, still stands sturdy.

**The Famine Statues** | Custom House Quay | D1
A predatory dog watches six skeletal souls clutching bundles and a child as, barefoot, they head for the docks. For £200–£750, which goes to charity, expat Irish can cast their names in the bronze plaques surrounding Rowan Gillespie's statues (1997).

**Floozie in the Jacuzzi** | O'Connell Street | D1
Dubliners, proud of their idiosyncratic wit, re-christen monuments and statues. Check out Molly Malone, the 'Tart With the Cart' (College Green); the 'Hags With the Bags' (Liffey Street); and the 'Floozie in the Jacuzzi', the bronze and granite Anna Livia who personifies the nearby Liffey.

**Four Courts** | Inns Quay | D1
Witness to countless trials and retrials, the large-drummed, shallow-domed Four Courts (1796) rose, phoenix-like, from their civil-war remains. Sculptures of Moses, Justice and Mercy by the prolific Edward Smyth deck the main pediment.

**General Post Office** | O'Connell Street | D1

On Easter Monday 1916, Patrick Pearse proclaimed Ireland a republic from the steps of the GPO. Gutted in the ensuing rising, the building retained its 1814 façade. Fidelity, Hibernia and Mercury, residing above the huge portico, oversee comparatively pedestrian activities today.

**Ha'penny Bridge**

Gracefully arching its way over the murky Liffey, the pedestrians-only Ha'penny Bridge is named after an old toll charged to cross it. Much beloved by Dubliners, the 1816 bridge sports three tenacious lamps held aloft by elderly curved ironwork.

**Irish Financial Services Centre**
Custom House Quay | D1

Bathed nightly in a green tinge, the IFSC, where native and international institutions nestle snugly together, was established by the Irish Government in 1987. It's full of gung-ho young things, vying to make a buck or a million.

**Leinster House** | Kildare Street | D2

Political heavyweights wheel and deal inside Richard Cassell's townhouse, built in 1745 as a family home for James Fitzgerald (subsequently Duke of Leinster). Flanked by the National Library and Museum, it encases the Dáil and Senate, which make up the Irish parliament.

**St Patrick's Cathedral** | St Patrick's Close | D8

Myths and monuments aplenty hide within this early English Gothic-style cathedral. Ireland's patron saint allegedly baptized on the site, centuries before the wayward Archbishop Comyn founded St Patrick's in 1192. Jonathan Swift, self-declared 'champion of liberty', became Dean in 1713.

**Trinity College** | College Green | D2

Four eventful centuries have made Trinity [→49] a veritable haven of classical and modern architecture. The place is teeming with life: students lean casually against the front gates, while the campanile, guardian of the college bell, beckons from within.

**Windmill Lane** | D2

In psychedelic, multilingual homage, U2 fans from Monaghan to Morocco have decorated the wall near the studio where Bono and the boys recorded their first albums. The Dublin Corporation has now sandblasted much of the graffiti, some of which hit a reportedly unmusical note, but the die-hard fans refuse to call it a day.

# the big four

## Christ Church Cathedral

Dusty cobwebs dangle spookily from the mega-thick stone ceilings of Christ Church's crypt. Seventeenth-century stocks, which once restrained many a fruit and veg-spattered deviant, lurk in the large, slightly sinister underbelly along with ancient carved stones, pewter candlesticks, countless monuments and a mummified cat and rat.

In 1172, Archbishop O'Toole and the Norman knight Richard de Clare, aka Strongbow, planned the cathedral on the site of a Viking church, though today's edifice owes more to the heady ambitions of Victorian architecture than to 12th-century ardour.

Full of semi-hidden chapels and quiet corners, the interior exudes high-minded holiness. Over the centuries, Christ Church has been renowned for the dulcet tones of its choristers, who still sing strong. An oft-played 1984 solid oak organ hovers under the arch of the central tower and annually, on New Year's Eve, thousands of revellers gather outside to share in a symphony of bell ringing before massacring a few bars of *Auld Lang Syne*.

The chameleon-like cathedral, which occupies an unusual niche, can readily tap into the growing penchant for ecumenism. A descendant of the Celtic and medieval Christian traditions, Christ Church breezed through the Reformation and is now a venerable Church of Ireland institution, welcoming all pilgrims.

Christ Church Place, D8
☎ 677 8099
**w** www.indigo.ie/~cccdub/
[ticket] £2 ◑ *10am–5pm daily (check for service times).* (Apr–Nov only).
**[→Temple Bar 10–15; West of Grafton Street 16–21]**

## Dublin Castle

An eclectic, semi-hidden gem just out of the hubbub of Dame Street, Dublin Castle has resolutely transcended a murky history including torture, imprisonment and British rule. Now an active government building, the Castle regularly hosts bashes for heavyweight politicos in its grandiose State Apartments, which proudly defy contemporary notions of chic. Minimalism it ain't. Waterford crystal chandeliers sway high above intricate, hand-woven Donegal carpets and ornate furniture, while mirrors and paintings of dour aristocrats flank the walls. Mandela and Mitterrand, among others, have kipped amid the opulence of the Queen's Bedroom, and Irish Presidents are inaugurated with due pomp in St Patrick's Hall.

Outside, the Lower Yard reveals a mix of architectural styles. A thoroughly 1970's office block – unafraid to boast the Revenue Commissioners as tenants – confronts the imposing 13th-century Record Tower and the Gothic Chapel Royal. The glitterati who attend corporate shindigs in the castle today dance near an ancient pulse of Dublin's history, for the gardens of Dublin Castle stand on the site of Dubhlinn, the dark pool which gave the city its name.

❶ Occasionally Dublin Castle may be closed for state functions. Access to the State Apartments is by guided tour only.
▶ The Chester Beatty Library, which includes Islamic and early Christian manuscripts, Western prints, Chinese, Japanese, Indian and other Oriental art, is moving to Dublin Castle and will open to the public around mid-2000.

Dame Street, D2
☎ 677 7129
**w** www.visit.ie/dublin
[ticket] £3 ◑ *10am–5pm Mon–Fri, 2–5pm Sat & Sun.*
**[→West of Grafton Street 16–21]**

## National Museum of Ireland

Cheek by jowl, the sordid and sublime live out their glass-cased confinement in the Kildare

Street branch of the National Museum. A fabulous collection of gold jewellery (from 2000 BC) including the ornate Tara Brooch shimmer provocatively, close to a long-deceased unfortunate who lay for aeons beneath a Galway bog before being transported to the capital to be gawped at by millions. Gaze at axe-heads, altar vessels, revered reliquaries and contraptions designed by clever Celts and Vikings, or artefacts dating from 7000 BC. Some of the garb donned by the rebels involved in the 1916 Easter Rising can be found in The Road to Independence, and Ancient Egypt pokes its somewhat anomalous head in too.

Up river, Collins Barracks is the newer, hipper kid on the block, hoarding a wealth of industrial and decorative arts. Overlooking the sizeable courtyard, the museum's rooms are filled with myriad examples of Irish silver and period furniture. Funky items, like a massive Scottish teapot from 1880, stand loftily in the Out of Storage exhibit.

Tara Brooch, Ardagh Chalice & Derrynaflan Hoard (Kildare St); Fonthill Vase from 14th-century China (Collins Barracks).
Textile exhibition in Collins Barracks (summer 99), featuring costumes, jewellery and accessories from the 1760s to the 1960s. The museum's jewellery collection, not exhibited since the 1960s, has special prominence.

Kildare Street, D2 6// /444
**w** indigo.ie/~nmi1/museum/index.html
free *10am–5pm Tue–Sat, 2–5pm Sun.*
(ground floor only)
[→Temple Bar 10–15; East of Grafton Street 22–25]

Collins Barracks, Benburb Street, D7
677 7444
37, 39, 70 free *10am–5pm Tue–Sat, 2–5pm Sun.*

## Trinity College ✓

Old-world erudition and contemporary chic coexist peacefully within the sandblasted walls of Trinity's city centre campus. Gowned lecturers breeze past throngs of chattering students who pause for hourly smokes outside the arts block, unfazed by the 400 years of history staring them in the face. Trinity is keen to stress its role as alma mater to the great and the good. Oscar Wilde, Samuel Beckett and Mary Robinson all regularly passed the campanile and walked the cobblestones of Front Square in

their day. When results are announced in summer, pasty faces can be seen drowning academic sorrows outside the Pavilion. Others disappear into the Buttery, a considerably darker option, in the cellars of the old Dining Hall.

Pockets of green are scattered among the medley of buildings which have emerged over the centuries. The elegant Rubrics, begun around 1700, is home to live-in lovers of college life and Trinity's oldest-surviving structure. Just around the corner, the spirited folk of the drama department let their creativity run riot in a wooden-stilted construction reminiscent of alpine chalets.

Hiding out in the Old Library, the *Book of Kells* (approx 800 AD) wows the masses who flock to gaze upon its hallowed pages. The barrel-vaulted ceiling, marble busts and gallery bookcases of the Long Room inspire awe and rose-tinted nostalgia for bygone times.

*Book of Kells*; Long Room; Front Square
The *Book of Kells*, Turning Darkness into Light exhibition (until Dec 2000) covers the making of the *Book of Kells* and the history of Ireland at the time.
There are several entrances to Trinity College. For the most spectacular introduction, enter through the Front Gate on College Green.

College Street, D2 608 2320 **w** www.tcd.ie

**Old Library and *Book of Kells* exhibition**: £4.50 **Dublin Experience** – a multimedia audiovisual presentation of the history of Dublin: £2.75 **Trinity Tours** – half-hour tours of the campus plus admission to Old Library and *Book of Kells* exhibition: £5
**Old Library & *Book of Kells***: *9.30am–5pm Mon–Sat, 12–4.30pm Sun (Jun–Sep: 9.30am–4.30pm Sun).* **Dublin Experience**: *late May–end Sep: hourly, 10am–5pm daily.*
**Trinity Tours**: *Easter–Sep: 10am–5pm daily.*
[→Temple Bar 10–15; West of Grafton Street 16–21; East of Grafton Street 22–25]





more sights, museums & galleries

# write on

## Dublin Writers Museum

Yeats, Synge, O'Casey and wild child Brendan Behan bask in the stained-glass glory of this restored Georgian building, while older and forgotten scribes battle for attention. Downstairs is loaded with facts 'n' figures; walls are splattered with biographies and welcome summaries for overwrought brains. Idiosyncratic knick-knacks, such as Oliver St John Gogarty's flying goggles, lie alongside typewriters galore and Beckett's Paris telephone. Upstairs, the high-ceilinged, book-laden library awaits. Painted door panels, ornamented colonnades and framed men of letters adorn the adjoining Gallery of Writers. In *Seomra na nóg*, enormous models of books and profiles of kids' authors greet young visitors, while next door a large dolls' house invites adults to release their inner child.

Combined tickets are available for the Dublin Writers Museum, the Shaw Birthplace and the James Joyce Museum.

18 Parnell Square, D1
872 2077
w www.visit.ie/dublin
£3 *Sep–May: 10am–5pm Mon–Sat, 11am–5pm Sun (Jun–Aug: 10am–6pm Mon–Fri, 10am–5pm Sat, 11am–5pm Sun).*
[→North of the Liffey 26–28]

## James Joyce Centre ✓

A generous jumble of books festoons the Guinness Library in the JJC. While swots pore over hefty German translations of *Ulysses*, dilettantes can listen to the master's voice swirling around the light mint walls. As much a tribute to Dublin's Georgian architecture as to the city's famous son, the centre shows off its restored plaster work, much of it the work of super-stuccadore Michael Stapleton. Mr Dennis J Maginni, immortalized in Joyce's classic work, once ran his dance academy here at No. 35 and the Maginni Room is littered with medallions of dancers looking suitably lithe. Pictures of Joyce's nearest and dearest line the stairwell and his descendants, alive, alive-o, can be found in every cranny of the centre, which they are actively involved in running. In the Tea Room, Paul Joyce – Jimmy's grand-nephew – has painted a mural depicting Leopold Bloom's much fêted stroll on June 16, 1904. The door of No. 7 Eccles Street, the fictional house of Leopold and Molly, stands nearby.

35 North Great George's St, D1
878 8547
w www.jamesjoyce.ie
£2.75 (house only), £6 (house & walking tour).
*Sep–May: 9.30am–5pm Mon–Sat, 12.30–5pm Sun (Jun–Aug: 9.30am–5pm Mon–Sat, 11am–5pm Sun).*
ground floor only
[→North of the Liffey 26–28]

## James Joyce Tower

'At present he is staying on sufferance with Gogarty in the Tower at Sandycove. Gogarty wants to put Jim out, but he is afraid that if Jim made a name some day, it would be remembered against him...' So wrote Joyce's brother of the author's short stay in the Martello tower at Sandycove – by far the finest of his Dublin residences. One of 15 such towers built as a defence against Napoleonic invasion, the bastion commands a spectacular view of the coast. Howth is to the north, Bray Head to the south, and just below lurks the 'Forty Foot', for many years the preserve of eager gentleman bathers, who would dive naked into 'the snotgreen sea, the scrotumtightening sea' *(Ulysses)*.

Today the tower is a museum, with Joyce's writing desk, letters, photos and other memorabilia – none of which beats the experience of simply being there.

Sandycove, Dun Laoghaire
280 9265 872 2077
to Sandycove
£2.60 [combined ticket available →Dublin Writers Museum]. *Apr–Oct: 10am–5pm Mon–Sat, 2–6pm Sun.*
[→The Coastal Towns 34–37]

## Shaw's Birthplace

With characteristic unconventionality, baby Bernard Shaw arrived feet first into No. 33 Synge Street in July 1856. Alas, the lad was to experience more neglect and poverty than childhood bliss in this modest terraced abode, his home for the next ten years.

Today, the house is carefully decked out in period clutter. Aficionados of the Victorian era will adore the acorn-patterned wallpaper, dark wood cabinets and age-old collectables of the downstairs parlour. The obligatory good book, lying open in the corner, belies the decidedly racy past of the Shaw residence. With her husband all too fond of the bottle, Mrs Shaw took to hosting musical soirées in the drawing room. So impressed was she by the conductor that she ran off to London with him. An appropriate *pièce de résistance* – the exquisite 1840 Broadwood piano – currently stands guard.

33 Synge Street, D8
475 0854
w www.visit.ie/dublin
16, 16a, 19, 19a, 83, 155
£2.60 [combined ticket available →Dublin Writers Museum] *May–Oct: 10am–5pm Mon–Sat, 11am–5pm Sun.*
[→Around Camden St 29–31]

# ↓ liquid inspiration

**Bewley's Oriental Café**

The second you step inside Bewley's Café, and sometimes long before, the tantalizing smell of coffee reaches you. From Terry Wogan to Ludwig Wittgenstein, millions have stopped by at Bewley's, stocking up on sticky buns, cooked breakfasts, pastries and, of course, endless pots of fresh coffee and tea.

Of four city-centre branches, Grafton Street, recent beneficiary of a £4 million refurbishment, is the flagship café. It is perhaps hard to believe that, in the run up to the 3rd millennium, you can still count on seeing sleepy old men, fledgling poets and, tucked into the corner, whispering conspiracies of handbags. Light beams on to this delightful medley through impressive panels of art-nouveau stained glass, by lauded artist Harry Clarke.

Bewley's still commands religious devotion in its regulars as well as in those belonging to the pushy-shovey breed. As Brendan Kennelly said with relish 'the man who doesn't enjoy a bit of Bewley jostling should be sentenced to some other kind of coffee.'

Each café has a shop selling tea, coffee and chocolates.

78 Grafton Street, D2 (other branches at Westmoreland St, George's St & Mary St)
☎ 677 6761 679 9237
*7.30am–11.30pm daily (from 10am Sun).*
[→West of Grafton St 16–21]

**Guinness Hop Store**

Arthur Guinness' black magic has been lining guts for over 200 years, and the beer is as much part of Ireland as the pubs which serve it. Ten million glasses are downed daily in almost 150 countries worldwide – not a bad return on a £45 annual lease.

Although access to the brewery proper has long ceased, the Hop Store nevertheless proffers all the smells, the vats, the barley and the facts you are likely to need. The three-tiered Guinness Experience is accomplished, comprehensive and witty. Interactive displays cover marketing and advertizing, transport and the brewing process. Quarter-hourly presentations make use of waxworks, scale models and 70 of those beer barrels.

Discovering how a widget works, designing your own stout ad and standing inside a settling pint adds up to indoctrination at its most enjoyable. You may be reassured to hear that the Guinness drinker 'is more discerning in terms of taste and perspective'. It'll put the thirst into you to boot so hurrah for that free beer voucher – you'll need it.

The Guinness shop is an intoxicating exercise in marketing with everything from pint-shaped mouse mats to Guinness clocks.

St James's Street, D8
☎ 408 4800 453 8364
w www.guinness.ie
51b, 78a £4 *Apr–Oct: 9.30am–5pm Mon–Sat, 10.30am–4.30pm Sun; Nov–Mar: 9.30am–4pm Mon–Sat, 12–4pm Sun.*

**Old Jameson Distillery**

Between the cobblestones and narrow streets of the market area of Smithfield is the Old Jameson Distillery. Old is right – whiskey was first made here in the 1780's and Jameson shares the tag (with Guinness) of Ireland's most recognized drink. Although the Old Distillery now exists solely as a museum, business and legal types from the nearby courts have transformed the Old Distillery's restaurant into a popular (liquid) lunching spot in recent years.

From the stone foyer, covered in whiskey paraphernalia which spins you back over the last 200 years, it's straight into a to-the-point promo video which gives the spiel on the Jameson family and their place in Irish history. The tour tracks over the entire hooch-making process, from grain delivery to malting and bottling. Each area has wax models, authentic fittings and yawn-free descriptions. Finally, in the Ball O'Malt Bar, you're treated to a whiskey and a tutored tasting session. The tour is short and sweet, like the drink. At least 20 pubs within walking distance allow you to pursue your acquaintance with Ireland's finest.

Bow Street, Smithfield, D7
☎ 807 2355
w www.irish-whiskey-trail.com
134 £3.50 *9.30am–6pm daily (last tour 5pm).*
[→North of the Liffey 26–28]

more sights, museums & galleries

# georgian splendour

Cradling a cocksure ascendancy and a semi-independent parliament, Georgian Dublin reflected its prosperity in its cityscape. In 1757, the Wide Streets Commissioners got the thumbs up to regulate the ongoing building spree, ensuring excellence, and creating vast boulevards and top residential areas such as **Merrion** and **Fitzwilliam Squares**. Dublin's architectural king was James Gandon who, in popular myth, was smuggled into Ireland to design the **Custom House** [→46]. He stayed for 42 years, creating the **Four Courts** [→46] and other edifices which continue to have kudos heaped upon them.

The 1960's and 70's were rife with city planners itching to deploy the wrecking ball. Elegant Georgian houses, often complete with fancy fanlights, luscious interiors and wrought iron foot-scrapers, were often seen as expendable obstructions, and uncomfortable reminders of British rule. However, many fine examples of this 18th-century construction orgy can still be found. Hanging onto bullet wounds from the 1916 Rising, the **Royal College of Surgeons**, with its distinctive round-headed windows, pumps would-be doctors full of medical know-how. **Mansion House** is the Lord Mayor's 1710 gaff, and **Tailors' Hall** is now the HQ of Ireland's National Trust. Thousands of Irish kids scream their first scream in the **Rotunda Hospital** and daily entertainment is provided by the nearby **Ambassador Cinema** and the **Gate Theatre** – former Rotunda rooms. The granite-faced **Newman House** is open to visitors for guided tours of its lavish interior. Also open for a look is **Number 29** which has been restored and packed brimfull of Georgian furniture by the Electricity Supply Board, in an attempt to atone for levelling a batch of neighbouring houses.

When the 1801 Act of Union abolished the Irish parliament, many aristocrats scarpered and **North Great George's Street** lost its status as one of the city's most prestigious addresses. The street has now waved a firm goodbye to its tenement phase, but the cobbled and largely dilapidated **Henrietta Street** has not fared so well. Once a row of swanky dwellings, Henrietta Street terminates in the Law Society's copper-domed **Kings Inns**, begun by Gandon in 1795.

**Ambassador Cinema**
Parnell Square, D1

**Custom House**
Custom House Quay, D1 ☎ 878 7660 (ring for opening times)

**Four Courts**
Four Courts, D7 ☎ 872 5555 (ring for opening times)

**Gate Theatre**
1 Cavendish Row, D1

**Kings Inns**
Henrietta Street, D1

**Mansion House**
Dawson Street, D2

**Newman House**
85 St Stephen's Green S, D2
☎ 706 7422 (ring for opening times)

**Number 29**
29 Fitzwilliam Street Lower, D2
☎ 702 6165 (ring for opening times)

**Rotunda Hospital**
Parnell Street, D1

**Royal College of Surgeons**
St Stephen's Green W, D2

**Tailors' Hall**
Back Lane, D8

# specialist museums

**Heraldic Museum**

The snooker-playing chimps carved on the pillars of this lesser-known museum give some idea of the building's history: this was the site of the legendary 19th-century fleshpot, Kildare Street Men's Club, where the degenerate of old unwound. The Office of the Chief Herald (1552) designs and grants coats of arms to Irish citizens, towns and universities. It now shares the same building as the museum (founded in 1911), itself consisting of examples from four centuries of the office's handiwork. Flags, plaques and exquisite heraldic gemstones compete for attention with an interesting collection of coins, insignias and proclamations.

2 Kildare Street, D2
☎ 677 7444 free
◑ *10am–8.30pm Mon–Wed, 10am–4.30pm Thu & Fri, 10am–12.30pm Sat.*
[→East of Grafton Street 22–25]

**Irish Jewish Museum**

Chock-a-block with bits and pieces, this museum affords 15 minutes' of fame to its sacred and secular objects. Upstairs, in the disused but intact synagogue, a mannequin couple in the process of getting hitched stand under the traditional *huppah* (canopy). What was the Ladies' Gallery now exhibits a seasoned *torah* scroll along with disconcerting circumcision instruments, shiny children's stickers and information pamphlets such as *The Jewish Woman's Guide to Lighting Shabbat Candles*.

Doing its best to record the history of a dwindling

community from the year dot, the museum doesn't try to whitewash Ireland's record. The government's stance during World War II and various instances of anti-Semitism are documented. In general though, upbeat photographs of grinning scouts and guides, letters, books and other pertinent paraphernalia fill the ground floor. A concealed table set for a turn-of-the-century Sabbath jumps out from among the glass cases as a bonus.

3–4 Walworth Road (off Victoria Street), D8
☎ 453 1797
14, 14a, 15a, 15b, 83 free
◑ *May–Sep: 11am–3.30pm Tue, Thu & Sun; (Oct–Apr: 10.30am–2.30pm Sun only).*
[→Around Camden St 29–31].

**Natural History Museum**

A taxidermist's idea of heaven – stuffed with birds, beasts and bumblebees on four cluttered levels, the collection is astonishing in its scope. From panthers to pickled fish, all manner of creatures are exhibited in the old cabinet style. On the ground floor, Ireland's wildlife lies frozen in time, behind glass, suspended in jars, and scowling beneath dog-eared leather covers. A motley collection of insects is pinned down in formal classifications. However, it's when you journey upwards that the fun starts. In a deeply Gothic display, the world's most fantastic animals are caught mid-prowl, from skyscraping giraffes to a selection box of Tasmanian Devils. Most impressive in terms of scale is the skeleton of a 20m fin whale stranded off the Irish coast in 1862. Hardly quintessential Dublin, but you'll be overawed by the sheer variety of creatures inhabiting the planet. Beats the zoo hands down.

Merrion Street Upper, D2
☎ 677 7444 free
◑ *10am–5pm Tue-Sat, 2–5pm Sun.* ground floor only
[→East of Grafton St 22–28]





# ↓ distinctly dublin

**Marino Casino**

Sandwiched between a retirement home, a housing estate and a Fire Brigade Training Centre, lies Dublin's most unusual site. From a distance, the building looks huge (stately even); get closer and it appears remarkably small. On entering you realize you've been fooled again.

The Casino was built in 1759 for James Caulfield, 1st Earl of Charlemont. The man was obsessed with all things Italian and tried to bring a little of the place to Ireland with the Casino. Guarded on the outside by lions and sculptures of Greek gods, it's one of the finest examples of neo-classical architecture in Europe. Winding staircases lead from the kitchens to the exquisite parquet floor of the Hall and eventually to Caulfield's over-the-top bedroom. The key to enjoying the place is to look up: exquisite carvings of Apollo, antique trophies and the signs of the zodiac decorate the ceiling.

❶ Videos and cameras not permitted on the guided tours.

off Malahide Road, Marino, D3
☎ 833 1618 661 3111
w www.heritageireland.ie
20b, 27, 27b, 42, 42b, 43 £2
◑ *Feb–Apr: 12–4pm Sun & Thu; May & Oct: 10am–5pm daily; Jun–Sep: 9.30am–6.30pm daily; Nov: 12–4pm Sun & Wed.*

**Dublin's Viking Adventure**

Pluck up courage and board the *Skadi* – a Viking longship – and be transported back 1,000 years to 'Dyflin', where locals outline the intricacies and indignities of daily life.

These high jinks give way to more subdued offerings – a layered historical wall and a model of Wood Quay – the archaeological jewel built on by Dublin Corporation, despite protests by heritage bodies. In the main hall the sail of a full-size longship is the screen for a film about ancient Scandinavian seafarers. A museum full of excavated artefacts from nearby digs deposits you firmly back in the terrestrial present.

Essex Street West, D8
☎ 679 6040
w www.visit.ie/dublin
£4.95 ◑ *10am–4.30pm Tue-Sat.*
[→Temple Bar 10–15]

**Kilmainham Gaol**

Kilmainham's fame as 'a machine for grinding rogues honest' lies chiefly in its political prisoners. An alarmingly comprehensive tour offers views of cells once occupied by characters like Emmet, Parnell, Pearse and de Valera. Also on view is the Victorian wing, the set for numerous films, including *In the Name of the Father*, *Michael Collins* and *The Italian Job*.

Revolutionaries weren't the only inmates – you can almost feel what it was like during the famine, when up to 9,000 prisoners were crowded into 400 cells. Graffiti peppers the walls, dating from the 1790's

more sights, museums & galleries

when it first opened, to 1926, when the gaol closed, and curiously, as recently as 1991. Playwright Sean O'Casey's 'empty, stony silence' still reverberates here, and it is always colder inside than out.

The experience is a sombre one. At the end one is left pondering the walls against which leaders of the Easter Rising were executed by firing squad.

Access is by guided tour only – approx 1 hr 15 min. Last admission is 1 hr 15 min before closing time.

South Circular Rd, Kilmainham, D8 453 5984 453 2037 68, 69, 79 £3 *Apr–Sep: 9.30am–6pm daily; Oct–Mar: 9.30am–5pm Mon–Fri, 10am–6pm Sun.* limited

**Malahide Castle & Fry Model Railway Museum**

Walking up the tree-lined lane leading to Malahide Castle, you might think you've stumbled on the set of a 60's horror film or a despot's country hideaway. The truth is only marginally less seductive. Built in 1180, the castle is allegedly haunted by a belligerent small ghost called Puck, and once had the unenviable task of playing host to enforcer Oliver Cromwell. The castle was owned by the Talbot Family for nearly 800 years, and their heritage shadows you from room to room. Carved Italian fireplaces and Irish period furniture are overlooked by rococo ceilings, while family portraits and exhibits from the National Gallery adorn the thick walls. Ascend more exquisite staircases to the family bedrooms, complete with four-poster beds and enchanting views of the 80-hectare estate. By far the most jaw-dropping room is the Great Hall. Furnished in the Irish Chippendale style, it still hosts banquets today.

Wander through Lord Milo Talbot's 8-hectare botanical garden, or the ruins of a 15th-century abbey. In a nondescript building in the grounds is Mr Fry's collection of Irish train memorabilia. The panelled doors at the end of the museum lead to a far greater locomotive treasure. Inside the darkened room is an elaborate model, which provides a fascinating account of Ireland's transport history, and also manages to tour the entire country within 230 sq m. Narrow gauge trains wind through valleys and picture-postcard towns, barges ferry provisions up and down a canal network, and trams bring you back to the early part of the century, while just a few feet away Dublin's DART system catapults you into the present.

Fry Model Railway is great for kids.

Malahide, Co Dublin
846 2228 (castle)
846 3779 (museum)
to Malahide (Mon–Sat).
Castle: £3.10 Museum: £2.85 *Castle: 10am–6pm Mon–Sat, 11am–5pm Sun.*
*Museum: Apr–Sep: 10am–5pm Mon–Sat, 2–6pm Sun; Oct–Mar: 2–5pm Sat & Sun only.* museum only
[→The Coastal Towns 34–37]

**Marsh's Library**

One of the few 18th-century buildings in Dublin still being used for its original purpose, Archbishop Marsh's library is a kind of time capsule for choice books of the 'don't touch' variety. Much the same rules apply as did 300 years ago – 'All Graduats and Gentlemen shall have free access... provided they behave themselves well, give place and pay due respect to their betters...'.

Dark oak bookcases flank the library wings, crammed with Marsh's 25,000 volumes. Just when you think you couldn't hack another book, it makes a change to turn a corner and come face to face with Swift's death mask and a mould of the skull of Stella, his alleged lover. The trail ends with three wired alcoves, into which, it is said, students were locked so they couldn't steal the treasured tomes.

Ireland's oldest public library can seem a little crusty. It oozes heritage however, and the building itself forms an integral part of this area – a stately oasis that includes St Patrick's Cathedral [→47] and the Iveagh Baths.

An on-site Conservation Bindery repairs and restores old books and manuscripts.
Photography is not permitted; there's almost no heating.

St Patrick's Close, D8
454 3511
w www.kst.dit.ie/marsh
16, 16a, 83, 155 £1
*10am–12.45pm & 2–5pm Mon, Wed–Fri, 10.30am–12.45pm Sat.*
[→West of Grafton St 16–21]

## taking a breather

**Glasnevin Cemetery**

Towers for 'dead watchers' in the walls of Glasnevin Cemetery hark back to the lawless days when body snatchers ran amok. Hoi polloi lie beside statesmen and legends in this wolfhound-, shamrock-and harp-laden graveyard which opened in 1832. A window on the soap opera of Irish history, the cemetery is the final resting place of lovers and enemies alike. Michael Collins and Eamon de Valera are interred here, as are Brendan Behan and his literary opposite, the poet/priest Gerard Manley Hopkins. In the Republican plot, Maud Gonne MacBride is buried near feisty souls like Countess Markievicz and O'Donovan Rossa.

Finglas Road, D11 ☎ 830 1133
w www.glasnevin-cemetery.ie
🚌 40, 40a, 40b 🎫 free ◑ *8am–5pm daily.* ♿ ☞ *2.30pm Wed & Fri.* ❑ flower shop

## Grand Canal & Royal Canal

'O commemorate me where there is water, canal water preferably', entreated Patrick Kavanagh. And so they did. A likeness of the Monaghan poet now sits solo on the towpath by the Grand Canal, awaiting kindred spirits. A walk by the waterway, beginning around Baggot Street Bridge, can be surprisingly tranquil, considering the proximity of the big smoke. Mute swans and cygnets intermittently strut their stuff – a particularly romantic sight at first light.

The Grand Canal's northside rival, the Royal, hasn't been left out in the literary cold, copping a mention in both *Ulysses* and a downbeat ode penned by Brendan Behan. Primped and prettified recently by the Office of Public Works, who belatedly recognized the leisure potential of both canals, the Royal, like the Grand, stretches way beyond Dublin. Some pleasant walks are signposted from Clonsilla.

🚌 10 (Baggot Street Bridge, Grand Canal); 39 (Clonsilla, Royal Canal) 🎫 free ◑ *all year round* (Waterways Visitors' Centre, Grand Canal Quay, D2 ☎ 677 7510 ◑ *May–Sep: daily; Oct–May: Wed–Sun*). ❑ ♿ to some sections

## National Botanic Gardens

Masses of pampered plants have taken root in the Botanic Gardens since its inception in 1795, and now over 20,000 exotic and lowly species rule the roost. At the grand old age of almost 400, the *Todea barbara* is the most senior inhabitant, currently living in the Fern House. With lofty leafery and pervasive humidity, the Great Palm House feels like a tropical rainforest. Richard Turner, iron-master supremo, designed the restored range of glasshouses which epitomize finer Victorian visions.

Glasnevin, D9 ☎ 837 4388
🚌 13, 19, 134 🎫 free ◑ *Mar–Oct: 9am–6pm Mon–Sat, 11am–6pm Sun; Nov–Feb 10am–4.30pm Mon–Sat; 11am–4.30pm Sun (glasshouses close from 12.45–2pm daily & at 3.15 on Thu).* ❑ ♿ limited

## Phoenix Park ✔

Over a million believers ebulliently flocked to Phoenix Park on 29 September 1979 to wave tricolours

and Vatican flags as the Pope said mass. A huge cross and a bewildering plaque, advising visitors to 'be converted every day', mark the spot.

As well as 710 hectares of wilderness, sports pitches and gardens, the park encircles Dublin Zoo [→58], Ashtown Castle and Áras an Uachtaráin – home to President Mary II. Fluttering stars and stripes line the driveway leading to the US Ambassador's residence and if you're lucky you may catch a glimpse of some shy fallow deer prancing in the shadow of Wellington's 63 m obelisk.

Nestling on the banks of the Liffey, the War Memorial Park, dedicated to the Irish casualties of two world wars, is less lush than its famous neighbour.

☞ Gaelic football, polo, cricket and concerts.

Phoenix Park, D8
☎ 821 3021 (general office) ☎ 677 0095 (Visitors' Centre) ☎ 677 0236 (War Memorial Park) 🚌 10, 25, 25a, 26, 66, 67, 68, 69 🎫 free (£2 to Visitors' Centre & Ashtown Castle).
◑ *park: 24-hours* ◑ *Visitors' Centre: mid-Mar–Oct daily; Nov–mid-Mar Sat & Sun.*
◑ *War Memorial Park: 8.30am–sunset Mon–Fri; 10am–sunset Sat & Sun.* ❑ ♿

## St Stephen's Green

At the first hint of a rare summer ray, the green is strewn with scantily-clad bodies and on the stroke of one o'clock tired office workers pour in to enjoy a spot of picnicing. Jam-packed with fancy flowers, the meandering park has its fair share of resident duck-feeders who hang around the ornate pond and fling their offerings at flurrying waterfowl. 'Tone-henge', a statue of nationalist Theobald Wolfe Tone, stands with other memorials among the bandstands and landscaped lawns.

☞ Braille garden; kids' playground.

St Stephen's Green, D2 ☎ 475 7816
🎫 free ◑ *8am–sunset daily (from 10am Sun).*
❑ ♿

[→West of Grafton Street 16–21; East of Grafton Street 22–25]

From the grand, state-owned collections to private commercial spaces, Dublin's galleries are always buzzing with a diverse range of exhibitions.

# ↓ well hung

### Arthouse

Arthouse is a truly multi-media space with banks of video screens in the windows and open plan interiors which are adapted to the artists' requirements. Since opening in 1995, it has steadily become a focal point for experimental and inspirational art, incorporating art exhibitions, CD rom classes, internet facilities, performance art, kids' stuff, bagels... it has the lot – and more, as long as it's in keeping with the zeitgeist.

Curved St, D2 ☎ 605 6800 **w** www.arthouse.ie free ◑ *9am–6.30pm Mon–Fri, 10am–5.30pm Sat.* [→Temple Bar 10–15]

### Douglas Hyde Gallery ✓

Situated in the Trinity College arts block area, this small space houses some of the most experimental art around. The gallery is a popular home for performance art as well as installation work so you probably won't be buying the pieces on display. As modern art goes it doesn't get much more conceptual than this.

Trinity College, D2 ☎ 677 2941 free ◑ *11am–6pm Mon–Fri (7pm Thu), 11am–4.45pm Sat.* [→West of Grafton Street 16–21; East of Grafton Street 22–25]

### Green on Red

Jerome O'Driscoll, the curator of this trendy warehouse gallery, has an eye for what's hip. The monthly exhibitions are full of variety: some are clever installation shows, others more sales-orientated. Showing predominantly Irish work, the gallery also coordinates talks and workshops for interested parties. Speaking of parties, the Thursday night openings are some of the most happening gatherings in town.

26–28 Lombard Street East, D2 ☎ 671 3414 free ◑ *10am–6pm Mon–Fri, 11am–5pm Fri & Sat.*

### Hugh Lane Municipal Gallery of Modern Art

A real smorgasbord of all art styles and disciplines, mostly from the 20th century. Of particular

interest is the stained-glass room – with some excellent Irish examples – and the forthcoming Francis Bacon studio which will give the gallery a global focus. Bacon's studio has been moved lock, stock and barrel and will be reconstructed by 2001, with a run-up of related exhibitions. In addition to the resident collection are rotating shows by contemporary artists.

Charlemont House, Parnell Square North, D1 ☎ 874 1903 free ◑ *9.30am–6pm Tue–Thu, 9.30am–5pm Fri & Sat, 11am–5pm Sun.* [→North of the Liffey 26–28]

### Ib Jorgensen Fine Art

More conservative in flavour but XL in the chic stakes, this is the place to go if you have wads of cash and fancy some tasteful 20th-century art. What Jorgensen lacks in adventure he makes up for in quality. Originally Ireland's most prestigious fashion couturier, Danish-born Ib developed the gallery from what was initially a personal passion. A perfectionist by nature, his exhibitions follow suit, and shows regularly sell out on opening nights.

29 Molesworth Street, D2 ☎ 661 9758 free ◑ *9am–5.30pm Mon–Fri, 9.30am–2pm Sat.* [→East of Grafton Street 22–25]

### Irish Museum of Modern Art

The Irish Museum of Modern Art is just what its name suggests. Housed in Ireland's most important 17th-century building, IMMA was inaugurated in 1990 and has since shown the museum's collection and acquisitions on a rotating basis along with shows of Irish and international provenance. At least three exhibitions run simultaneously. Annual highlights include the Glen Dimplex Awards in Irish art each June.

Kilmainham Hospital, Kilmainham, D8 ☎ 612 9900 🚌 68, 68a, 69, 78a, 79, 90 free ◑ *10am–5.30pm Tue–Sat, 12–5.30pm Sun.* ☐ (2.30pm Wed & Fri, 12.15 pm Sun)

### Kerlin Gallery

In this John Pawson-designed gallery, even the walls are cooler than cool. With a policy that concentrates on the conceptual and innovative end of modern art, the Kerlin includes some of Ireland's most renowned contemporary artists. The gallery never fails to get viewers drooling. Prices vary hugely, but those who simply want some visual stimulation are left to look in peace.

Anne's Lane, D2 ☎ 670 9093 **w** www.kerlin.ie free *10am–5.45pm Mon–Fri, 11am–4.30pm Sat.* **[→East of Grafton St 22–25]**

### National Gallery

Probably the most conventional gallery on the list, the National is impressive, even by global standards. The ground floor houses Irish paintings and the Jack B Yeats' Museum, a fantastic display of work by Ireland's most famous turn-of-the-century artist. Upstairs the international collection includes work by Rembrandt, Rubens, Titian, Uccello, Goya and Vermeer. The gallery's extensive collection of Turners is on show every January.

Merrion Square West, D2 ☎ 661 5133 **w** www.nationalgallery.ie free *10am–5.30pm Mon–Sat (8pm Thu), 2–5pm Sun.* **[→East of Grafton Street 22–25]**

### RHA Gallagher Gallery

One of Dublin's best spaces, the gallery consists of several large rooms which exhibit the Royal Hibernian Academy annual restrospective, as well as other landmark shows. This is also the chosen venue for the National College of Art and Design summer show in June, where the names of tomorrow get their first airing. A new curator, Pat Kelly, has already instigated some interesting changes in exhibitions upstairs. The basement cellars are often used as a theatre and party venue.

Royal Hibernian Academy, 15 Ely Place Upper, D2 ☎ 661 2558 free *11am–5pm Tue–Sat (9pm Thu), 2–5pm Sun.* (on request) **[→East of Grafton Street 22–25]**

## in the picture

Temple Bar isn't just known for its Rabelaisian excesses – thankfully there's some culture going on too. The **Gallery of Photography** exhibits a well-selected mix of new and established names over four floors, whilst keeping an excellently stocked book and card shop. The neighbouring **Temple Bar Gallery** defies type, bringing a wide variety of art to its single room. Upstairs, resident artists work out of subsidized studios, some of which have the best views in Dublin. Next door, the **Original Print Gallery** is an excellent place to find affordable pieces by Irish and foreign artists. Flick through racks of unmounted work or oggle over the ever-changing displays on the walls.

Popular culture buffs will find the **Apollo Gallery** of particular interest. Amongst the artists represented is Graham Knuttel whose harsh cubist compositions caught the eye of Sylvester Stallone in the early 1990's and have since rocketed in value. Popular in restaurants and bars around the world, Knuttel may be an acquired taste, but his pointy people and social settings seem to be seducing those in the know. For more interesting bargains try the **Kevin Kavanagh Gallery**, a new space opened by the owner/curator of the former Jo Rain Gallery. Once again, he goes for the new, unexhibited artist as well as interesting Irish names on the up. Exhibitors in the **Rubicon Gallery** are often young, but many are already established thanks in no small part to the tireless work of owner Josephine Kelleher. Work on show is contemporary, innovative and often abstract.

If you're looking for art, but not necessarily of the framed variety, the **Solomon Gallery** shows a wide variety of glass, ceramic and metal pieces. Managing to stay on the arty side of craft, the work comes from all over the world and many fit neatly into a suitcase. Noelle Campbell Sharp has been known for many things in Irish society – a publisher and band manager to name just two – but her latest project is the **Origin Gallery**. Though governed strongly by her own personal taste, it has seen some interesting exhibitions since opening in 1997. The work is mostly Irish, with a generous quantity of sculptural pieces for fans of the third dimension.

**Apollo Gallery**
17–18 Duke Street, D2
☎ 671 2609

**Gallery of Photography**
Meeting House Square, D2
☎ 671 4654

**Kevin Kavanagh Gallery**
66 Strand Street Great, D1
☎ 874 0064

**Origin Gallery** 83 Harcourt St, D2 ☎ 478 5159

**Original Print Gallery**
4 Temple Bar, D2 ☎ 677 3657

**Rubicon Gallery**
10 St Stephen's Green, D2
☎ 670 8055

**Solomon Gallery**
Top Floor, Powerscourt Townhouse, William St South, D2 ☎ 679 4237

**Temple Bar Gallery**
5–9 Temple Bar, D2
☎ 671 0073

There are anomalies in the Dubliners' attitudes to children. Many city-centre pubs and some restaurants won't allow them, while others may fail to provide the required equipment and menus. On the other hand, entertainment for kids, such as The Ark and the Lambert Mews Puppet Theatre, are superb, and the quality of Irish-made toys and clothes is excellent. So it's a mixed bag – but by no means actively hostile towards children.

# ↓ kiddies' corner

## great adventures

**The Ark ►**

The Ark provides plays, art workshops, exhibitions and interactive concerts for kids. There are no permanent shows or exhibitions, so phone to check for activities to suit your child's interest and age. A wonderful place in a fantastic building that includes mini-size loos and a stage area that opens out onto Meeting House Square for special plays and events.

11a Eustace Street, D2
☎ 670 7788
w www.ark.ie
£3–£6 ◑ *9.30am–5.30pm Mon–Fri (weekends variable).*
4–14

**Dublin Zoo**

Now bigger and better, and doing its best to cope with changing attitudes towards keeping animals in captivity. Some of the larger animals have gone, and enlarged grounds have been built for the rest. The World of Primates, the Fringes of the Arctic and the World of Cats have recently been completed, while African Plains – a 13-hectare enclosure for the giraffes, rhinos and hippos – is next for development as the zoo plans to double in size.

Phoenix Park, D8
☎ 677 1425
w www.dublinzoo.ie
10 £5.90 adults; £3.20 kids (under 3's free)
◑ *9.30am–4.30pm Mon–Sat (to 5pm Sat), 10.30am–5pm Sun.*
all ages

**LeisurePlex**

This leisure centre is one of a chain scattered around the Dublin area that targets all ages by offering wide-ranging activities. There's something for everyone from Zoo Adventure through to Quasar, bowling, snooker, billiards and a whole galaxy of video machines. And if you find yourself spending all day here, it's even got its own restaurant.

Malahide Road, Coolock, D17
☎ 848 5722 27 vary from £2 plus ◑ *24 hours daily.*
3 and over

## kid's portions

**Botticelli**

Large joint run by real Italians with a genuine enthusiasm for children. They will make pizzas to suit individual tastes, but also serve fantastic pizza slices (herbs and potato, aubergine and mozzarella) that are perfect for kids, and pretty good for adults too!

3 Temple Bar, D2
☎ 672 7289
◑ *12pm–midnight daily.*
all ages limited

**Café Rouge**

French bistro chain that gets top marks for effort with the best kids' menu in town and a really imaginative children's pack, with colours, puzzles, stickers and masks, etc. There are two children's menus – one for young kids and another for those with more sophisticated tastes, including a vegetarian option. A warning: the 'grown up' food can vary hugely in quality and the service can be erratic. But when it all works it's wonderful.

1 St Andrews' Street, D2
☎ 679 1357
◑ *10am–11pm daily (to 10.30pm Sun).* all ages

## *bray*

*A seaside town in County Wicklow, Bray [→37] is a wonderful spot to bring children of all ages for the day, and a place they will clamour to revisit. First there is the DART ride [→6] out along the coast, a treat in itself. The entire seafront is lined with entertainments, including* ***Dawson Family Fun*** *and* ***Star Amusements****, offering dodgems, slot machines, whirligigs, horse-racing machines, a spiralling snake slide and a funfair. There's* ***Bray Bowl****, which, as well as bowling, has a restaurant, and the* ***High Jinks Club*** *where children can climb net frames, bounce with giant balls, plunge into vats of smaller balls and run through tunnels into net cages. The* ***Bray Royal Cineplex*** *has six screens, while the* ***National Sealife Centre*** *offers an interactive journey through the aquatic world. Children will see octopus, sea horses and sharks – even getting to touch some of them. Then there are quizzes and tricks to spot along the way to an entertaining, but expensive, souvenir shop. Kids can also enjoy the* ***Bray Seaside Road Train****, which leaves the centre every 15 minutes and takes them along the seafront, around Bray Head and back again. After all that adventure,* ***Pizzas 'n' Cream*** *offers pizzas, pasta and ice-cream, with a patio for pleasant summer dining, and staff who go out of their way to make a fuss of the young ones.*

**Bray Bowl**
Quinnsboro Road ☎ 286 4453
**Bray Royal Cineplex**
Quinnsboro Road ☎ 286 8686
**Bray Seaside Road Train**
Bray Beach ☎ 286 3750
**Dawson Family Fun**
Strand Road ☎ 286 0974
**High Jinks Club**
Quinnsboro Road ☎ 286 5677
**National Sealife Centre**
Strand Road ☎ 286 1299
**Pizzas 'n' Cream**
9b Albert Walk ☎ 286 1606
**Star Amusements**
Strand Road ☎ 286 3540

**Captain America's Cookhouse**

Longstanding, reliable burger joint, this Dublin landmark has a good, varied children's menu for £3, non-alcoholic cocktails, colour-in menus, crayons, high chairs and a clown on Sundays who does balloon sculpture.

44 Grafton Street, D2
☎ 671 5266
◑ *12–11.30pm daily.* all ages

**The Good World**

One of the best Chinese restaurants in town, it's always packed with Chinese kids tucking into noodles and dim sum. High chairs available.

18 South Great George's St, D2
☎ 677 5373 ◑ *12.30pm–3am daily.* all ages

**Gotham City**

A busy, city-centre pasta and pizza joint, Gotham [→82] is cool enough for adolescents and the food is good enough for adults. High chairs are available, including one for tiny babies, but space doesn't allow for buggies. Crayons and colouring books are provided and children's requests will be willingly accommodated. Booking is advisable on Saturdays.

8 Anne Street South, D2
☎ 679 5266
◑ *12–midnight Mon–Sat, 12–4pm & 5–10.30pm Sun.*
all ages ♿ limited

## toys galore

**Early Learning Centre**

Quality toys – safe, hard-wearing, with age ranges carefully marked, and a leaning towards the educational, creative and PC.

3 Henry Street, D1
☎ 873 1945
◑ *9am–5.30pm Mon–Sat (to 8pm Thu), 1–5pm Sun.*
up to 8 ♿

**Nimble Fingers**

No Barbie dolls here, just helpful staff and old-fashioned arts, crafts and educational toys. This is where Mia Farrow buys for her youngsters.

Stillorgan, Co Dublin
☎ 288 0788
🚌 46, 46a, 62, 63, 84 ◑ *9am–6pm Mon–Sat (from 9.30am Sat).* all ages

**Rainbow Crafts**

Specialists in handmade wooden toys, rubber-stamp art and, at the top of the range, bespoke teddy bears.

Westbury Mall, Harry Street, D2
☎ 677 7632
◑ *9am–6pm Mon–Sat.*
all ages ♿

**Smyths**

A vast toy superstore that stocks an enormous range of the usual, much-hyped toys and fads, including computer games and equipment.

Jervis Street, D1 ☎ 878 2852
◑ *9.30am–6pm Mon–Sat (to 9pm Thu), 2–6pm Sun.*
all ages ♿

## top-to-toe

**Arnott's**

This store has a huge childrenswear department with a section for all the big names – Adams, Benetton, Clarks, Laura Ashley, Ladybird, Lego, Osh Kosh and Timberland – as well as their own Arnott's area. Size often matters, and 7,300 sq m ensures the widest choice in the country.

12 Henry Street, D1
☎ 805 0400
◑ *9am–6.30pm Mon–Sat (to 9pm Thu), 12–6pm Sun.*
all ages ♿

**Dunnes Stores**

It may be the cheap end of the market, but those living abroad pine for their good-value, warm, colourful children's clothes. You won't be handing them down to the third generation, but then you can hardly expect to for the price.

St Stephen's Green Centre, D2
☎ 478 0188
◑ *8.30am–7pm Mon–Sat (to 9pm Thu), 12–6pm Sun.*
all ages ♿

**Gymboree**

The Dublin outlet of an American chain in an accessible location. The clothes are brightly coloured and hard-wearing – ideal for climbing trees, building dams and having a good time. Also some pretty party pieces.

75 Grafton Street, D2
☎ 670 3331
w www.gymboree.com
◑ *10am–6pm Mon–Sat (to 8pm Thu), 12–6pm Sun.*
up to 7 ♿

**Jacadi**

The only Irish outlet of this super-chic French chain – for children who like a fully coordinated look, never get dirty, and have well-off, indulgent parents. They will look delightful, though.

33 King Street South, D2
☎ 671 1418
◑ *9.30am–6pm Mon–Sat.*
up to 12

## *show time*

*Pantomimes are a crucial part of the traditional Dublin Christmas. The sumptuous **Gaiety Theatre**, complete with its red velvet and sparkling chandeliers, was once the only place to go, but now the **Olympia Theatre** also runs a panto every year. Well worth a trip is Ireland's only puppet theatre, the enchanting **Lambert Mews Theatre**, which is run by Eugene Lambert, his wife and their ten children.*

*Among the wide range of large cinema complexes, the **Virgin Multiplex** cinema is one of the most accessible and best geared towards children, offering always at least one children's film and a non-smoking milk bar specially for kids. But the newest sensation is the **Sheridan IMAX** cinema (next to the Virgin Multiplex), which has a giant wrap-around screen, a well-policed games arcade, a simulator ride, fast food and a family restaurant based on a sports theme. The **Junior Dublin Film Festival** takes place in the last week of November and first two weeks of December at different venues around town.*

**Gaiety Theatre**
King Street South, D2
☎ 677 1717

**Sheridan IMAX**
Parnell Centre, Parnell St, D1
☎ 817 4222

**Junior Dublin Film Festival**
☎ 671 4095

**Lambert Mews Theatre**
Clifton Lane, Monkstown, Co Dublin ☎ 280 0974

**Olympia Theatre**
72 Dame Street, D2
☎ 677 7744

**Virgin Multiplex**
Parnell Centre, Parnell St, D1
☎ 872 8444

A weird and wonderful range of activities and experiences awaits you. From belly dancing or cruising around in a limo, to the more traditional pub crawl, if you want something a bit different, you'll find it in Dublin.

# ↓ game for a laugh

### Belly Dancing

Sample another culture. If you want to wiggle like Marilyn Monroe, try belly dancing. It's graceful, fun and easy to learn and it's great exercise for body and mind. You tie a scarf round your hips to highlight the moves and to make sure you're doing them right. The weekly classes – open to all – are run by Bellydance Ireland and held in Outhouse, the Dublin resource centre for gays and lesbians. Private classes can also be organized for groups of six or more.

**Outhouse**
William Street South, D2
☎ 679 1306 £5 per class
◑ *6.30–7.30pm Mon.*
❶ Wear loose comfortable clothing and bring a scarf to tie around your hips.

### Greyhound Racing

Go to the dogs, a traditional night out in Dublin with a difference. Dog breeding is very popular in the city with owners as young as ten at the tracks. As the stadium is flood-lit it makes a better winter pursuit than a summer night out. Corporate suites are available for parties of 20 or more, and booking is advisable for these. Posh three course dinners, or burgers on the hop, are served during the races.

**Shelbourne Park**
Lotts Road, Ringsend, D4
☎ 668 3502
1, 3 £4 ◑ *8pm onwards Wed, Thu & Sat.*

### Early Houses

Drink at dawn in some of the city's famous Early Houses – a practice popular with clubbers and party animals. These pubs traditionally opened at about 7am to serve the dockers and market wholesalers who didn't work nine to five. They also pull some of the finest pints of Guinness to be found in the capital. Grab the opportunity to rub shoulders with real Dubs. Favourite early-morning haunts include Delaney's and Slattery's [→96] the Dockers, Windjammer and Ned Scanlans.

**The Dockers**
5 Sir John Rogersons Quay, D2
☎ 677 1692 ◑ *from 7am.*

**Windjammer**
111 Townsend Street, D2
☎ 677 2576 ◑ *from 7.30am.*

**Ned Scanlans**
44 Townsend Street, D2
☎ 677 9507 ◑ *from 7am.*

### Go Karting

Kart City is the biggest karting facility in town, with three tracks – two outdoor and one indoor. Make like Eddie Jordan and go for the 'Pro-Track Grand Prix'. You really need a minimum of eight to ten people to make the most of the racing. Food can be organized and tailored to suit your needs – anything from chip-van fast-food to a four-course meal. Mini-bus hire can also be arranged if required.

**Kart City**
Old Airport Road, Santry, D9
☎ 842 6322 41, 41b
vary (Pro-Track costs £30 per person) ◑ *12–10pm daily.*
❶ Advance booking is essential. Alcohol is not served.

### Horse Riding

Horse ride in Phoenix Park [→55], the biggest urban green space in Europe. The Ashtown Riding Stables ride out from the Castleknock Gates. The stables offer hour-long lessons and/or rides, and you can also experience an exhilarating gallop through the herds of Sika deer that roam the park.

**Ashtown Riding Stables**
Ashtown, Castleknock, D15
☎ 838 3807 37, 38, 39
£12/hour ◑ *9.30am–5.30pm Sat & Sun.*
❶ Wear boots and non-restrictive clothing. Hats are supplied.

### Hiring a Boat

Ride the waves, race the wind and have the time of your life on the Dublin Bay Sea Thrill. Get a group together and you'll be kitted out in high-chest trousers and life jackets and then taken out past Dalkey Island, the Muglins, around Killiney Bay and back to the Kingston Hotel for a barbecue. Not for the faint-hearted.

**Dublin Bay Sea Thrill**
Carlisle Terminal, East Pier, Dun Laoghaire
☎ 230 1230
to Dun Laoghaire
£160 per boat
◑ *subject to group booking.*
❶ Wear warm clothing. Waterproofs provided.

### Hiring a Limo

The Limousine Company offers a variety of services. All cars seat seven and have not one but two champagne bars, multi-media system, telephone and – most essential of all – an ice box. If you simply want to arrive in style they offer a direct transfer from the airport. For half- or full-day scenic trips they will customize the tour to suit you. A great – if pricey – alternative to the taxi crisis that holds the city to ransom.

**The Limousine Company**
☎ 843 9055 from £65 for direct transfers, £156 for 4 hours, £390 for the night
◑ *24 hours.* ❶ Credit card payments only.

### Horse & Cart/Rickshaw

Since taxis can be difficult to find on weekend nights, an alternative and entertaining way to get home is either in a cycle rickshaw or on one of the city's many horse-drawn carts. Temple Bar is Rickshaw Central; most rickshaw drivers are students and will, if bribed appropriately, give you an unofficial tour of the inner city sights. Hail them as you would a taxi, or try a traditional horse-drawn carriage. The carriages are scruffy and the drivers may be gruff but they are bona fide Dubs who will give an insight into the city. There's a carriage 'rank' at the Grafton Street corner of St Stephen's Green.

£ vary ◑ *up to seven nights a week in the high summer season, & Thu–Sun in winter.* ❶ Establish an estimated fare before setting off.

## Ice Skating

The only rink in the city, the Silver Skate Ice Rink attracts a mixed crowd of rough-and-ready regulars and groups who are there for a laugh. The locals are pretty nifty on their skates, so unless you're Torvill or Dean you may feel slightly inadequate. Your friends will probably enjoy the floor show though. Dress down and wear lots of layers as it is freezing. The place has great kitsch appeal.

**Silver Skate Ice Rink**
372b North Circular Road, D7
☎ 830 4405 🚌 10 £ £3
◑ *2.30–5pm & 8–10.30pm daily.* ❶ Boot hire included.

## Spinning Yarns & Set Dancing

Become Irish – learn how to spin yarns without ever kissing the Blarney Stone. There are story-telling sessions on the second Thursday of every month at Club Na Muinteoiri. You get the opportunity to hear real experts expound on life, love and the world. If you've got a really good story to tell you might even get the chance to share it.

Also at Club Na Muinteoiri is set dancing, the origin of the ceilidh species and a traditional activity that is enjoying an ironic renaissance. Do you know how to do the 'Walls of Limerick'? They also have occasional ceilidh nights. These are irregular so be sure to call ahead. Alternatively there is dancing every night at O'Shea's Merchant [→93] – quite touristy but a great craic nonetheless.

**Club Na Muinteoiri**
36 Parnell Square, D1
☎ 280 8322
£ £4 ◑ *5–11pm Mon–Sat.*

## Paragliding

Learn how to paraglide in two days. The training is weather-dependent, but if you're in the city for more than a few days and want to feel the wind in your hair and enjoy the beautiful scenery in the 'Garden of Ireland,' this is the most unusual way to do it. If there's not much time, forget it, since Kilmacanogue is quite off the beaten track.

**Paragliding Centre**
Kilmacanogue, Bray, Co Wicklow
☎ 830 3884
Ⓓ to Bray where a van will collect you. £ £120 for a two-day course not including food or accommodation (booking essential) ◑ *Mar–Sep.*
❶ Wear layers and ankle-supporting boots.

## Pub Crawling

Try the literary or music pub crawls. The Jameson Literary Pub Crawl tours are conducted by thesps who will regale you with the antics of the city's best-loved writers and trawl the haunts of Behan *et al.* The Musical Pub Crawl tends to be a rowdier evening out. Top-class traditional musicians accompany you on a tour of the city's best musical pubs whilst entertaining you with some of their finest ballads.

**Jameson's Literary Pub Crawl**
☎ 454 0228
Meet in the Duke pub, Duke Street, D2 £ £6 ◑ *phone for details.*

**Musical Pub Crawl**
☎ 478 0193
Meet in the Oliver St John Gogarty pub, 18–21 Anglesea Street, D2 £ £6 ◑ *phone for details.*

## Snooker

For a ballsy evening head for Jason's for Snooker. A smoky, atmospheric place open 24 hours a day this is *the* southside place to hang out in the wee hours. As the former training ground of one-time world champion Ken Doherty, there's every chance that you might bump into him fine-tuning his skills. He's also open to being challenged to a game.

**Jason's for Snooker**
56 Ranelagh Road, D6
☎ 497 5983
🚌 44, 44b, 86 £ £4.80/hr (4am–6pm); £6.80/hr (6pm–4am) ◑ *24 hours daily.*

## Swimming

DART to Killiney and scramble down the cliffs from the Vico Road to White Rock where you can take the plunge or – on a good day – sun yourself on the rocks. To join the northsiders and feel the sand beneath your feet, Dollymount Strand on North Bull Island is a beautiful white sandy beach backed by dunes which form a bird sanctuary for several rare species. Anyone with a car wishing to splash around in Wicklow [→38–41] should head for Nun's Head at Brittas Bay – head south on the N11.

**White Rock**
off Vico Rd, Killiney, Co Dublin
Ⓓ to Killiney

**Dollymount Strand**
North Bull Island, Co Dublin
🚌 130

**Nun's Beach**
Brittas Bay, Co Wicklow
🚌 2 from Busaras

## Ten-Pin Bowling

If you're still buzzing after the clubs, go ten-pin bowling. At this time of night most of the clientele are like-minded clubbers who aren't quite ready to go home. Food is available and the mini-breakfast should provide the required 'soakage' to help you get through your game.

**Stillorgan Bowling Centre**
Stillorgan, Co Dublin
☎ 288 1656 🚌 Nitelink route K
£ £13 per lane plus £1 entrance fee & 60p shoe hire
◑ *24 hours daily.*

## Windsurfing

Being a coastal city there are numerous locations around Dublin where you can surf and sail. Surfdock is located in Ringsend, one of the most photographed areas of the city, which was used as a location for movies such as *The General* and *In the Name of the Father.* Windsurfing, sailing and canoeing are all on offer. It's a wonderful, central location to indulge in the great outdoors.

Surfdock also organizes party nights for groups of ten or more. Learn how to windsurf, canoe or sail and then enjoy a barbecue followed by the mandatory visit to the pub.

**Surfdock**
Grand Canal Dock Yard, South Dock, Ringsend, D4
☎ 668 3945
🚌 1, 3 £ £25 for a 3-hour session (day/weekend rates available) ◑ *summer: 10am–sundown.*
❶ Wetsuits, lifejackets and insurance cover provided.

## Theatrical Walking Tour

Expose yourself to the Zozimus Experience: a theatrical walking tour of medieval Dublin that is a fascinating cocktail of street theatre, entertainment, ghosts and murder mystery. Inspired by a blind 17th-century Dublin character, it is an atmospheric after-dark encounter with much of Dublin's past. The tour concludes in a pub where you take part in a mini-wake.

☎ 661 8646
£ £6 ◑ *varies: meet daily at nightfall at the main gate of Dublin Castle, D2.*
❶ Dress warmly. Advance booking essential.

When your tense body screams 'enough', chilled-out practitioners with honeydew hands and vats of sweet-smelling oils are just around the corner. So, have a detoxifying facial, lift the spirit with a spot of quiet meditation or subject yourself to a strenuous stretching session.

# ↓ the feelgood factor

## all-rounders

**Powerscourt Springs**

This live-in health spa does luxurious one day packages as well as longer stays. Surrendering your body to the joys of a peppermint twist is just as encouraged as going hell-for-leather on the exercise bikes. A well-stocked wine cellar means that you can knock back the bevvies afterwards. A place for total indulgence.

Coolakay, Enniskerry, Co Wicklow ☎ 276 1000 to Bray then Mulvey's bus £40–£100/day; £95–£110/overnight; £249–£279/weekend; £450–£525/week ◑ *24 hours daily.*

## beauty treatments

**Anne McDevitt**

Since 83, this high-tech salon, has been curing skin complaints and conditions, in addition to providing the usual treatments to help achieve a general state of loveliness.

13 Wicklow Street, D2 ☎ 677 7962 aromatherapy £39; reflexology £30; diathermy (30 min) £20; massage £20–£40 ◑ *9.30am–6pm Mon–Sat (to 6.30pm Tue, 9pm Thu).*

**Buttercups**

A busy city centre salon with myriad sumptuous products, therapies and methods to rid the body of noxious city fumes. Flouncy, frilly cubicles separate clients who pop in for quick fix-its and day-long sessions.

26a Powerscourt Townhouse, D2 ☎ 679 4866 facials from £30; full body massage from £32 ◑ *9am–7pm Mon–Wed, 9am–8.30pm Thu, 9am–7.30pm Fri, 9am–6pm Sat.*

**Cherry Coogan**

Serene and discreet, Cherry Coogan's no-nonsense salon is a comfortable, old-world place for a spot of self-improvement. The regal Shelbourne offers appropriate surrounds for this salubrious parlour popular with both men and women.

Shelbourne Hotel, St Stephen's Green, D2 ☎ 676 1358 massage £30; facial £14 ◑ *9am–6pm Tue–Sat (to 8pm Thu).*

**Gillian Fox Chiropody Health & Beauty Clinic**

The best of holistic and high-tech treatments including aromatherapy, reflexology, hair removal and anti-aging. Gillian also runs a thriving fashion consultancy business from these airy turn-of-the-century rooms. Glorious foot massages are included in the price of facials.

38–39 Morrison Chambers, 32 Nassau Street, D2 ☎ 670 9324 full body massage £35; one-hour facial £35 ◑ *10am–6pm Tue–Sat.*

**Tethra Spa**

Treatments in the neo-Roman Tethra Spa may be pricey, but their clever stress-busting techniques and fancy Espa products send the senses soaring. A 'flight reviver' and various cosmetic touch-ups are also available.

Merrion Hotel, Merrion Street Upper, D2 ☎ 603 0600 treatments from £4–£60 ◑ *9am–8pm daily.* in hotel

## alternative therapies

**Holistic Healing Centre**

Dame Street's answer to nasty modern stresses, with Indian head massages, reflexology and two-hour aromatherapy treatments – all devilishly pleasurable.

38 Dame Street, D2 ☎ 671 0813 reflexology £25; aromatherapy £40 ◑ *9am–7.30pm Mon & Tue, 9am–6pm Wed–Fri, 10am–6pm Sat.*

**Melt, Temple Bar Natural Healing Centre**

An oasis of calm amid Temple Bar's dens of iniquity. At an iridology session, an iris analyst will gaze into your eyes and reveal all. Kinesiology, acupuncture and Zen shiatsu are among the other delights.

2 Temple Lane South, D2 ☎ 679 8786 treatments from £20 ◑ *10am–9.30pm Tue–Sat.*

**Tony Quinn Health Centre**

Health guru Tony Quinn's centres do a rip-roaring trade. Try a bout of Ki massage therapy to replenish that misplaced zest.

9–11 Grafton Street, D2 ☎ 671 2788 Ki massage

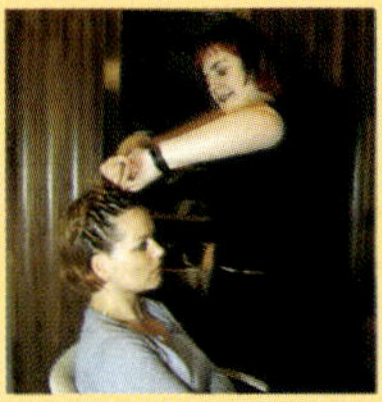

## *hairdos*

*If a blowdry or trim is in order, Dublin's copious coiffeurs will willingly oblige.* David Marshall Hair Studio *is home to Ireland's first superstar stylist. A session in the maestro's palace doesn't come cheap, but the glamour pusses remain undeterred.* Peter Marks Hair & Beauty *is a less expensive safe bet. Down the road, the young, funky* Lunatic Fringe *specializes in dreadlocks, hair extensions and creative colouring, while* Zoo ✓ *offers loads of remedies and treatments. For some ultra-individual attention and a bit of hair philosophy to boot, try* The Natural Cut*. Believing in 'maintenance-free hairdressing', the professionals here will wet rather than shampoo your hair. Oh, and forget about the blowdry.*

## directory

**David Marshall Hair Studio**
6 Dawson Street, D2
☎ 677 0106
**Lunatic Fringe**
69 Grafton Street, D2
☎ 679 3766
**The Natural Cut**
First Floor, 34 Wicklow St, D2
☎ 679 7130
**Peter Marks Hair & Beauty**
St Stephens Green Centre, D2
☎ 478 0362
**Zoo**
25 Exchequer Street, D2
☎ 672 5177

therapy from £17; nutritional consultation £60 ◑ *9am–7pm Mon–Fri (to 9pm Tue & Thu), 10am–4pm Sat.*

## meditation/yoga

**Dublin Meditation Centre**

Run by the friends of the Western Buddhist Order, and swaddled in mellowness, the DMC draws you away from the lunacy of the street. On weekdays, anyone interested in karma, dharma and such can use the meditation room for 50p. Drop-in yoga, workshops and seminars are sometimes available too.

2 Essex Street East, D2
☎ 671 3187 🎫 vary ◑ *vary.*

## fitness & dance

**Litton Lane**

A real 'kids from Fame' kinda place where all the teen bands, Riverdancers and pantomime extras audition and rehearse. The venue hosts plenty of classes from step to specialist dance. Pay as you go.

2–4 Litton Lane, D1.
☎ 872 8044 🎫 classes £2.50–£3.50; day pass £10 ◑ *vary.*

**Pulse Fitness Workshop**

A sweat-box of a gym with a good vibe for those into working out rather than posing in lycra. Power-step, body sculpt and cardio-funk to your heart's content.

1–2 Temple Bar, D2 ☎ 679 9620
🎫 classes £3–£3.50 (membership not needed) ◑ *varies* ♿

## body piercing

**Body Shock**

If studs and rings are your game, this is the place to play. Exuding hygiene, this piercing parlour smells comfortingly of disinfectant. They've bedecked the navel, lips, nose and dangly bits of many an intrepid soul here. As long as you're over 18, they'll punch a hole just about anywhere.

11 Fownes Street Upper, D2
☎ 672 7602 🎫 ear/nose/eyebrow from £12; navel from £18
◑ *12–6pm Tue–Sat.*

Whether it's a flutter on the horses or the frenetic energy of hurling, Dubliners just live for sport.

# ↓ match of the day

**Boxing**

The thriving amateur scene has its home in the National Stadium. With a capacity of 2000, you're close enough to smell the sweat and it's the perfect spot to catch emerging talent. If you're after the heavy hitters, the Point Depot occasionally hosts title fights. A new venue, Vicar Street, will hold professional fights in the future.

**National Stadium**, 145 South Circular Road, D8 ☎ 453 3371
🚌 19 🎫 £6–£10 ♿ limited
**Point Depot**, East Link Bridge, D1 ☎ 836 3663 🚌 53, 53a ♿
**Vicar Street**, Thomas Street, D7
☎ 609 7788 🚌 51b, 78a
🎫 from £15 ♿

**Football**

The national team play their home games at Lansdowne Road. Tickets for qualification matches go fast, but you should be able to pick up a ticket for a friendly on the day. Domestic-league games between Dublin clubs such as Shelbourne and St Patrick's Athletic are worth a look. Season: Aug–May (domestic); all year (international).

**Lansdowne Road Stadium**, Lansdowne Road, D4
☎ 676 6864 ⓓ to Lansdowne Road 🎫 from £14
**St Patrick's Athletic**, 125 Emmet Road, D8
☎ 453 6332 🚌 51b, 78a ♿ limited
**Shelbourne**, Tolka Park, Richmond Rd, D9 ☎ 837 5536
🎫 £4–£7 🚌 3, 11, 11a, 13a, 16, 16a ♿

**Gaelic Games**

An absolute must. Gaelic football is the national game, while hurling is probably the fastest sport in the world. Dublin plays its home games at Parnell Park. The home of the Gaelic Athletics Association in Ireland is Croke Park, a magnificent stadium. The top-level county games are held here. Tickets are always scarce so be prepared to pay over the odds. Season: all year (club); Mar–Sep (inter-county).

**Croke Park**, Jones' Road, D9
☎ 836 3222 🚌 3, 11, 11a, 16, 16a, 51a 🎫 £25
**Parnell Park**, Collins' Avenue East, Donnycarney, D5
☎ 851 0650 🚌 27, 42 🎫 £26

**Horse Racing**

As you would expect from a country world-renowned for breeding and training horses, there are plenty of places to go if you fancy a flutter. All the racecourses below are outside the city, so plan for a full-day trip. Buses operate from Busaras coach station on race days (check for details).

**Fairyhouse** (steeplechase), Fairyhouse Road, Rathoath, Co Meath ☎ 825 6167
🎫 £8–20 ♿
**The Curragh** (flat), The Curragh, Co Kildare
☎ 045 441 205 🚆 from Heuston station 🎫 £8–13 ♿
**Leopardstown** (flat & national hunt), Foxrock, D18
☎ 289 3607 🎫 £8–15 ♿
**Naas** (flat & national hunt), Pipper Road, Naas, Co Kildare
☎ 045 897 391 🎫 £7–8 ♿
**Punchestown** (national hunt), Naas, Co Kildare
☎ 045 897 704 🎫 £7–£13 ♿

**Rugby Union**

Two of the five nations championship matches (Jan–Mar) are guaranteed to be held at Lansdowne Road. But beware: tickets sell fast and you'll find yourself paying a small fortune on match day. The stronghold of club rugby is on the south side of the city – watch out for teams like Blackrock and Lansdowne. Season: Oct–May.

**Blackrock College RFC**, Stradbrook Rd, Blackrock, Co Dublin ☎ 280 0151 🚌 45 ♿
**Lansdowne Road Stadium**, Lansdowne Road, D4
☎ internationals: 668 4601; club: 668 9300
ⓓ to Lansdowne Rd 🎫 internationals: from £14; club: £4

## what's on & booking tickets

Check the national newspapers (*Evening Herald, Irish Times, Irish Independent*) for events for the week ahead. They also give listings for minority sports. *Aertel* (RTE's on-screen magazine) also lists sporting fixtures.

For many of the minor sporting events, simply turn up on the day. Phone the venue in advance for major events. Try a ticket agency such as Ticketmaster ☎ 456 9569 or go to the Ticket Shop in the HMV music store on Grafton Street. For disabled access phone ahead.

# dublin's shopping zones

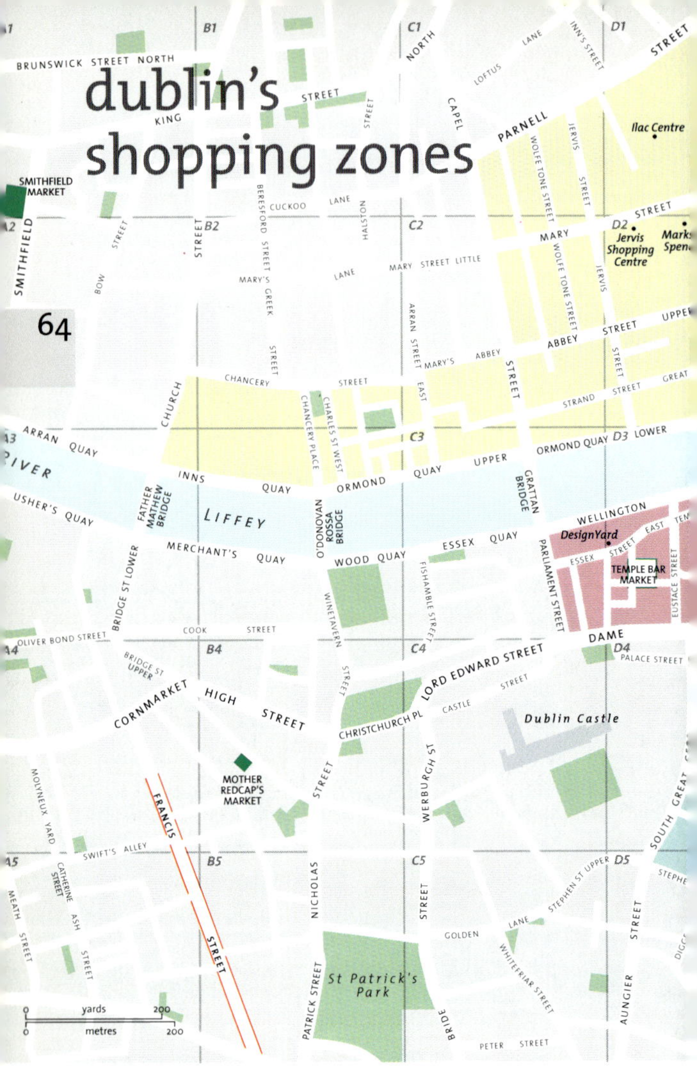




## directory

**Arnotts** D1: Arnotts has shaken off its dowdy image by revamping, and luring stylish names: Mango, Kookai, Benetton and others attract the young and zesty in droves [→72].

**Brown Thomas** E4: Long established plush store for the well-to-do. Where to find lionized international names and Irish designers like John Rocha and Louise Kennedy. Upstairs nifty, costly kitchen gadgets and lots of Denby crockery abound [→72].

**BT2** E5: Brown Thomas's kid sister for the teenage and twenty-something offspring of seasoned BT shoppers: Polo, Prada, D&G, CK etc rule the roost [→70].

**Dawson Street** E5: A few Aran jumpers, posh interior outlets and clothes shops for the well-heeled lady or gent. Bookstores Hodges Figgis and Waterstone's [→75] offer floors of weighty tomes and lighter stuff.

**Castle Market** D4: A short stretch where clothes stores Harlequin [→70] and Costume [→66] are the main attractions.

**DesignYard** D3: A must for those with a penchant for silver, gold, chunky rings and one-off chokers. Be prepared to shell out for the spectacular contemporary Irish jewellery [→71].

**Exchequer Street** D4: Rapidly changing area with, as yet, just a smattering of shopping options including home-grown street-wear favourite Hobo [→69].

**Francis Street** A4: An antique hoarder's utopia and one of Dublin's only definite shopping 'districts.' Spend hours sifting through priceless piles, and a fortune on final purchases [→74].

**George's Street Arcade** D4: A mix of shops and stalls offer funky secondhand garb, bargain music, delectable food, and fortune-telling. Pop into Jenny Vander [→70] for far-out and age-old fashion delights.

**Grafton Street** E5: Dublin's most famous shopping street bar none, teems with bodies, buskers and street artists. High street stores are interspersed with swankier boutiques.

**Henry Street** D1: An atmospheric pedestrianized stretch littered with cut-price, department and chain stores. It has more of a down-beat charm than its south-side cousin, Grafton Street, and draws the punters en masse.

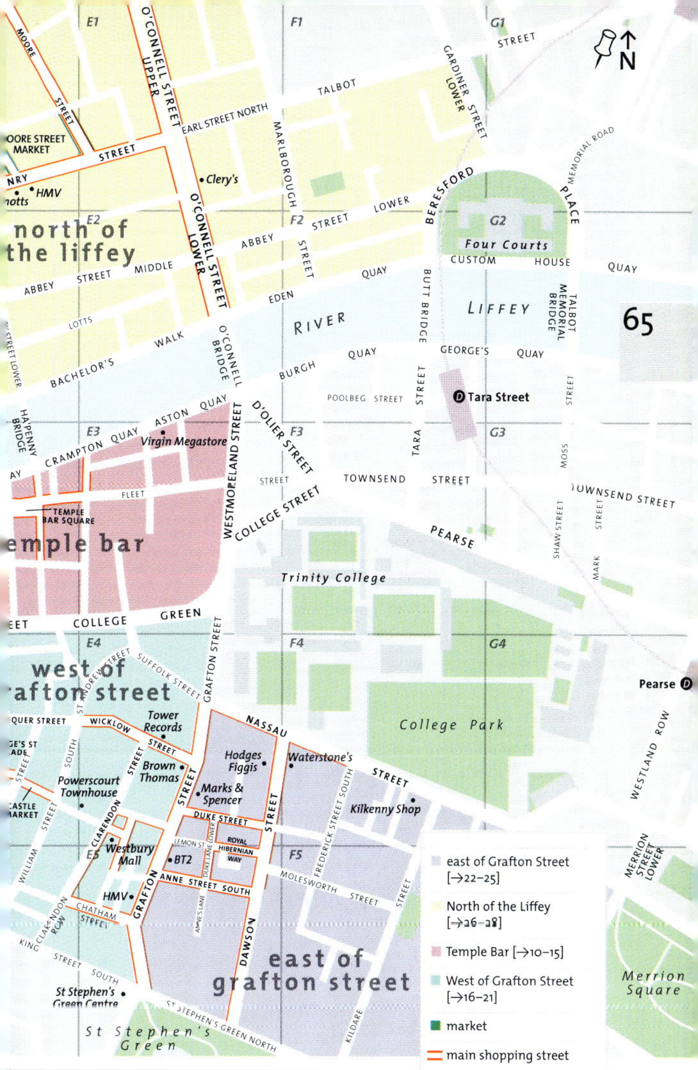


**HMV** D1 & E5 [→76]

**Ilac Centre** D1: Hot and busy hub with mainly chain and cut-price stores.

**Jervis Shopping Centre** D2: Jam-packed with recognizable bigwigs – Debenhams, the Body Shop and Tescos – from across the water.

**Kilkenny Shop** F4: Hoards of superb pottery and native craft. Showcases extol Irish clothes designers such as Lainey Keogh, Lynn Mar and Paul Costelloe [→66, 68].

**Moore Street Market** D1: Fruit, flower and veg stalls are backed by butcher shops in this utterly unique market. Don't leave Dublin without a trip through the strewn cabbage leaves and ever-eager echoing cries of traders [→77].

**Mother Redcap's Market** B4: A motley crew of new and worn clothes, intriguing paraphernalia, music and heaps of books [→77].

**O'Connell Street** E1: Easons bookshop [→76] and Clery's department store stand out among O'Connell Street's infamous fast food eateries.

**Powerscourt Townhouse** E4: Wonderfully elegant setting for a morning's browsing. The Design Centre [→66] is the undisputed crowning glory here. FCUK garishly proclaims its presence while Lipsy and Karen Millen vie to attract the young and style-conscious.

**St Stephen's Green Centre** E5: Lots of places to buy cards and wind chimes with paintings and hipper apparel on the top floor. The shopping centre is also home to Dunnes, a massive department store.

**Smithfield Market** A1: Good place to stock up on fruit and veg or, once a month, a piebald pony or two [→77].

**Temple Bar Square** D3: Voguish clubwear and unusual sets of threads.

**Temple Bar Market** D3: The place to buy mouthfuls of scrumptious sweet 'n' savoury morsels every Saturday [→77].

**Tower Records** E4 [→76]

**Virgin Megastore** E3 [→76]

**Westbury Mall** E4: Worth a look for rugs, jewellery and exclusive leather.

**Wicklow Street** E4: A handful of shoe shops and clothes stores for lithe girls.

Modern emporiums, kooky off-beat shops, old-world service and charm, innovative designs, ultra-hip urban trends, Dublin shopping is breathtakingly fresh.

# retail therapy

## ↓ fashion

### womenswear

**Airwave**

A brightly designed interior houses a broad spectrum of European daywear with a contemporary feel from the likes of In-Wear and Matinique, as well as more obscure labels. Suitably stylish footwear range to match. ££

36 Grafton Street, D2 ☎ 679 8374 ◑ *9.30am–6pm Mon–Sat (to 8pm Thu).* 💳 AE/MC/V

**Brown Thomas**

[→department stores]

**Cocoon**

Cocoon is a one-stop emporium for grown-up underwear, graceful nightwear and indulgent bathroom treats – with fairly fancy prices to match. ££–£££

26 Royal Hibernian Way, D2 ☎ 679 5916 ◑ *10am–6pm Mon–Sat (to 8pm Thu).* 💳 AE/MC/V

**Costume ✓**

A paradise for sassy modernists and lovers of chic tailoring. French styling in avant-garde fabrics takes pride of place alongside traditional Irish suits. They also have a glitzy range of evening wear. ££–£££

10 Castle Market, D2 ☎ 679 4188 ◑ *10am–6pm Mon–Sat (to 7pm Thu).* 💳 AE/MC/V

**Design Centre**

An impressive showcase for 30-odd Irish designers. The mix of established names and new kids on the scene always yields gems in the form of stunning knitwear, timeless tailoring and ravishing eveningwear. ££–£££

Powerscourt Townhouse, William Street South, D2 ☎ 679 5718 ◑ *9.30am–6pm Mon–Sat (to 7pm Thu).* 💳 all

**Fogal**

An intimate shop (more than four customers and it's a squeeze) full of hosiery and underwear to suit all tastes from marabou-trimmed chiffon slips to exquisite French-lace dressing gowns. ££

19 Creation Centre, D2 ☎ 677 4525 ◑ *10am–6pm Mon–Sat (to 7pm Thu).* 💳 all

**Kilkenny Shop**

This excellent source of contemporary Irish fashion, specializes in sleek designs, drop-dead gorgeous knitwear (Lainey Keogh, Glynis Robins and Elaine Curtis) and zingy outfits for the evening. Their own-label suits and snappy separates are keenly priced. [→menswear 67–68] ££

5–6 Nassau Street, D2 ☎ 677 7066 ◑ *9am–6pm Mon–Sat (to 8pm Thu).* 💳 all

**Peekaboo**

Strictly for extroverts, Peekaboo is a temple to the dedicated clubber or exhibitionist. Lycra, fun-fur, PVC, distressed denim and neoprene are all fashioned here into eye-catching well-priced one-offs. Special commissions are also welcome. £–££

7 Crow Street, D2 ☎ 670 3253 ◑ *10am–6pm Mon–Sat (to 7pm Thu).* 💳 none

**Pia Bang**

Exclusive design without the price tag has been the 30-year mission of Pia Bang, which never fails to surprise. Well-cut and exquisite French designs fill the carefully colour-coordinated rails. Upstairs is a stunning selection of mostly Italian shoes. ££

46 Grafton Street, D2 ☎ 671 5065 ◑ *10am–6pm Mon–Sat (to 8pm Thu), 1.30–5.30pm Sun.* 💳 all

## irish fashion designers

*Shrugging off the familiar, traditional Irish fashion legacy (Aran cardigans, linens and tweeds), young Irish designers have burst fast-forward into the international fashion arena. Defining Irish design for over ten years,* ***John Rocha*** *➘ continues to capture his customers at home and abroad with his loose silhouettes and stunning fabrics for men and women, and is now turning his talents successfully to homeware. Award-winning designer* ***Lainey Keogh*** *► produces the most talked about (and worn) knitwear for her international clientele, which includes Naomi Campbell, Madonna and Marianne Faithfull. Effortless style is always on the cards with* ***Louise Kennedy****. Her smart classic suits have become chic wardrobe-staples in Europe and the US.*

*New directions in Irish fashion thrive on the vibes from the street and a discerning youth market.* ***Philip Treacy****'s extraordinary millinery creations have made him a household name, while young blood* ***Orla Kiely*** *puts a spin on the traditional bag – her witty urban designs ricochet from Japan to New York and back again. Inspiring Irish fashion comes from* ***Marc O'Neill*** *with edgy modern separates; well-cut, well-priced suits from* ***Quinn & Donnelly*** *and* ***Pat McCarthy;*** *and frothy romantic evening wear from* ***Lyn Mar***, ***Brid Nihill***, ***Elaine Curtis*** *and* ***Ciáran Sweeney****. Unlike the UK and the US, very few Irish designers have their own shops. Their clothes will mostly be found in the bigger department stores like the Kilkenny Shop and Brown Thomas, as well as being showcased in the Design Centre.*

### Platform

This small boutique has been sourcing young, off-beat Irish and European design talent for over a decade. Their avant-garde and unusual range attracts an impressive showbiz clientele. There isn't a boring item on the rails. ££–£££

8 Duke Lane, D2 ☎ 677 7380 ◑ *10am–6pm Mon–Sat (to 7.30pm Thu).* ▭ AE/MC/V

### Richard Alan

A two-storey boutique full of old-world charm and service. From the marble foyer to the deep-pile carpeted staircase, this quietly elegant, upmarket store is a magnet for the refined label-conscious shopper. Expect Escada and Valentino rather than Prada or Gucci. £££

58 Grafton Street, D2 ☎ 677 5149
◑ *9am–5.30pm Mon–Sat (to 7pm Thu).* ▭ all

### Susan Hunter

A tiny shop which flaunts the finest, most delicate lacy lingerie imaginable – with exclusive price tags. This is the place to blow your budget – and indulge. ££

Unit 13, Westbury Mall, Grafton Street, D2 ☎ 679 1271 ◑ *10am–6pm Mon–Sat (to 7pm Thu).* ▭ all

### Whistles

As well as its own innovative label, Whistles is also home to the best of dressy European design from the likes of Helmut Lang and John Rocha. ££–£££

18 Balfe Street, D2 ☎ 670 5520 ◑ *10am–6pm Mon–Sat (to 8pm Thu).* ▭ AE/MC/V

## menswear

### Alias Tom ▼

Few can rival this shop's range of contemporary designer menswear – Issey Miyake, Prada, Comme des Garçons, Helmut Lang and John Rocha. Prepare to dig deep into those pockets for sharp suiting, hedonistic casual/clubwear and an ultra hip selection of shoes. ££–£££

Duke House, Duke Lane, D2 ☎ 671 5443
◑ *9.30am–6pm Mon–Sat (to 8pm Thu).*
▭ AE/MC/V

### Brown Thomas

[→department stores]

### Custom Store

Shelves piled high with shirts dominate this unique store. Any shape, size, style – no shirt is too unusual or intricate for the custom-made service available here for both men and women. That's if you're not already tempted by the shop's own range of off-the-peg shirts. £–££

20 Royal Hibernian Way, D2 ☎ 677 4086
◑ *9am–6pm Mon–Sat (to 8pm Thu).* ▭ all

➔ more shops

### Massimo

What this shop lacks in size it makes up for in content with a strong emphasis on Italian styles – and at competitive prices. At any time expect to see a well-sussed men's fashion pack trawling through the rails of snappy shirts, informal suits and fitted sweaters. ££

1 Creation Arcade, D2 ☎ 670 5227 ◑ *9.30am–6pm Mon–Sat (to 8pm Thu).* ▤ all

### FX Kelly ▲

This three-level store is a paradise for label-conscious boys. Every style dilemma is catered for, from slick Italian suits (Armani, Hugo Boss and Zegna) on the upper level, to the funked-up streetgear in the basement. It's up-to-date without drowning in the avant-garde. ££–£££

48 Grafton St, D2 ☎ 677 8211 ◑ *9.30am–6pm Mon–Sat (to 8pm Thu), 1–5.30pm Sun.* ▤ all

### Kilkenny Shop

Kilkenny's innovative buying policy represents the way forward in Irish fashion, combining traditional styles with a modern twist. As well as chenille sweaters and snazzy linen suits, their own Art of Menswear label takes care of the urban uniform whilst competing well on price. [→womenswear] ££–£££

5–6 Nassau Street, D2 ☎ 677 7066 ◑ *9am–6pm Mon–Sat (to 8pm Thu).* ▤ all

### Louis Copeland

A Dublin icon, Louis Copeland holds the most comprehensive range of off-the-peg suits in the city catering for all tastes, shapes and prices. A made-to-measure service is also available. ££–£££

39 Capel Street, D1 ☎ 872 1600 ◑ *9am–5.30pm Mon–Fri (to 8pm Thu).* ▤ AE/DC/V

### Michael Barrie

A reassuringly old-fashioned ambience permeates this large menswear outlet, but thankfully without the sniffy sales staff. Upstairs is home to a wide range of well-priced, sober European suits, while downstairs clubbers are spoilt for choice with the usual treats from D & G, Moschino et al. ££–£££

20 Duke Street, D2 ☎ 671 5265 ◑ *9.30am–6pm Mon–Sat.* ▤ AE/DC/V

### Monaghans

You can't fail to find something among the refined collection of menswear designs from the UK, Germany, Ireland, Italy and the US, including a kicking Calvin Klein section. Topnotch for cashmere and lambswool knitwear. ££

2 Royal Hibernian Way, D2 ☎ 679 4451 ◑ *9am–6pm Mon–Sat (to 8pm Thu).* ▤ AE/MC/V

### Thomas Pink

Even the pickiest shirt shopper will find solace in Thomas Pink. The flagship store for this Irish-owned international brand, there is a myriad of styles and colour combinations both traditional and up-to-date. Their affordable range also includes accessories like ties, cufflinks, boxer shorts and a small collection of women's shirts. £–££

29 Dawson Street, D2 ☎ 670 3647 ◑ *9.30am–6pm Mon–Sat (to 7pm Thu).* ▤ all

## custom tailoring

True style-setters (with cash and a fair amount of time) who are seeking to make a more exclusive fashion statement, are spoilt for choice among the city's numerous bespoke designers. Indulgent fabrics and seductive design combine to create covetable clothes for every special occasion. Reassuringly expensive, couturiers such as **Pat Crowley** (who designs some stunning bridalwear) and **Jen Kelly** (maker of the clothes for Riverdance) operate from sumptuous salons catering to a select clientele. So does **Richard Lewis** who dresses his well-heeled clients in signature fabrics of jersey and silk crepe. **Thomas Wolfangel** has a dedicated following of mature men who rely on his couture to smooth any ruffled edges and turn them out impeccably. Unique customized off-the-peg womenswear is the calling-card of the **Oakes** label. Choose a style from the current collection and the order will be made to fit.

**Jen Kelly**
38 Molesworth Street, D2
☎ 676 9844 ◑ *9.30am–5.30pm Mon–Fri (appointment preferred), Sat by appointment only.* ▤ V

**Oakes**
8 Dawson Street, D2
☎ 670 4178 ◑ *10am–6pm Mon–Sat (to 5pm Sat).* ▤ MC/V

**Pat Crowley**
3 Molesworth Place, D2
☎ 661 5580 ◑ *9.30am–5.30pm Mon–Fri.* ▤ AE/V

**Richard Lewis**
22 Frederick Street South, D2
☎ 679 7016 ◑ *10am–6pm Mon–Fri (to 5pm Fri).* ▤ none.

**Thomas Wolfangel**
158 Pembroke Road, D4
☎ 660 4069 ◑ *9am–5.30pm Mon–Fri, 9am–1pm Sat (appointment preferred).* ▤ V

## chain stores

*Henry Street and the Jervis Shopping Centre on the north side and Grafton Street – the south side's rather more chichi shopping zone – are the main hubs for affordable chain stores. Sharp bargain-hunters will find many a treat in Irish outlets and franchises such as* ***Pennys, Dunnes Stores, Sasha, A-Wear*** *and* ***Vero Moda****, while British chains like* ***Top Shop*** *and* ***Dorothy Perkins*** *– with their capsule collections by catwalk creators – and* ***Oasis, Warehouse*** *and* ***Karen Millen*** *can all be relied on to keep up with current trends and deliver the goods for young and discerning women. The European style flag is held by the ever-colourful* ***Benetton****. More dependable than the weather,* ***Marks & Spencer*** *which stands for classic fashion (and reliable undies), has become a firm conservative favourite with Dublin shoppers. Quiet sophistication at affordable prices also comes in the form of* ***Principles, Wallis*** *and* ***Jigsaw****, while popular unisex casualwear rules the roost at* ***Next****, and the far from racy* ***Racing Green****.*



## streetwear

### Cuba

The newest kid on the designer style block, Cuba is the perfect stomping ground for the truly discerning streetwear guru. Less sweatshirts and baggy pants and more high-tech nylons and utility gear from exclusive cult labels like Born Free, Conscious Earthwear, Evisu and the home-grown Optix. £–££

13 Trinity Street, D2 ☎ 672 7489
◑ *9.30am–6pm (to 8pm Thu).* ▭ AE/MC/V

### Genius

This small store is crammed with an inspiring choice of top unisex labels like Diesel and French Connection. The result is an eclectic blend of workwear and kitsch urban chic. £–££

6a Clarendon Street, D2 ☎ 679 7851 ◑ *9.30am–6pm Mon–Sat (to 8pm Thu).* ▭ AE/MC/V

### Hobo ▼

Hobo has become synonymous with well-priced, durable unisex style. Snowboarding-influenced performance baggies and some Beastie Boys imports add to the mix, but expect mostly cosy hooded tops, work-pants and T-shirts in what is essentially the Irish Carhartt of the 90's. £

6–9 Trinity Street, D2 (& 4 Exchequer St, D2) ☎ 670 4869 ◑ *9am–7pm Mon–Sat, 12–6pm Sun.* ▭ MC/V

### O'Connors

Denim heaven, populated by a steady stream of school kids and European exchange students who regularly check out the designer threads. Top favourites include the ever-kooky Red or Dead and hard-as-steel G-Star. £–££

23 Grafton St, D2 ☎ 677 1763 ◑ *9.30am–6pm Mon–Sat (to 8pm Thu), 2–5pm Sun.* ▭ AE/MC/V

### Raidar

Though the site is outwardly unimpressive (second floor of a shopping centre), it belies the wealth of style gems hidden within. Raidar is one for the label conscious, who will feel at home among old friends like Hamnett, Stussy and Maharishi. £–££

106 St Stephen's Green Centre, D2 ☎ 478 3221
◑ *9.30am–6pm Mon–Sat (to 8pm Thu).* ▭ all

### Sabotage

An excellent source of affordable, edgy urban style from the less well-known names on the scene. The outlets for men and women are separate, but both carry a range of funky accessories. Check out Pauric Sweeney's ingenious perspex chokers and computer key rings. £

men's: 14 Exchequer Street, D2 ☎ 670 4789
women's: 23a George's St Arcade, D2 ☎ 677 0299
◑ *10am–6pm Mon– Sat (to 7.30pm Thu).* ▭ V

### Tribe

Dublin's mecca for urban fashion, Tribe consistently offers an excellent variety of streetgear and accessories from the giants of casualwear. The place for big pants and snowboard chic from the likes of Mambo, Quiksilver and Psycho Cowboy. £–££

209 St Stephen's Green Centre, D2.
☎ 475 0311 ◑ *10am–6pm Mon–Sat (to 8pm Thu).* ▭ AE/MC/V

### Urban ▲

A tiny space crammed with exclusive street labels, this is aimed squarely at the highly individual youth market. The prices are competitive and rails sag under the weight of leftfield brands like Haze and Fresh Jive. £–££

30 Drury Street, D2 ☎ 670 4757 ◑ *10am–6pm Mon–Sat (to 8pm Thu).* ▭ AE/MC/V

➔ more shops

# ↓ sportswear

Things are looking good for die-hard sportswear fans. Aside from the familiar sports labels which fill the branches of the popular **Marathon Sports, Lifestyle** and **Champion Sports**, Dublin's upmarket shops have also redefined the choice of designer sportswear. Join the throngs of sassy shoppers who strut through Brown Thomas' oasis of modern shopping, **BT2**. The eye-piercing white interior reflects the shelves of shining international brands such as Moschino, Prada Sport and Versace Jeans.

For a more comprehensive collection of sportswear, the trail leads to **Arnotts** [→72], where you can pick up competitively priced Nike, Adidas and Reebok. The truly sportif need look no further than **The Great Outdoors** which has hoards of equipment and an impressive range of activewear. State-of-the-art high-tech fabrics are the order of the day at **Patagonia** which offers the ultimate combination of maximum style with minimum fuss.

**BT2**
28–29 Grafton Street, D2
☎ 605 6666
◑ *9am–6pm Mon–Sat (from 10am Tue, to 8pm Thu), 12–6pm Sun.* ▭ all

**Champion Sports**
Unit 16, Jervis Shopping Centre, D1
☎ 878 1292
◑ *10am–6pm Mon–Fri (to 9pm Thu, 7pm Fri), 9am–6.30pm Sat, 12–6pm Sun.*
▭ MC/V

**The Great Outdoors**
Chatham House, Chatham Street, D2
☎ 679 4293
◑ *9.30am–5.30pm Mon–Sat (to 8pm Thu).*
▭ AE/MC/V

**Lifestyle**
St Stephen's Green Centre, D2
☎ 478 3366 ◑ *9am–6pm Mon–Sat (to 8pm Thu, 6.30pm Fri), 12–6pm Sun.* ▭ AE/MC/V

**Marathon Sports**
28 Henry Street, D1
☎ 872 9808 ◑ *9am–6pm Mon–Wed & Sat, 9am–8pm Thu & Fri.* ▭ AE/MC/V

**Patagonia**
24–26 Exchequer Street, D2
☎ 670 5748 ◑ *10am–5.45 Mon–Sat (to 9.30am Sat).*
▭ AE/MC/V

# ↓ secondhand & vintage clothing

Dublin is a treasure-trove of secondhand and antique clothing shops, with serious gems for the bargain-hunter and label-conscious shopper alike. At **A Store is Born, Harlequin** ▲ and **Jenny Vander**, celebs and the odd supermodel (Naomi and Christy) have been known to queue eagerly for items such as beautiful vintage beaded tops, fuchsia-pink 50's swing frocks or even the perfect James Bondesque white tuxedo. The fine collections of jewellery, shoes and accessories at Harlequin and Jenny Vander also make for rich pickings.

A more streetwear approach can be found in kooky secondhand emporiums like **Wild Child, Flip, SéSí** ◥ and the various stalls in the bustling Victorian George's Street Arcade (off South Great George's Street). Here you can rummage happily through rails crammed with original Levis in a rainbow of colours, leathers and suedes in every style, 50's dresses and original Mary Quant make-up. For dedicated label-lovers, head for the mecca of secondhand style in **Stock Exchange**. Top Irish names and international brands fill this small shop, which boasts fashion from nearly 1,000 private suppliers and boutiques around the country.

**A Store is Born**
34 Clarendon Street, D2
☎ 679 5866
◑ *10am–6pm Sat only.* ▭ MC/V

**Flip**
4 Fownes Street Upper, D2
☎ 671 4299
◑ *9.30am–6pm Mon–Sat.*
▭ MC/V

**Harlequin**
13 Castle Market, D2
☎ 671 0202
◑ *10.30am–6pm Mon–Sat (to 7pm Thu).* ▭ MC/V

**Jenny Vander**
20 George's Street Arcade, D2
☎ 677 0406
◑ *10am–6pm Mon–Sat.*
▭ MC/V

**SéSí**
13 Temple Bar Square, D2
☎ 679 0523 ◑ *10am–6pm Mon–Sat (to 8pm Thu, 7pm Fri & Sat).* ▭ MC/V

**Stock Exchange**
8 Baggot Street Upper, D2
☎ 668 8010 ◑ *10am–6pm Mon–Sat.* ▭ MC/V

**Wild Child**
61 South Great George's St, D2
☎ 475 5099 ◑ *10am–6pm Mon–Sat (to 7pm Thu).* ▭ MC/V

# jewellery & accessories

## eyewear

**Eyecon**

A huge range of stylish eyewear without a hefty price tag. Quirky shades in yellow and pink are displayed beside ultra-sleek steel glasses and outrageous sports shades. ££

11 Fownes Street Upper, D2
☎ 670 9183 ◑ *10am–6pm Mon–Sat.* AE/MC/V

**Optica**

Extroverts and lovers of modern design will adore this completely glass-fronted shop. It is home to old faves like Gucci, Dolce & Gabbana and Cutler & Gross, as well as more avant-garde designs from Oakley and Diesel. ££–£££

1 Royal Hibernian Way, D2
☎ 677 4705 ◑ *9.30am–5.30pm Mon–Fri (to 6.30pm Thu), 9.30am–6pm Sat.* AE/MC/V

## hats

**The Hat Studio**

Fancy an ostrich-feathered extravaganza or pearl-inlaid funky tiara for that special occasion? Showy headgear in every imaginable shape and texture covers the walls of this tiny treasure trove. ££

33 Clarendon Street, D2
☎ 679 7988 ◑ *9.30am–6pm Mon–Sat (to 7.30pm Thu).* MC/V

## jewellery

**Angles**

Funky silver jewellery packs the glass shelves in this miniature shop. The emphasis is on clean, sleek designs from mostly Irish and some European designers. Worth a visit for the men's collection alone which includes cufflinks and chunky chains. £–££

10 Westbury Mall, D2
☎ 679 1964 ◑ *10am–6pm Mon–Sat (to 7pm Thu).* AE/MC/V

**DesignYard**

This stunningly designed space (with iron-gated frontage and colourful mosaic floors) showcases the best of contemporary Irish and international jewellery. An ever-changing rota of 120 new and established designers serves up ingenious gems such as Wendy Ramshaw's silver ring sets fashioned onto perspex, Arline Fisch's elaborate silver and gold woven Elizabethan collars and Selina Coyle's silver and rubber sphere on a chain. £–£££

12 Essex Street East, D2
☎ 677 8453 ◑ *10am–5.30pm Mon–Sat (from 11am Tue).* AE/MC/V

**Hervé Coulon**

Situated in the 'jewellery lane' of Dublin, Hervé Coulon's fine jewellery, in the style of Boucheron or Cartier, makes for serious nose-pressing at the window of his small shop. Equally eyecatching prices reign. £££

Unit 9, Westbury Mall, D2
☎ 670 8212
◑ *10am–6pm Tue–Sat (to 7pm Thu)* AE/MC/V

**John Farrington**

Simple wooden trays in this small shop exhibit a range of antique jewellery which is eminently wearable if not immediately affordable (prices range from £2,000 to £100,000 plus). Try and tear your eyes away from the rows of stunning engagement rings, diamond-set bracelets, elegant stud earrings, pearl necklaces, high-quality loose diamonds and much much more. £££

32 Drury Street, D2
☎ 679 1899 ◑ *10.30am–5pm Tue–Sat.* MC/V

**National Museum Shop**

Irish jewellery collectors will find ample treasures in the National Museum Shop. Quality modern silver and gold jewellery pieces have been modelled on awe-inspiring historical pieces like the Ardagh Chalice. £–£££

Kildare Street, D2 ☎ 677 7444
◑ *10am–5pm Mon–Sat, 2–5pm Sun.* AE/MC/V

**Rhinestones**

The sister duo here focus on serving an eclectic mix of well-priced vintage and costume jewellery as well as shelves of quirky ornaments and glass objets d'art. Join the regular crew of customers from 12 year-old girls rifling through the box of 40's clip-on earrings to the serious collectors eyeing up the Venetian beaded jewellery. £–££

18 St Andrew Street, D2
☎ 679 0759 ◑ *9.30am–6pm Mon–Fri (to 7pm Thu).* AE/MC/V

**Vivien Walsh**

Accessory nirvana with pride of place going to Vivien Walsh's own unique costume jewellery. Effortless well-priced style comes in the form of hip contemporary silver and costume jewellery, tiaras, gorgeous scarves, an ultra-chic range of shoes and a small exclusive collection of European designer clothes. ££

24 Stephen Street Lower, D2
☎ 475 5031 ◑ *9.30am–6pm Mon–Sat (to 7pm Thu).* AE/MC/V

**Weir & Sons**

It's easy to lose track of time in this smart three-storey shop, which is devoted to a hedonistic selection of jewellery, fine china, glass, leather, antiques and silverware. Helpful staff are equally at home discussing the merits of 70's Casio watches as they are gift-wrapping a £50,000 diamond ring. ££–£££

96 Grafton Street, D2 (& Ilac Centre, D1)
☎ 677 9678
◑ *9am–5.30pm Mon–Sat.* all

## make-up

**Make Up Forever**

Step into this smart oasis of wooden floors and gentle lighting where a cool posse of knowledgeable staff guides you through the array of brightly coloured make-up. Essential tricks of the trade can be gleaned through a professional makeover session at £25 an hour. £–££

38 Clarendon Street, D2
☎ 679 9043
◑ *9.30am–6pm Mon–Sat (to 7pm Thu).* AE/MC/V

more shops

# shoes

Whatever your footwear fetish of the moment, it can be found in Dublin: from ultra-hip to elegant classics and top-of-the-range designer numbers.

Chain stores are the best bet for affordable, middle-of-the-road footwear, while for more outlandish and imaginative designs **Korky's** is a well-priced option with an excellent range. **DV8** can always be relied upon for a fab and funky selection and the loud and exuberant **Buffalo Boots** usually come up with a few surprises. For catwalk styles at high-street prices, head for the playfully-named **Schuh** ✓ and take your pick from a dizzying array, ranging from thigh-high boots to the zaniest of trainers.

European, mostly Italian, collections fill the capital's more upmarket shoe shops; **Cinders, Fitzpatricks** and the medium-priced **Carl Scarpa** provide timeless classics for the smart set. **Brown Thomas** [→department stores] remains the place for serious shoe-aholics – slip into some Gucci slingbacks or zip into a pair of Prada's perfect boots. Also worth investigating are the small, exclusive ranges of must-have footwear which can be found in the city's definitive fashion boutiques: **Vivien Walsh**, Alias Tom [→67], Whistles [→67] and Pia Bang [→66] to name a few.

**Buffalo Boots**
16 Exchequer Street, D2 ☎ 671 2492 ◑ *10am–6pm Mon–Sat (to 8pm Thu).* 💳 AE/MC/V

**Carl Scarpa**
25 Grafton Street, D2 ☎ 677 7846 ◑ *9.30am–6pm Mon–Sat (to 8pm Thu).* 💳 AE/MC/V

**Cinders**
22 Wicklow Street, D2 ☎ 677 7491 ◑ *9.30am–6pm Mon–Sat (to 8pm Thu).* 💳 all

**DV8**
4 Crown Alley, D2 ☎ 679 8472 ◑ *10.30am–6pm Mon–Sat (to 7.30pm Thu).* 💳 AE/V

**Fitzpatricks**
76 Grafton Street, D2 ☎ 677 2333 ◑ *9.30am–6pm Mon–Sat (to 8pm Thu), 1.30–5.30pm Sun.* 💳 all

**Korky's**
55 Grafton Street, D2 ☎ 873 1359 ◑ *9.30am–6pm Mon–Sat (to 8pm Thu)* 💳 AE/MC/V

**Schuh**
Unit 5, Jervis Shopping Centre, D1 ☎ 873 0433 ◑ *10am–6pm Mon–Fri (to 9pm Thu, 7pm Fri), 9.30am–6.30pm Sat, 12–6pm Sun.* 💳 MC/V

**Vivien Walsh**
Powerscourt Townhouse Centre, D2 ☎ 677 5449 ◑ *9.30am–6pm Mon–Sat (to 7pm Thu)* 💳 AE/MC/V

# department stores

**Arnotts**

Ireland's oldest department store, now hugely expanded with a smart new extension. A long-term home for affordable if safe furnishings, cosmetics, electronics and fabrics. Still excellent value, the store's familiar Irish and international clothing labels hang comfortably alongside the funkier new-generation collections.

12 Henry Street, D1 ☎ 805 0400 ◑ *9am–6.30pm Mon–Sat (to 9pm Thu), 12–6pm Sun.* 💳 all

**Brown Thomas** ↗

Glamour and sophistication oozes from this plushly designed shopping mecca. Imaginative window displays are a consistent magnet for style-setters who beat a path to this inspiring store. All that is exclusive, expensive and covetable can be snapped up here, from designer fashion and accessories to high-tech electronics. Top Irish fashion labels are much in evidence, from Lainey Keogh to Louise Kennedy, Philip Treacy, Paul Costelloe and John Rocha. An impressive cosmetic hall houses Ireland's only MAC counter as well as other leading brands. Fantastic contemporary and conservative homeware and furnishings include Rocha's sophisticated lights made from Waterford Crystal. You'll also find trad Irish linens, Ferguson's coveted damasks, voluptuous fur-edged throws, suede and leather cushions, and sofas, all befitting a palace.

Grafton Street, D2 ☎ 605 6666 ◑ *9am–6pm Mon–Sat (to 8pm Thu), Sun 12–6pm.* 💳 all

# interiors

**Brown Thomas**

[→see department stores]

**Crate & Barrel**

Large pine tables, deep custom-made sofas and wooden beds, plus hand-painted pieces, all imported from the US and France, are the hallmark of this large homestore. The kitchen accessories room stocks a myriad of useful items from egg beaters to table mats. The ground floor is almost exclusively devoted to that absolutely necessary accessory, the candle, and irresistible ceramics – allowing you to spend without breaking the bank. £–£££

56–57 George's Street Upper, Dun Laoghaire, Co Dublin ☎ 280 5965 Ⓓ to Dun Laoghaire ◑ *9.30am–6pm Mon–Sat.* 💳 AE/V

**Enclosure**

Enclosure shines as a beacon of style in the middle os Dublin's mainstream suburb of Blackrock. This smart store stocks a concise range of modern furniture and accessories including all the Alessi favourites and cool Irish ceramics. Check out the corrugated cardboard chairs! ££–£££

8 Main Street, Blackrock ☎ 283 6310 ◑ *9am–6pm Mon–Fri (from 10am Sat).* 💳 MC/V

**Foko**

Spacious and hip, Foko stocks house and office furniture at affordable prices. Tables sell alongside a quirky range of custom-made sofas; contemporary chairs and storage units complete the cyber look. You can fill your basket with lots of bright plastics, desk must-haves and bathroom accessories to die for. £–£££

66–67 South Great George's Street, D2 ☎ 475 5344 ◑ *9.30am–6pm Mon–Sat (to 8pm Thu), 2–6pm Sun.* 💳 A/V

**Haus**

Garret O'Hagan, the man behind this exclusive designer shop, has an ever-expanding business and contract design company. Haus stocks eyecatching 20th-century design classics – Eames chairs,

Eileen Gray tables, Philippe Starck lighting and accessories, and pieces by Le Corbusier. Expect prices to match. ££–£££

3–4 Crow Street, D2 ☎ 679 5155 ◑ *10am–6pm Mon–Sat (to 7pm Thu).* 💳 MC/V

**Minima**

Ultra-chic shop with, as the name suggests, minimalist tendencies. Think cool whites, sharp lines, elegant lighting and funky accessories. Items like textured handmade papers amid the leather sofas mean that every wallet can afford a splurge on something. £–£££

35–38 St Stephen's Green N, D2 ☎ 662 7894 ◑ *9.30am–6pm Mon–Sat (to 8pm Thu), 2–6pm Sun.* 💳 AE/MC/V

**The Natural Interior**

A compact shop that made its name in the heyday of seagrass flooring and terracotta walls, and still commands a devout following. All the basics for decoration, from handmixed paint to fabric and floorings, plus a slicker look with groovy lamps, mirrors, hand-carved finials and curtain poles. ££

46 Dawson Street, D2 ☎ 677 1666 ◑ *10am–5.30pm Mon–Sat (from 11am Sat).* 💳 MC/V

**Pad**

A tiny shop brimming with cheap and cheerful kitsch. If your heart beats faster at the sight of garden gnome candles, amoeba-shaped place mats and swirly 70's standard lamps, then this is your spiritual pad. £

20 Stephen's Street Lower, D2 ☎ 478 1080 ◑ *10am–6pm Mon–Sat (to 7pm Thu).* 💳 MC/V

**Reverie**

Owner and interior stylist Laura George sources shabby chic French furniture at bargain prices. The result is romantic carved Louis XVI four-posters, cast-iron day beds, chandeliers with purple or amber-coloured crystal, antique linens and crockery, as well as contemporary lighting from Tse Tse. £–££

19 Sandycove Road, Sandycove, Co Dublin ☎ 086 260 5850 Ⓓ to Sandycove ◑ *9.30am–5.30pm Mon–Sat.* 💳 AE/MC/V



more shops

### Solo

A little off the main shopping route, this compact shop, jam-packed with sophisticated ethnic furniture in teak and rattan, handwoven throws and cushions, wall hangings, candle holders and chunky picture frames, is worth the diversion. The owners travel regularly to the Far East, so stock changes regularly. £–££

153 Capel Street, D1 ☎ 872 1052 ◑ *11.30am–5.30pm Mon–Fri, 10am–6pm Sat.* 💳 MC/V

### Urbana

An eclectic mix of shops in a funky warehouse, trading under the umbrella name of Urbana. The soft romanticism of Lavender & Linen lies alongside antique stoves, ensuring there is something for everyone. Try SKK for innovative lighting, the Source for gimmicky budget buys, District for surreal handmade furniture and Grimes & Co for sharp contemporary houseware. £–££

43–44 Temple Bar, D2 ☎ 670 3083 ◑ *10am–7pm Tue–Sat (to 8pm Thu); 12–6pm Sun.* 💳 vary

# ↓ antiques & salvage

The majority of Dublin's antique shops are clustered along Francis Street in the Liberties [→8] one of the oldest parts of the city. Don't be put off by the locked doors and air of exclusivity, once inside browsing is encouraged. Opening prices can be high, but dealers are not averse to friendly negotiation. Most can also issue certificates of antiquity for customs and will organize shipping at competitive rates.

**Fleury Antiques** has a vast selection of gilt mirrors and statuary, and also imports French antiques, while **O'Sullivan Antiques** specializes in Georgian and Victorian furniture, paintings, mantelpieces and mirrors. Nineteenth-century furniture and other pieces can be found at **Roxanne Moorhead Antiques**. For traditional pub posters and old shop fittings, as well as a good range of brass period lighting, try **Lantern Antiques**. If it's art deco you're after, **Odeon Decorative Arts** has amazingly affordable chrome and bakelite wall-lights and cocktail cabinets. Beautiful crafted silver (plus some glass and fine porcelain) is found at **Delphi Antiques, The Silver Shop, JW Weldon's** and **H Danker. Anthony Antiques** deals in fine 18th-century furniture and brass lighting. There are several antique rug shops, but the best known is **Peter Linden**, with a big selection of high-quality oriental carpets, kilims and tapestries. Finally, **Christy Bird**, at the cheaper end of the market, has an abundance of charm and a hotchpotch of goodies including Czech coffee cups, old pine furniture, stuffed animals and brass fenders. Next door, Mrs Bird's son has an architectural salvage shop specializing in church pieces. Other salvage places worth exploring are **Mac's Salvage Warehouse** and **Architectural Salvage & Supply**.

**Anthony Antiques**
7–9 Molesworth Street, D2
☎ 677 7222 ◑ *9am–6pm Mon–Sat.* 💳 AE/DC/V

**Architectural Salvage & Supply**
5a Gloucester Street South, D2
☎ 0872 551299 ◑ *8.30am–5pm Mon–Fri, 9am–2pm Sat.* 💳 V

**Christy Bird**
32 Richmond Street South, D2
☎ 475 4049 🚌 14, 14a, 15a, 15b, 83 ◑ *10am–6pm Mon–Sat.* 💳 none

**Delphi Antiques**
Powerscourt Townhouse, William St South, D2
☎ 679 0331 ◑ *10.30am–5.30pm Mon–Sat.* 💳 MC/V

**Fleury Antiques**
57 Francis Street, D8
☎ 473 0878 ◑ *9am–6pm Mon–Sat.* 💳 AE/V

**H Danker**
10 Anne Street South, D2
☎ 677 4009 ◑ *9am–5.30pm Mon–Fri, 9.30am–5pm Sat.* 💳 DC/MC/V

**J W Weldon's**
55 Clarendon Street, D2 (& 18 Anne Street South, D2)
☎ 677 1638 ◑ *10am–5.30pm Mon–Sat.* 💳 all

**Lantern Antiques**
56 Francis Street, D8
☎ 453 4593 ◑ *10am–5.30pm Mon–Sat.* 💳 none

**Mac's Salvage Warehouse**
749 South Circular Road, Islandbridge, D8 ☎ 679 2110
🚌 25, 25a, 26, 68, 69
◑ *9am–6pm Mon–Sat, 9am–3pm Sat.* 💳 none

**Odeon Decorative Arts**
69 Francis Street, D8
☎ 473 2384 ◑ *9.30am–5pm Mon–Sat.* 💳 AE

**O'Sullivan Antiques**
43–44 Francis Street, D8
☎ 454 1143 ◑ *9am–6pm Mon–Sat (from 10am Sat).* 💳 AE/MC/V

**Peter Linden**
George's Avenue, Blackrock, Co Dublin ☎ 288 5875
to Blackrock ◑ *10am–5.30pm Mon–Sat.* 💳 MC/V

**Roxanne Moorhead Antiques**
First Floor, 65–66 Francis St, D8
☎ 453 3962 ◑ *10am–5.30pm Mon–Sat.* 💳 MC/V

**The Silver Shop**
Powerscourt Townhouse, William St South, D2
☎ 679 4147 ◑ *11am–6pm Mon–Sat.* 💳 AE/MC/V

# auctions

Dublin auctions often yield unexpected bargains. Most of the auction rooms hold a viewing the day before the sale and will put in a bid for you if you are unable to attend in person. Check with them in advance for charges. For silver, china and antiques, **James Adams** is tops, and also run sales of big-name Irish art. **Town & Country** have a wider range of artefacts and hold antiques auctions and household sales every week. They sometimes also auction ecclesiastical furnishings. South of the city at Sandycove, **Buckley Galleries** has a weekly auction with bargains in contemporary and antique furniture, while **Thomas P Adams & Co** has fortnightly auctions of good Georgian and Victorian furniture and fine art. At **Herman & Wilkinson Auction Rooms** in Rathmines you'll find a mixed bag with some treasures to be picked up – the odd art deco piece or a classy table.

**Buckley Galleries**
27–28 Sandycove Road, Dun Laoghaire, D1 ☎ 280 5408
to Sandycove *viewing 9am–2pm Thu; auction 2pm Thu.* none

**Herman & Wilkinson Auction Rooms**
161 Rathmines Road Lower, D6
☎ 497 2245
14, 14a, 15a, 15b, 83
*viewing 2–6.30pm Wed; auction 10am Thu.* none

**James Adams**
26 St Stephen's Green D2
☎ 676 0261
*phone for times and contents of monthly auction.*
MC/V

**Thomas P Adams & Co**
38 Main Street, Blackrock, Co Dublin ☎ 288 5146
to Blackrock
*viewing 10am–1pm Sat, 2–5pm Sun, 10am–7pm Mon; auction 11am on alternate Tue.* MC/V

**Town & Country**
4 Ormond Quay Lower, D1
☎ 872 8300
*viewing 10am–6pm Wed, 10am–6pm Sat, 10am–12pm Sun; antique auction 2pm Sun; household 6pm Wed.*
none

# crafts

Irish crafts have well and truly shaken off their plastic leprechaun image. Especially worth seeking out are chunky Donegal tweeds – chic used as upholstery – ceramics and beautifully handturned wooden bowls.
First stop should be the **Crafts Council** at Design Yard, a national showroom for crafts, where top-quality furniture, glass, tableware and ceramics are on display. Staff are well-informed and can organize commissions. On the more traditional side, the **Kilkenny Shop**[→66 & 68] represents all the well-known potters including Stephen Pearce, Nicholas Mosse and **Louis Mulcahy**, who has a dedicated retail outlet nearby. There are also wood carvings by Con Doyle, sturdy Jerpoint glass and craft staples like Irish linen and the knits and weaves of Blarney Woollen Mills. The **Crafts Centre of Ireland** has a collection of ceramics and glassware by a number of artists. Further out-of-town, in an unprepossessing tower block, the **Tower Craft Design Centre** houses a warren of workshops for craftspeople. Most are happy to demonstrate techniques and even happier to sell you their creations. Many Dubliners head out to **Avoca Handweavers** [→39] in Wicklow to browse through their imaginative collection of goods – pottery and glass are the mainstays, but there are woollens and smart tweeds too.

**Avoca Handweavers**
Kilmacanogue, Bray, Co Wicklow ☎ 286 7466
tours from city centre
*9.30am–5.30pm Mon–Sat; 9am–4.30pm Mon–Fri workshop.* all

**Crafts Centre of Ireland**
Top Floor, St Stephen's Green Centre, D2
☎ 475 4526
*10am–6pm Mon–Sat, 2–6pm Sun.*
AE/MC/V

**Crafts Council**
Design Yard, 12 Essex Street East, D2
☎ 677 8467 *9am–5pm Mon–Fri.*
AE/MC/V

**Louis Mulcahy**
51c Dawson Street, D2
☎ 670 9311
*10am–6pm Mon–Sat.*
DC/MC/V

**Tower Craft Design Centre**
Enterprise Centre, Pearse St, D2
☎ 677 5655
*9am–5.30pm Mon–Fri.*
AE/MC/V

more shops

# books, magazines & comics

Ireland is historically renowned as the Land of Saints and Scholars, so it seems fitting that Dublin should be virtually awash with bookshops. The high-brow collector can pick treasures from the many nook-and-cranny type bookstores, while those interested in Irish heritage can while away hours in dedicated shops. A few creaky old secondhand shops and market stalls litter the north side – mostly around the quays – where you'll find the wonderfully authentic and atmospheric **Winding Stair**, which has an appealing café overlooking the river. Every magazine under the sun fills the racks in **Easons**, the home of school books, newspapers, bestsellers and art supplies. Across the river, **Greene's** near Trinity exudes old-fashioned eccentricity. It also has a useful post office service. **Books Upstairs** imports books from the US which can be snapped up at heavily discounted prices. A modern, bustling flavour can be found in the mainstream outlets like **Waterstone's, Dublin Bookshop** and **Hodges Figgis**, where Agatha Christie vies for space with John Grisham and Delia Smith. For an Irish literature fix, **Cathach Books** is home to the work of every famous Irish writer, including a good selection of coveted limited editions. While American thriller addicts will find **Murder Ink** a haven of flashy pulp thrillers and crime novellas. Comic heaven is attained in **Forbidden Planet**, where die-hard Star Trek collectors mingle easily with Manga fans and cult film buffs.

**Books Upstairs**
36 College Green, D2
☎ 679 6687 ◑ *10am–7pm Mon–Sat, 1–6pm Sun.*
AE/MC/V

**Cathach Books**
10 Duke Street, D2 ☎ 671 8676
◑ *9.30am–5.45pm Mon–Sat.*
AE/MC/V

**Dublin Bookshop**
24 Grafton Street, D2 ☎ 677 5568 ◑ *9am–7pm Mon–Sat (to 9pm Thu & Fri, 6pm Sat), 11am–6pm Sun.* all

**Easons**
40 O'Connell Street Lower, D1
☎ 873 3811 ◑ *8.30am–6.45pm Mon–Sat (to 8.45pm Thu), 1–6pm Sun.* V

**Forbidden Planet**
5–6 Crampton Quay, D2
☎ 671 0688 ◑ *10am–6pm Mon–Sat (to 7pm Thu), 12–5pm Sun.* AE/MC/V

**Greene's**
16 Clare Street, D2
☎ 676 2554 ◑ *9am–5.30pm Mon–Sat (to 6pm Sat).* all

**Hodges Figgis**
57 Dawson Street, D2
☎ 677 4754 ◑ *9am–7pm Mon–Sat (to 8pm Thu), 12–6pm Sun.* AE/MC/V

**Murder Ink**
15 Dawson Street, D2
☎ 677 7570 ◑ *10am–5.30pm Mon–Sat.* V

**Waterstone's**
7 Dawson Street, D2
☎ 679 1415 ◑ *9am–8pm Mon–Sat (to 8.30pm Thu, 7pm Sat), 11am–6pm Sun.* all

**Winding Stair**
40 Ormond Quay, D1
☎ 873 3292 ◑ *10am–6pm Mon–Sat, 1–6pm Sun.*
AE/MC/V

## ↓ cd's, records & tapes

From small market stalls to grand superstores, record shopping in the city centre can be a mesmerizing experience. The choice is great, the prices are competitive and many surprises come to hand. Old-skool staples **Comet** ↖ and **Freebird** started out as the chief indie mecca and secondhand rock superstore respectively, but they have taken account of changing times and added hip-hop, techno and house to their already overcrowded rosters. Both will also be able to give you a handle on those early U2 singles which are always available, at a price.

If you want global sounds, or even just an Irish jig or three, **Claddagh** is the one. Those seeking indie solace should check out **Road Records**, while DJs favour **Abbey Discs** where elusive white labels are available from behind the counter to the chosen ones. Secondhand joints tend to be a mixed bunch. George's Street Arcade is home to a few, but only the long-running **Macs** really cuts the mustard. Head across the road instead to **Smile Records** or across town to **Chapters** where there are bargains aplenty in the basement. **HMV** plays it safe with the Top 40, best-selling back-catalogue and little else. The **Virgin Megastore** is better with a good classical section, but **Tower Records** is really the pick of the multiples: cool classical and jazz sections, a great soul/dance selection, an ever-growing vinyl mountain under the stairs, and it's open until 10pm.

**Abbey Discs**
19 Liffey Street Lower, D1
☎ 873 3733 ◑ *10am–7pm Mon–Sat (to 8pm Thu & Fri), 2–6pm Sun.* MC/V

**Chapters**
54 Abbey Street Middle, D1
☎ 872 3297 ◑ *10am–6pm Mon–Sat (8pm Thu), 2–6pm Sun.* none

**Claddagh**
2 Cecilia Street, D2 ☎ 677 0262 ◑ *10am–6pm Mon–Sat, 2–6pm Sun.* AE/MC/V

**Comet**
5 Cope Street, D2 ☎ 671 8592
◑ *10am–6pm Mon–Sat (to 8pm Thu), 2–6pm Sun.* MC/V

**Freebird**
1 Eden Quay, D1 ☎ 873 1250
◑ *10am–6pm Mon–Sat (to 8pm Thu), 2–6pm Sun.*
MC/V

**HMV**
65 Grafton Street, D2
☎ 679 5334 ◑ *9.30am–6pm Mon–Sat (to 8pm Thu), 2–6pm Sun.* AE/MC/V

**Macs**
George's Street Arcade, South Great George's Street, D2
☎ none ◑ *10am–6pm Mon–Sat.* none

**Road Records**
16b Fade Street, D2
☎ 671 7340 ◑ *10am–6pm Mon–Sat (to 8pm Thu), 2–6pm Sun.* none

**Smile Records**
59 South Great George's Street, D2 ☎ 478 2005
◑ *10am–6pm Mon–Sat (to 8pm Thu), 2–6pm Sun.*
none

**Tower Records**
16 Wicklow Street, D2
☎ 671 3250 ◑ *9.30am–10pm Mon–Sat, 2– 6pm Sun.*
AE/MC/V

**Virgin Megastore**
14–18 Aston Quay, D2
☎ 677 7361 ◑ *9.30am–6pm Mon–Sat (to 8pm Thu), 2–6pm Sun.* AE/MC/V

# food & drink

**Big Cheese Company**

Large, spotless, laboratory-type shop dedicated to cheeses. Over 250 varieties are stocked, and the staff are very knowledgeable. The only stockist of American foods (Hershey Bar addicts take note), plus spices, olives and patés. ££–£££

St Andrew's Lane, D2
☎ 671 1399 ◑ *10am–6pm Mon–Sat (from 9.30am Sat).* ▭ MC/V

**Cooke's Food Hall ✓**

An Aladdin's cave of own-brand and internationally renowned delicacies: jams, pastries, confectionery and breads to give you a taste of wicked indulgence. There's a stand-up counter plus a couple of tables outside. £££

15 Castle Market, D2 ☎ 679 9923 ◑ *10am–6pm Mon–Sat (to 7pm Thu).* ▭ AE/MC/V

**The Gallic Kitchen**

Hand-prepared and stylish, homely concoctions with superbly fresh ingredients, this is a fantastic place for take-away lunches. Brioches, quiches, flans and strudels are served warm. ££

49 Francis Street, D8
☎ 454 4912. ◑ *9am–5pm Mon–Fri.* ▭ none

**The Good Food Store**

Full of straight-from-the-farm organic goodness, a tiny, bulging cornucopia of delicious fruit and veg plus luxury items like foie gras, organic truffles and Skelligs. ££

7 Pembroke Lane, D4 ☎ 667 5656 ▣ 10, 11, 11a, 13b, 46a, 46b ◑ *9am–7pm Mon–Sat.* ▭ none

**Magills**

Dublin's first deli, and still going strong. This family-run shop offers consistency and quality with a good range of Irish cheeses, beautifully presented charcuterie, oils, spices and locally-made sausages. £–££

14 Clarendon Street, D2
☎ 671 3830 ◑ *9am–6pm Mon–Sat.* ▭ MC/V

**Mitchell & Son**

This traditional wine merchant has been around since 1805 and knows its business. They offer a good range of Irish whiskies – some of which are very rare.££

21 Kildare Street, D2 ☎ 676 0766 ◑ *10.30am–5.30pm Mon–Sat (to 8pm Thu).* ▭ all

**Sheridan's Cheesemongers**

A tiny cheese shop offering a superb, personal service. It

specializes in Irish and European farmhouse produce, especially cheeses, but also meat and charcuterie from Italy. ££–£££

11 Anne's Street South, D2
☎ 679 3143 ◑ *9am–6pm Mon–Sat.* ▭ MC/V

**Temple Bar Market**

Smoked haddock from Hederman's in County Cork; organic veg; homemade pâtés and terrines such as duck and lemon; oysters to sample (cooked and *au naturel*); breads; eggs; venison; sausages; cheeses (heaps of them); chocolates; dips; olives and dried lavender – this is a showhouse of Ireland's superb raw ingredients and the talent with which they are being used. ££–£££

Meeting House Square, D2
◑ *9am–5pm Sat.*

# markets

Dublin is surprisingly short on street markets. The city's best flea market used to be in the atmospheric surroundings of the Victorian Iveagh Market in the Liberties. A refurb is in the pipeline, so check with Dublin Tourism [→121] for an update.

Soak up the atmosphere at the northside's two fruit & veg markets, **Moore Street** – where the stallholders' wry banter is legendary – and **Smithfields**. The latter incorporates a flower market and each month is home to an intriguing horse sale. A horse may not be on your shopping list, but this fascinating place oozes downbeat charm.

The centrally located **Mother Redcap's Market**, sells delicate wood-turned bowls and some stylish knits, mixed with the usual chaotic jumble of second-hand clothes and worn paperbacks. Tucked behind the green-domed church on Rathmines Road is **Blackberry Fair** where huts painted with their proprietors' names huddle round a water fountain. It is chock-full of old furniture, three-piece suites, second-hand sound systems and a host of ancient bicycles. South of the city, the **Blackrock Market** does a rip-roaring trade with an ever-changing stream of smart stallholders, selling a mish-mash of anything from beanbags to carved wood wall-hangings or handmade candles.

**Blackberry Fair**
Rathmines Road Lower, D6
☎ 496 3172 ▣ 14, 14a, 15a, 15b, 83
◑ *11am–6pm Sat & Sun.*

**Blackrock Market**
19a Main Street, Blackrock, Co Dublin ☎ 283 3522
Ⓓ to Blackrock ◑ *11am–5.30pm Sat, 12–5.30pm Sun.*

**Moore Street Market**
Moore Street, D2
◑ *9am–4pm Mon–Sat.*

**Mother Redcap's Market**
Back Lane, Christ Church, D8
☎ 454 0656
◑ *10am–5pm Fri–Sun.*

**Smithfield Market**
Smithfield, D7
☎ 872 1248
▣ 39 ◑ Fruit market: *6.30am–4pm Mon–Wed; 6.30am–4.30pm Thu, 6.30am–5pm Fri; 6.30am–1pm Sat.*
◑ Horse market: *10am–2pm first Sun of every month.*

# dublin night-time hot spots

## *directory*

### restaurants

Ar Vicoletto B2 [→89]
Botticelli B1 [→89]
Bruno's B2 [→83]
La Cave C3 [→82]
Chameleon B1 [→85]
The Commons C5 [→86]
Cooke's Café B3 [→90]
Dish B2 [→83]
Eden B2 [→83]
Les Frères Jacques A2 [→87]
Good World B3 [→85]
Gotham Café C3 [→82]
Jacob's Ladder D3 [→83]
Kapriol B6 [→89]
The Lord Edward A2 [→85]
Mao B3 [→83]
Mermaid Café B2 [→84]
Monty's of Kathmandu B2 [→86]
Restaurant Peacock Alley C4 [→87]
QV2 B2 [→90]
Rhino Room B3 [→84]
Saagar B5 [→86]
Shalimar B2 [→86]
The Side Door D4 [→82]
Steps of Rome C3 [→89]
The Tea Room A2 [→87]
Unicorn D4 [→89]
Wagamama B4 [→86]
Zafraan B3 [→86]

### cafés

Joy of Coffee B2 [→91]
Café Gertrude B1 [→90]
Il Baccaro B2 [→90]
Kaffe Moka B3 [→91]

### pubs & bars

Bleeding Horse B6 [→95]
Café en Seine C3 [→94]
Chocolate Bar B6 [→94]
Dawson Lounge C4 [→96]
Devitt's B5 [→93]
Dicey Reilly's B5 [→97]
Drumm's Emporium B2 [→94]
Foggy Dew B2 [→95]
Front Lounge A2 [→97]
The George B2 [→97]
The Globe B2 [→94]
Hairy Lemon B3 [→94]
Hogan's B3 [→95]
International Bar C2 [→92]
Jute B3 [→94]
Keating's B1 [→93]
Kehoe's C3 [→96]
The Long Hall B3 [→96]
McDaid's C3 [→96]
Mulligan's D1 [→92]
Odeon B6 [→94]
O'Donoghue's D4 [→93]
O'Neill's C2 [→96]
Out on the Liffey A1 [→97]
Porterhouse A2 [→96]
Pravda B1 [→94]
Renard's D3 [→93]
Stag's Head B2 [→95]
Thomas Read A2 [→95]
Thing Mote C2 [→95]
Turk's Head A2 [→96]
Whelan's B5 [→93]
Zanzibar B1 [→95]

### entertainment venues

Andrew's Lane Theatre B2 [→105]
Da Club B3 [→101]
Gaiety Theatre C3 [→105, 107]
Ha'penny Bridge Inn B1 [→104]
International Bar C2 [→101, 104, 105]
Irish Film Centre B2 [→103]
The Mean Fiddler B5 [→101]
Murphy's Laughter Lounge C1 [→104]
National Concert Hall (NCH) C6 [→102, 106, 107]
Olympia Theatre A2 [→101, 105, 106]
The Screen D1 [→103]
Temple Bar Music Centre B2 [→101]
Whelan's B5 [→101, 102]

### clubs

Club M B2 [→98]
Gaiety Theatre C3 [→98]
The Kitchen A2 [→98]
Lillie's Bordello C2 [→98]
PoD B6 [→98]
Red Box B6 [→98]
Renard's D3 [→99]
Republica D3 [→99]
Ri-Ra B2 [→99]
Temple Bar Music Centre B2 [→99]
Velvet B6 [→99]

DART station
Taxi rank
Nitelink stop
restaurant or café
pub or bar
club
entertainment venue
Around Camden Street [→29–31]
East of Grafton Street [→22–25]
North of the Liffey [→26–28]
Temple Bar [→10–15]
West of Grafton Street [→16–21]

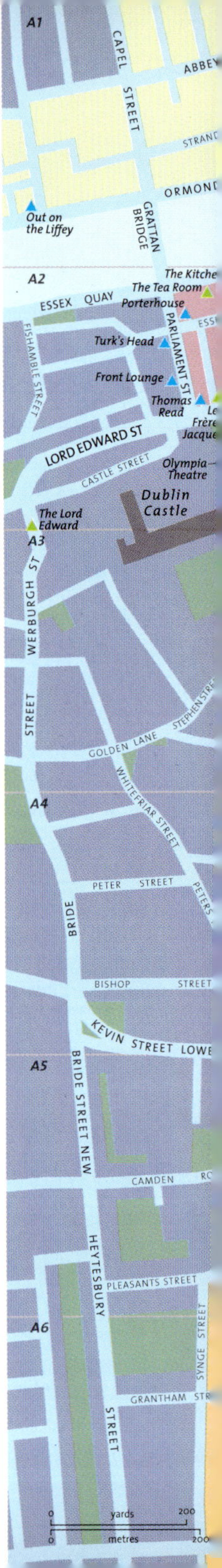

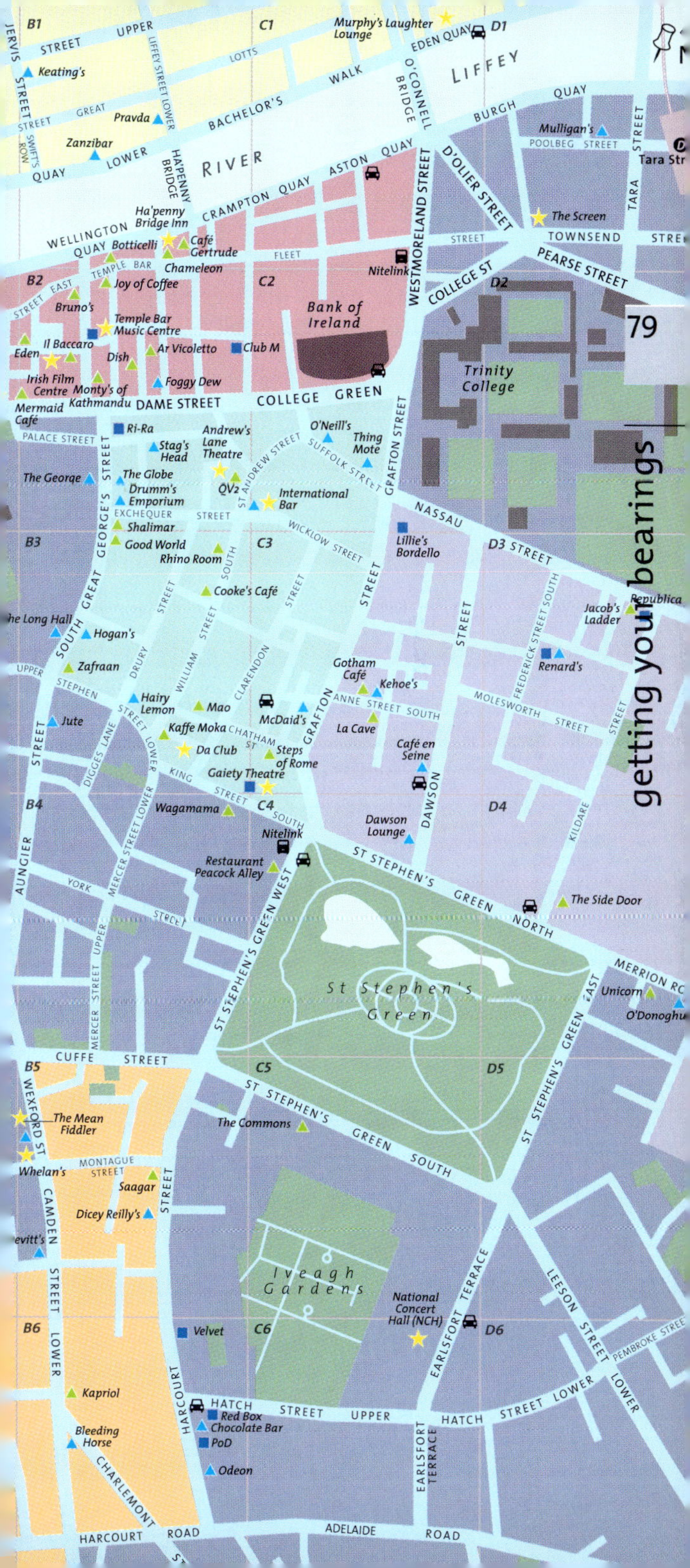
B1
C1
D1
B2
C2
D2
B3
C3
D3
B4
C4
D4
B5
C5
D5
B6
C6
D6
Murphy's Laughter Lounge
Eden Quay
Liffey
Jervis Street
Upper
Street
Liffey Street Lower
Lotts
Keating's
Walk
O'Connell Bridge
Bachelor's
Great
Street
Pravda
Swift's Row
Zanzibar
Lower
Quay
River
Ha'penny Bridge
Burgh
Quay
Mulligan's
Poolbeg Street
Street
Tara Str
Aston
Quay
Crampton Quay
Ha'penny Bridge Inn
Wellington Quay
Botticelli
Café Gertrude
Chameleon
Fleet
Temple Bar
Joy of Coffee
East
Street
Bruno's
Temple Bar Music Centre
Eden
Il Baccaro
Dish
Ar Vicoletto
Club M
Irish Film Centre
Monty's of Kathmandu
Foggy Dew
Mermaid Café
Dame Street
College Green
Bank of Ireland
Nitelink
Westmoreland Street
D'Olier Street
The Screen
Tara
Street
Townsend
Stre
Pearse Street
College St
Trinity College
Palace Street
Ri-Ra
Stag's Head
Andrew's Lane Theatre
O'Neill's
Thing Mote
Suffolk Street
St Andrew Street
Grafton Street
The George
The Globe
QV2
Drumm's Emporium
International Bar
Exchequer
Street
Shalimar
Good World
Rhino Room
Wicklow Street
Nassau
Street
Lillie's Bordello
Great George's Street
South
Cooke's Café
Street
Street
William
Jacob's Ladder
Republica
Frederick Street South
he Long Hall
Hogan's
South
Upper
Zafraan
Stephen
Drury
Clarendon
Gotham Café
Kehoe's
Renard's
Anne Street South
Molesworth
Street
Street
Hairy Lemon
Mao
McDaid's
Grafton
La Cave
Jute
Street
Kaffe Moka
Chatham St
Steps of Rome
Café en Seine
Digges Lane
Da Club
Lower
King
Gaiety Theatre
Dawson
Street
Street
Wagamama
South
Aungier
Nitelink
Dawson Lounge
Kildare
Restaurant Peacock Alley
York
Mercer Street Lower
Street
St Stephen's Green North
The Side Door
Upper
St Stephen's Green West
Merrion Ro
Unicorn
O'Donoghu
St Stephen's Green
Mercer Street
East
Cuffe Street
St Stephen's Green South
St Stephen's Green
The Mean Fiddler
Wexford St
The Commons
Whelan's
Montague Street
Saagar
Street
Camden
Dicey Reilly's
evitt's
Street
Iveagh Gardens
National Concert Hall (NCH)
Earlsfort Terrace
Leeson
Street
Lower
Pembroke Stree
Velvet
Lower
Kapriol
Harcourt
Hatch
Red Box
Street
Upper
Hatch
Street
Lower
Chocolate Bar
Bleeding Horse
PoD
Earlsfort Terrace
Odeon
Charlemont
Harcourt
Road
Adelaide
Road

# from dusk til dawn

## what's where

### ↓ off baggot st lower

Blue Room | ££–£££ [→91]
Dobbins Wine Bistro | ££–£££ [→84]
Doheny & Nesbitt [→92]
L'Ecrivain | £££ [→87]
Lloyd's Brasserie | ££–£££ [→82]
Mangetout | ££ [→88]
O'Donoghue's [→93]
The Pembroke | ££ [→88/96]
Restaurant Patrick Guilbaud | £££ [→87]
Toner's [→93]
Unicorn | ££ [→89]

### ↓ off baggot street upper

Caffola's | £ [→89]
Le Coq Hardi | £££ [→87]
Langkawi | ££ [→85]
Smyth's [→97]

### ↓ ballsbridge

Roly's Bistro | ££ [→88]

### ↓ blackrock (co dublin)

Ayumi-Ya | ££–£££ [→85]

### ↓ bray (co wicklow)

Tree of Idleness | ££ [→83]

### ↓ around camden street

The Barge [→97]
Bleeding Horse [→95]
Devitt's [→93]
Kapriol | £££ [→89]
Thornton's | £££ [→88]
Whelan's [→93]

### ↓ east of city centre

Beshoffs | £ [→89]
Dockers [→92]
Ferryman [→93]
Fitzsimons [→92]
The Funnel [→98]
Messrs Maguire [→95]
Mulligan's [→92]

### ↓ west of city centre

Leo Burdock's | £ [→89]
The Lord Edward | ££ [→85]
O'Shea's Merchant [→93]
Vicar Street [→95]

### ↓ dalkey (co dublin)

Queens [→97]

### ↓ around dawson street

Café en Seine [→94]
Dawson Lounge [→96]
Jacob's Ladder | ££–£££ [→83]
Renard's [→93/99]
Republica [→99]

### ↓ glasnevin

Addison Lodge [→97]
Grave Diggers [→92]

### ↓ off grafton street

Bewley's Oriental Cafe | £–££ [→90]
Browns | £ [→90]
Café Java | £ [→91]
La Cave | ££ [→82]
Eddie Rockets | £ [→91]
Gaiety Theatre [→98]
Gotham Café | £–££ [→82]
Kehoe's [→96]
Lillie's Bordello [→98]
McDaid's [→96]
O'Neill's [→96]
Steps of Rome | £ [→89]
Thing Mote [→95]
Wagamama | £ [→86]

### ↓ harcourt street

Chocolate Bar [→94]
Dicey Reilly's [→97]
Odeon | ££ [→84/94]
PoD [→98]
Red Box [→98]
Saagar | £–££ [→86]
Velvet [→99]

### ↓ howth (co dublin)

Summit Inn [→97]

### ↓ king street north

Delaney's [→96]

Ta Sé Mahogani Gaspipes | ££ [→84]

↓ around leeson street upper

Annabelle's [→98]
O'Brien's [→96]

↓ malahide (co dublin)

Gibney's [→97]

↓ around merrion square

O'Dwyer's [→92]

↓ around the north quays

Keating's [→93]
Life [→94]
101 Talbot | £–££ [→82]
Out on the Liffey [→97]
Panem | £ [→91]
Pravda [→94]
The Winding Stair | £ [→91]
Zanzibar [→95]

↓ northumberland road

Schoolhouse [→97]

↓ around parnell street

Bangkok Café | £ [→85]
Chapter One | £££ [→88]
Conway's [→92]
Harry Ramsden | £ [→89]
Slattery's [→96]

↓ near phoenix park

Ryan's [→93]

↓ ranelagh

Nectar | £ [→84]

↓ sandycove (co dublin)

Caviston's | £–££ [→84]
Morel's Bistro | ££ [→90]

↓ st stephen's green

The Commons | £££ [→86]
The Dome | £ [→91]
Restaurant Peacock Alley | £££ [→87]
The Side Door | ££ [→82]
Shelbourne Hotel | ££ [→91]

↓ around south great george's street

Drumm's Emporium [→94]
The George [→97]
The Globe [→94]
Good World | ££ [→85]
Hogan's [→95]
Juice | ££ [→91]
Jute [→94]
The Long Hall [→96]
Odessa | ££ [→84]
Ri-Ra [→99]
Shalimar | ££ [→86]
Simon's Place | £ [→91]
The Stag's Head [→95]
Zafraan | ££ [→86]

↓ temple bar

Ar Vicoletto | £–££ [→89]
Il Baccaro | £–££ [→90]
Botticelli | ££ [→89]
Bruno's | ££ [→83]
Café Gertrude | £ [→90]
Chameleon | £££ [→85]
Club M [→98]
Dish | ££ [→83]
Eden | ££ [→83]
Elephant & Castle | ££ [→84]
Foggy Dew [→95]
Les Frères Jacques | £££ [→87]
Front Lounge [→97]
Joy of Coffee| £ [→91]
The Kitchen [→98]
Mermaid Café | ££ [→84]
Monty's of Kathmandu | ££ [→86]
Porterhouse [→96]
Temple Bar Music Centre [→99]
The Tea Room | £££ [→87]
Thomas Read [→95]
Turk's Head [→96]

↓ around william street south

Cooke's Café | £££ [→90]
Hairy Lemon [→94]
International Bar [→92]
Kaffe Moka | £ [→91]
Mao | £–££ [→83]
QV2 | ££ [→90]
Rhino Room | ££–£££ [→84]
Trocadero | ££ [→91]

**Key**

restaurant/café
bar/pub
club

# dublin dining

Eating out in Dublin has been transformed: Cal-Ital, Mediterranean, Asian fusion and hearty Italian restaurants can be found on every corner, and a new generation of Irish chefs combines flavours and ingredients in irresistible, innovative ways. What's more, the service is often the most charming, friendly and attentive you'll find anywhere.

## ↓ chew & chat

**La Cave** 28 Anne Street South, D2 (off Grafton Street)

Straight out of a 40's gangster movie, this tiny bar-cum-restaurant-cum-nightclub is bathed in a red smoky glow, complete with willowy blondes, fast-talking poseurs and mellow music. The food is basic bistro fare, but the atmosphere is the main attraction. You could lose years of your life in here.

**££** (£7.95–£14.95)

12.30pm–2.30am Mon–Sat, 6pm–2.30am Sun.

☎ 679 4409

45 all

**Gotham Café** 8 Anne Street South, D2 (off Grafton Street)

Quietly confident, and attracting a mixed crowd with its laid-back approach and appealing menu, Gotham is just right for those who want more than a burger, but who don't want to dress for dinner. As well as top-drawer Cal-Ital pizzas, there's a wide selection of pastas and an irresistible dessert menu.

**£–££** (£4.95–£10.95)

12pm–midnight Mon–Sat, 12–10.30pm Sun.

☎ 679 5266

65 AE/MC/V V

**Lloyd's Brasserie** 20 Merrion St Upper, D2 (off Baggot St lower)

Lloyds is one of a trio of restaurants owned by Conrad Gallagher, whose name is synonymous with modernist food in the city. Cuisine is a mix of Italian, French, Californian and Thai, with an emphasis on clean flavours. With a cool design, Lloyd's is sometimes more about style than substance, but remains a favourite among hacks, minor celebs and wannabes who make the adjoining Blue Room 'members club' a popular late-night hangout.

**££–£££** (£13.95–£16.95)

12.30–2.30pm & 6–11pm Mon–Sat, 1–3.30pm & 6–10pm Sun.

☎ 662 7240

110 all

**101 Talbot** 100–102 Talbot Street, D1 (around the north quays)

For diners who like a damn good time with no fuss or frills, Margaret Duffy and Pascal Bradley's 101 Talbot is Mecca. This quirky restaurant, loved by thousands for its complete unpretentiousness and sheer confidence, serves chunky, inventive, unique food packed with taste. The wine list includes some of the very best that the Pays d'Oc has to offer, all at surprisingly good-value.

**£–££** (£4.95–£10.75)

5–11pm Tue–Sat.

☎ 874 5011

90 all V

**The Side Door** Shelbourne Hotel, 27 St Stephen's Green North, D2 (St Stephens Green)

A recent addition to the delights of Dublin's premier hotel, The Side Door pulls in film makers, rock stars, lunching ladies, country gentry and dodgy dealers passing through the capital. It is a fun, up-beat international bistro with flexible lunch hours, bold colours, mellow lighting, and a broad-ranging menu from pizzas and pasta to solid meat dishes. Languid afternoons merge into buzzy evenings as the punters drift in from the hotel's two splendid bars to seal deals over dinner.

**££** (£8.25–£11.75)

7.30–10.30am & 12–11pm Mon–Fri, 8.30–10.30am & 12–11pm Sat & Sun.

☎ 676 6471

70 all

**Prices quoted correspond to the cost of a main course in Irish pounds**

**Tree of Idleness** Seafront, Bray (Co Wicklow)

A gem of a restaurant with exceptional hospitality, offering a mix of Greek-Cypriot and European delights to a diverse clientele. The decor is old-fashioned, the portions enormous, and the classic wine list lovingly chosen. Leave room for the suckling pig, which is the stuff of legend, and the most interesting desserts in the capital. If you need to work up an appetite, go for a pre-dinner stroll along the seafront.

££ (£9.95–£16.50)
7.30–11pm Tue–Sat, 7.30–10pm Sun.
286 3498
to Bray
50 AE/MC/V

## ↓ where it's at

**Bruno's** 30 Essex Street East, D2 (Temple Bar)

A favourite haunt of Dublin's Bright Young Things whose chatter bounces off the high, architect-designed curved ceilings, painted in five different shades of white. But the BYTs know a thing or two, because here is professional French food served with a modern twist (the chef was trained at Restaurant Patrick Guilbaud). Excellent value for lunch, and a lively dinner venue, where booking is essential at the weekends.

££ (£9.95–£13.95)
12–5pm Mon–Fri; 6–11pm Mon–Sat.
670 6767
55 all

**Dish** 2 Crow Street, D2 (Temple Bar)

The latest restaurant to attract the attentions of the city's trendy diners, Dish is one of the more adventurous Temple Bar newcomers. While many swear by its Sunday brunch affairs, Dish is perhaps at its best in the evening when the ambience is relaxed, some funky blends come out to play, and the kitchen alway tries something a little bit different. International in scope, this restaurant is proudly new-skool in every sense.

££ (£7.95–£15.95)
12–11.30pm daily.
671 1248
55 all

**Eden** Meeting House Square, D2 (Temple Bar)

One of Dublin's essential restaurants to be seen in. Chef Eleanor Walsh cooks good, honest food brilliantly. The menu offers dishes such as corn-fed chicken with mash, organic steak Béarnaise with matchstick-thin chips, black pudding salad, and tuna steak with salsa. Everything is spanking fresh, full of flavour and presented in a modern way, echoing the restaurant's airy, minimalist design. The wine list is short, fairly priced and strong on the unusual, like riesling from Coonawarra and offbeat bottles from the Pays d'Oc.

££ (£9.50–£16.50)
12–10.30pm daily.
670 5372
120 AE/MC/V V

**Jacob's Ladder** 4–5 Nassau Street, D2 (around Dawson Street)

Jacob's Ladder is a food-snob-free zone, in spite of some exceptional cooking skills, imagination and creativity on the part of chef Adrian Roche. It's a very relaxed restaurant, offering a keen quality-to-price ratio while eschewing the hype surrounding food fashion: pheasant sausage with pea purée and fried quail's eggs, salmon with pearl barley stew, and goat's cheese soufflé are all wonderful. The wine list is particularly strong on New World oddities – and the view over Trinity College is fab.

££–£££ (£13.50–£18)
12.30–2.30pm Tue–Sat, 6–10pm Tue–Thu, 6–10.30pm Fri & Sat.
670 3865
60 all V

more restaurants & cafés

**Mao** 2–3 Chatham Row, D2 (around William Street South)

Mao's funky Asian fusion cooking set taste buds racing when it opened in 98. This outbreak of Maoism was a welcome one, bringing the flavours, tastes and blends of southeast Asia in a manner that was both affordable and chic. You can't book, so there are often queues of trendy Dubliners eager to stuff their faces with tangy Thai fish cakes, fierce *soba* noodles and the yummy natural yoghurt mousse. That was then, but this is Mao.

£–££ (£5.95–£9.95)
12–11pm Mon–Thu, 12–11.30pm Fri & Sat, 12–10pm Sun.
670 4899
110 MC/V V

**Mermaid Café** 69–70 Dame Street, D2 (Temple Bar)

On one of Dublin's busiest street corners, the Mermaid Café remains a haven of peace, tranquillity and some truly inspired cooking. The calm ambience is complemented by the unfussy wooden furniture and restrained marine touches. Ben Gorman has an unerring palate for complementary tastes and textures. Regulars plump for his crab cakes, while the rib-eye steak with caramelized onions and mustard mash is hard to pass over. Wacky but wonderful wine list.

**££** (£10.95–£16.95)

12.30–2.30pm & 6.30–11pm Mon–Sat, 12.30–3pm & 6–9pm Sun.

670 8236

50 MC/V

**Rhino Room** 14a William Street South, D2 (around William St Sth)

The Rhino Room is an airy venue above the mother restaurant, Cooke's Café. Much depends on the chargrill and Johnny Cooke's eclectic brand of cooking, with its insistence on first-class raw materials served simply but stylishly. The menu changes daily, dishing up treats such as spiced tuna with pineapple salsa, and duck confit with mixed leaves, asparagus and Thai-style dressing. Laid-back and informal, this is one of the city's prime people-watching locations.

**££–£££** (£14–£18.50)

6.30–10.30pm Thu–Sat, 12.30–3pm Sat.

670 5260

55 all (Fri & Sat)

## let's do lunch

**Caviston's** 58 Glasthule Road, Sandycove (Co Dublin)

A pure joy, and perhaps the best place in Greater Dublin to eat fish. Since this eight-table restaurant opened up off Caviston's fishmongers and deli, they have been block-booked for all three lunch-time sittings. The fish just sings off the plate, exquisitely fresh and flawlessly sensual with minimal sauces. Families, romancing couples, pearl-draped ladies and Bono have all been here in search of fishy perfection. Wonderfully relaxed and effortlessly brilliant.

**£–££** (£6.95–£14.95)

12–4pm Tue–Sat.

280 9120

D to Glasthule

24 MC/V only

**Dobbins Wine Bistro** 15 Stephen's Lane, D2 (off Baggot St Lower)

They say Dobbins invented the concept of lunch, and the activity is positively thriving in this melting pot of well-to-do ladies, politicians, business men and illicit lovers. The who's who of Irish public life conduct their affairs, in semi-private, behind Dobbins' hallowed walls, and gossip is savoured between nibbles of the finest international cuisine, from baked fillet of red mullet with lobster and bacon potato, to basil risotto. It's a perfect spot for hedonists wishing to while away the hours between lunch and dinner.

**££–£££** (£13.50–17.50)

12.30–3pm Mon–Fri, 7.30–10.30pm Tue–Sat.

676 4679

120 all (piano Wed–Sat)

## brunch

**Elephant & Castle** 18 Temple Bar, D2 (Temple Bar)
Truly American-style brunch: eggs, burgers and the best chicken wings in town.
679 3121 *brunch: 10.30am–5pm Sat, 12–5pm Sun.* 90 all ££

**Nectar** 53 Ranelagh Village, D6 (Ranelagh)
Funky juice bar offering smoothies, sarnies, salads and wraps. Fresh as fresh can be.
491 0934 *brunch: 10.30–4pm Sun.* 28 MC/V £

**Odeon** 57 Harcourt Street | D2 (Harcourt Street)
Sundays kick off with all-day brunch, followed by a 6pm classic movie and some laid-back tunes.
478 2088 *brunch: 1pm–1am Sun.* 220 MC/V ££

**Odessa** 13 Dame Court, D2 (around South Great George's Street)
Hang with the club crowd over huevos rancheros and brilliant Bloody Marys. Book in advance.
670 7634 *brunch: 12–4.30pm Sat–Sun.* 120 MC/V ££

**Tá Sé Mahogani Gaspipes** 7 Manor Street, D1 (King Street North)
Upmarket and pricey, this American/Irish brunch experience comes complete with live jazz.
679 8138 *brunch: 1–9pm Sun.* 52 MC/V/D ££

**Prices quoted correspond to the cost of a main course in Irish pounds**

**The Lord Edward** 23 Christchurch Place, D8 (west of city centre)

An institution in olde Dublin dining that boasts a huge dedicated and often suited clientele at lunch. The haute-service and 'character' waiters are only part of the attraction of this first-class seafood restaurant. The vintage-sized portions of ultra-fresh fish with brilliant sauces should carry a government warning. Ask for tables four or six, both of which overlook Christ Church Cathedral.

££ (£9.95–£15.95)

12.30–2.30pm & 6–10.45pm Mon–Sat.

☎ 454 2420

45 all

## ↓ ethnic spice



**Ayumi-Ya** Newtown Park Avenue, Blackrock, D2 (Co Dublin)

Ayumi-Ya prides itself on being the only 'classical' Japanese in town. It offers formality and theatricality, complete with the option of *ozashiki* seating. The food is exciting, varied and stimulating, the chief delight being lots of starters that display the artistry and intense flavour of Japanese cuisine. The raw fish, sushi and sashimi should be sampled. A less formal sister restaurant resides in Baggot Street Lower. [ >24].

££–£££ (£5.95–£21.95)

6–11pm Mon–Sat, 5.30–9.45 pm Sun.

☎ 283 1767

to Blackrock

65 AE/MC/V

**Bangkok Café** 106 Parnell Street, D1 (around Parnell Street)

Shabby appearances can be deceptive: this is one of the best-value restaurants in the city. Bustling with an evening crowd of streetwise musicians, media folk and foodies, it's difficult to get a table after 9pm. The atmosphere is mellow, the food genuine Thai – delicious marinated chicken, delicately spiced, and fiery, aromatic green and red curries. Now open for lunch, it is still more conducive to after-dark experiences.

£ (£5.95–£10.95)

12.30–2.30pm & 5.30–10.30pm daily.

☎ 878 6618

55 none

**Chameleon** 1 Fownes Street Lower, D2 (Temple Bar)

What Chameleon has done with basic Indonesian cooking is a joy to behold, and even better to taste. In unpretentious and comfortable surroundings, a few mouthfuls will transport you to a warmer, more relaxed world. The speciality is the Indonesian *rijstafel*, a choice of meat, fish, noodles and rice, with veggie alternatives. A well-kept secret for locals, this is a place that most of its easy-going regulars treat as a culinary best mate.

£££ (£13.50–£21.50)

5.30–11pm daily.

☎ 671 0362

50 DC/MC/V

**Good World** 18 Sth Grt George's St, D2 (around Sth Grt George's St)

Charming and stylish it ain't, but the real thing it certainly is. At weekends huge Chinese families cram in to eat delicacies you cannot find on the menu. It is a familiar Dublin hangover cure to come here and eat the best dim sum in the country – from won tons and spare ribs to delicacies like ducks' feet and steamed tripe. The opening hours facilitate late-night drinkers who need some soakage. So whether it's the night before or the morning after, you'll have a great ethnic experience.

££ (£7.50–£8.50)

12.30pm–3am daily.

☎ 677 5373

100 all (Fri & Sat)



more restaurants & cafés

**Langkawi** 46 Baggot Street Upper, D4 (off Baggot Street upper)

Dublin's original ethnic restaurant, affectionately referred to as the 'Lankers', is a seasoned slice of life in the city's culinary scene. Its location is local rather than central, and the Lankers reflects that in its laid-back approach, serving an excellent blend of spicy curries with milder, south Indian influences – try *gulai daging lembu*, beef in a subtly spiced coconut sauce garnished with chillies, tomatoes, potatoes and aubergines. A steady stream of regulars ensures the restaurant is always full, so book ahead.

££ (£10.50–£13.50)

12.30–2pm Mon–Fri, 6–11.30pm Mon–Sat.

☎ 668 2760

60 all

**Monty's of Kathmandu** 28 Eustace Street, D2 (Temple Bar)

The menu here may read like any ordinary Indian, with the usual *tikka masalas* and tandooris, but the dishes are all cooked with an intriguing Nepalese twist. Flavours have depth and fragrance and the breads are utterly delicious. Try the *hasani*, a Nepalese mega-kebab with exquisite, tender chunks of marinated lamb. Mellow and relaxed with attentive service, Monty's offers good value, especially for lunch.

££ (£8–£14)

◑ 12–2.30pm & 5.30pm–midnight Mon–Sat, 5.30pm–midnight Sun.

☎ 670 4911

100 ▭ DC/MC/V £ ♿ ▤ V

**Saagar** 16 Harcourt Street, D2 (Harcourt Street)

Hidden away in a basement, Saagar is shrouded in the scent of spices. Decor is plain, but the cuisine is stunning – a broad range of taste sensations with lots of vegetarian options. The chilli-fried prawns, with an order of the house lemon rice or their coriander nan bread, is unforgettable. Since the restaurant is located in a business area, lunchtimes attract their fair share of suits.

£–££ (£5.50–£13)

◑ 12.30–3pm & 6–11.30pm daily.

☎ 475 5012

14, 14a, 15a, 15b, 48a

70 ▭ all £ V

**Shalimar** 17 Sth Grt George's St, D2 (around Sth Grt George's St)

This is a big, bustling, mainly Punjabi restaurant where the welcome is understated but warm, and the service friendly, efficient and never intrusive. It has a mouth-watering selection of vegetarian dishes, and the menu extends beyond the usual *rogan josh* and *korma*. Chicken with ginger is a reminder of how hot this spice can be, and lamb cooked with pickle is something that makes the taste buds emulate the finale of *Riverdance*.

££ (£9.50–£13.75)

◑ 12–2.30pm Mon–Fri, 12.30–3pm Sat, 6pm–midnight Mon–Thu, 5pm–1am Fri & Sat, 12pm–midnight Sun.

☎ 671 0738

110 ▭ all £ ♿ ▤ V

**Wagamama** King Street South, D2 (off Grafton Street)

London's favourite fast-food ramen bar has made the transition to Dublin with ease. The minimalist design, slinky benches, no-smoking and no-booking policies, brisk staff with those electronic gizmos – even the tangy juices – will all be familiar to the initiated. For newbies and those searching for noodle nirvana, come on down and join the crowd, and enjoy the way of the noodle. Recommendation: order some *yasai yakitori* – chargrilled veg in *yakitori* sauce – and then slurp your way through one of their excellent ramen bowls. Bodacious.

£ (£3.95–£7.95)

◑ 12pm–midnight daily.

☎ 478 2152

136 ▭ all £ throughout ▤ V

**Zafraan** 41 Sth Grt George's St, D2 (around Sth Grt George's St)

A new, innovative restaurant serving Asian fusion food in a cutting-edge environment. The aim seems to be to assault every sense with the food, blending Goanese, Indian, Thai and Malaysian to create a sophisticated mix of all the best elements of Asian cooking. Chargrilled duck with ground, roasted spices and their sticky banana-leaf-wrapped rice must be sampled to be believed. A mixed crowd includes streetwise students and rich trendies.

££ (£9.50–£14.50)

◑ 12.30–10.30pm daily.

☎ 677 0999

150 ▭ AE/MC/V ♿ ▤ V

## ↓ out of this world

**The Commons** 86 St Stephen's Green Sth, D2 (St Stephen's Green)

Luxury without ostentation, the spacious dining room of The Commons is favoured by corporate diners. Tables are so far apart, the waiters should be kitted out with rollerblades. The menu is modern and innovative, making the most of seasonal and fresh produce, with dishes such as loin of rabbit with Dublin Bay prawns and savoy cabbage. Portions are delicate, which means there's room for dessert, coffee and petits fours. In summer the open French windows and billowing breezes are particularly conducive to lingering lunches.

£££ (£20–£24)

◑ 12.30–2.15pm Mon–Fri, 7–10pm Mon–Sat.

☎ 478 0530

Ⓓ to Pearse Street

60 ▭ all £ ▤

**Le Coq Hardi** 35 Pembroke Road, D4 (off Baggot Street upper)

Charming, old-fashioned and geared towards the old boys' brigade, Le Coq Hardi is often referred to as Dublin's best restaurant. And if traditional with a twist is your bag, then it possibly is. The main dining room is sumptuously decorated and there are private rooms available. Service is attentive and discreet; dishes are a sophisticated take on nursery favourites, and the wine list offers vintages that compete with Dublin's soaring house prices. Chef John Howard is convivial, welcoming and of international repute. The lunchtime set menu is excellent value.

£££ (£18.80–£28)

◑ 12.30–2pm Mon–Fri, 7–10.30pm Mon–Sat.

☎ 668 4130

Ⓓ to Lansdowne Road

50 all

**L'Ecrivain** 109a Baggot Street Lower, D2 (off Baggot St lower)

Derry Clarke is one of Dublin's unsung culinary heroes. His menus are always inventive but never gimmicky, chock-a-block with different flavours, textures and styles, while the room is so appealing you'll have trouble leaving after your meal. Despite the restaurant's name, the cooking makes excellent use of Ireland's native fish, meat and vegetables. It's dished up and served, without any fuss, by the superb staff in a way that looks effortless, but certainly isn't. Good wine list, very strong on Californian

£££ (£19.50)

◑ 12.30–2pm Mon–Fri, 7–11pm Mon–Sat.

☎ 661 1919

120 all (Thu–Sat)

**Les Frères Jacques** 74 Dame Street, D2 (Temple Bar)

This is the real thing when it comes to high-class French cuisine in the Irish capital. Long a bastion of traditional values, serving the classics (and that includes the exemplary service and perfectly crisp dining room), Les Frères Jacques takes a wide, enticing route through the possible options, from simple soups to extravagant desserts via some delightful main courses. Francophiles will not believe their luck; the rest will just sigh with contentment.

£££ (£15–£25)

◑ 12.30–2.30pm Mon–Fri, 7.30–10.30pm Mon–Sat.

☎ 679 4555

60 all (Fri & Sat)

**Restaurant Patrick Guilbaud** 21 Merrion Street Upper, D2 (off Baggot Street lower)

The place for full-on foodie theatre. Guilbaud's is smart, sophisticated and special – features reflected in its two Michelin stars. Though the atmosphere is ultra-formal, the menu is unfussy, uncheffy and wonderfully pure. The French service is meticulous, and main courses come under silver cloches, lifted simultaneously to reveal marvellous interpretations of French and Irish favourites. The beautiful dining room is filled with 20th-century Irish art, and the wine list is equally impressive

£££ (£23–£29)

◑ 12.30–2pm & 7.30–10.15pm Tue–Sat.

☎ 676 4192

80 all

**Restaurant Peacock Alley** 109 St Stephen's Green West, D2 (St Stephens Green)

Conrad Gallagher's 'new Irish' cooking really is unlike anything you have tried before. Though his detractors may accuse him of being unable to stop with the flavour combinations, a certain refinement has been introduced while retaining a mind-boggling array of tastes, textures and ingredients. Seafood is particularly good; there's plenty of excellent wine by the glass and service is charming. Hence his first Michelin star at the age of 26.

£££ (£19–£25)

◑ 12.30–2.30pm & 6.30–11pm Mon–Sat.

☎ 478 7015

110 all

➔ more restaurants & cafés

**The Tea Room** The Clarence, 6–8 Wellington Quay, D2 (Temple Bar)

Whether you're here to appreciate chef Michael Martin's extraordinary way with food, or on a celeb-spotting spree, a table at The Tea Room is one to savour. The menu is light with plenty of flavoursome veggie options such as a zingy mushroom risotto or *millefeuille* of aubergine with couscous. Martin's creations please the eye as well as the palate and will take your tastebuds to another culinary level. The dining room does the superlative food justice, coming into its own at night when the blue lighting transforms it into something mysterious and wonderful.

£££ (£15–£18.50)

◑ 12.30–2.30pm Mon–Fri, 6.30–10.30pm daily.

☎ 670 7766

120 all

**Thornton's** 1 Portobello Road, D8 (around Camden Street)

Diners may be divided as to whether they enjoy the attitude and ambience at this small restaurant, but everyone is unanimous in the belief that Kevin Thornton is not just a culinary genius, he's a devoted one. The dining room is undesigned and understated, and food is refreshingly informal and unpretentious. Thornton focuses on traditional Irish recipes with the best of local ingredients, carefully balancing intense flavours. His fillet of John Dory is served with a thick, rich bisque made from sautéed langoustines and a light and delicate *sabayon*, pungent with the aroma of truffles.

£££ (£21–£24)
12.30–1.45pm Fri & 7–10.30pm Tue–Sat.
454 9067
16, 16a, 19, 19a
45 all

## ↓ home-grown

**Chapter One** 18–19 Parnell Square, D1 (around Parnell Street)

A jewel in the otherwise bare crown of northside fine dining, Chapter One is a modern Irish experience in a formal environment. Seafood is a favourite on the ever-changing menu, with dishes such as seared scallops and fennel, and compote of artichokes with saffron cream and French beans. The Gate and the Abbey theatres are close by, making this popular with thesps taking advantage of the two-course pre-theatre menu; it also attracts the barrister brigade from the nearby Four Courts and lunch times bring out a substantial crew of sober suits.

£££ (£14–£15.50)
12.30–2pm Tue–Fri, 6–10.30pm Tue–Sat.
873 2266
120 all (Sat)

**Mangetout** Basement, 112 Baggot St Lwr, D2 (off Baggot St lower)

In the recent past Derry Clarke and Conrad Gallagher started their careers here, and so it comes as no surprise that standards and traditions remain intact under the helm of the recent incumbent Brian Beatty. Food is fresh with many interesting and innovative flavour combinations, and the menu appeals to diners of all persuasions – vegetarian, low-fat, gourmet and carnivore. Best experienced in the evening when the ambience, cooking and charming service combine to offer an excellent evening out.

££ (£8–£16.50)
12.30–2.15pm Tue–Fri, 7–11pm Tue–Sat.
676 7866
35 DC/MC/V

## ↓ comfort cuisine

**The Pembroke** 31 Pembroke St Lower, D2 (off Baggot Street lower)

It's comfortable, it's in good taste, it's self-assured – nothing flash, the cosy Pembroke offers a good French bistro, with its modern Irish menu packed with homely favourites to fill and satisfy. They rustle up a powerful steak here and the fish is always excellent. Puds are a particular joy, and by the time you polish off your last mouthful you'll feel like you've just eaten at a favourite friend's pad. The interior is nothing special, but don't let appearances deceive you – this is one of Dublin's best-kept secrets and is always packed with hungry hordes.

££ (£9.95–£12.95)
12.30–3.30pm & 6–11.30pm Mon–Sat.
676 2994
65 all (Fri & Sat)

**Roly's Bistro** 7 Ballsbridge Terrace, D4 (Ballsbridge)

Roly's is one of those places that attracts devotees rather than just regulars. The experience begins when you're greeted by Roly Saul at the door and ends when you struggle past him a few hours later, full to the gills with the classic bistro creations of an adventurous kitchen. The seafood dishes, in particular, are worth the trawl to Ballsbridge and, for those of you who judge a restaurant by the quality of its bread, you'll be licking your lips from the start.

££ (£9.50–£14.95)
12–3pm & 6–10pm daily.
668 2611
to Lansdowne Road
150 all

**Prices quoted correspond to the cost of a main course in Irish pounds**

## ↓ the italian connection

**Ar Vicoletto** 5 Crow Street, D2 (Temple Bar)

£–££ (£5.50–£10)

A non-touristy oasis in the heart of Temple Bar, this tiny trattoria, with 80's-style decor, serves simple no-fuss Italian food. Their *bresaola* with rocket and parmesan starter is a meal in itself. Leave some space for the *saltimbocca alla Romana* (veal with sage, parma ham and wine). The service is attentive but unobtrusive; the wine list is basic but reliable and the atmosphere spot on for long lazy lunches.

1–4pm & 6pm–midnight Mon–Sat, 1pm–midnight Sun.
☎ 670 8662
30 DC/MC/V

**Botticelli** 3 Temple Bar, D2 (Temple Bar)

££ (£7.95–£11.95)

Always busy, the service in this light and airy hot spot is fast and furious. While the flirtatious waiters banter with each other in Italian, bask in some of the best, simple dishes Italy has to offer. The gnocchi with basil or wild mushrooms is particularly delicious; there's a good choice of pizzas, meat and chicken dishes, and the tiramisu is simply sublime.

10am–midnight daily.
☎ 672 7289
100 MC/V (Mon)

**Kapriol** 45 Camden Street Lower, D2 (around Camden Street)

£££ (£12–£20)

Punters fill the wooden booths which line this intimate, cosy dining room, the walls of which are covered with patterned plates and ornaments. Adding to the charm are the old-skool waitresses who offer suggestions and reel off the specials night after night. Seafood is ultra-fresh; pasta comes in Trojan portions; veal and chicken appear in numerous guises and you couldn't find a better wine list in the big boot of Italy. Pricey enough, you pay for all this authenticity, but after a few flaming sambucas no one seems to care.

6.30pm–midnight Tue–Sat.
☎ 475 1235
35 all £19.95 (dinner)

**Steps of Rome** 1 Chatham Street, D2 (off Grafton Street)

£ (£5–£9)

With all the friendly, chattering, chain-smoking Italians packed into this quaint café-cum-eaterie, it's amazing that they find room for the myriad of toppings for their glorious pizzas. Sold by the slice, the potato and rosemary version is a particular house favourite. The wonderful waitresses, reasonable prices, fruity house red, and quite possibly the best coffee in town, make this a great daytime hang-out or evening pit stop.

10.30am–midnight daily.
☎ 670 5630
20 none

**Unicorn** 12b Merrion Crt, Merrion Row, D2 (off Baggot St lower)

££ (£7.50–£17.80)

A bastion for what masquerades these days as Dublin 'society', the Unicorn hosts an unbeatable Saturday lunch when the great and good gather to eat somewhat hackneyed but well-executed Italian food, chew the fat of the week's political and social events and linger lazily until late afternoon. Airy, interlinking dining rooms, very helpful staff and a bubbling, comfortable ambience make this something of a lush lunchtime experience, but you will find it just as convivial late into the night.

12.15–3.30pm & 6–11pm Mon–Sat.
☎ 662 4757
80 all (Thu–Sat)

more restaurants & cafés

## ↓ fish & chips

**Beshoffs** 14 Westmoreland Street, D2 (east of city centre)
Trad fish and chips served in posh marble surroundings. Extensive menu to eat in or take away.
☎ 677 8026 *11am–11pm Mon–Sat (3am Fri–Sat), 12–11pm Sun.* 60 none £

**Leo Burdock's** 2 Werburgh Street, D8 (west of city centre)
Massive fish menu matched only by the huge portions of chips. Mmmmmmmm....
☎ 454 0306 *12pm–midnight Mon–Sat, 4pm–midnight Sun.* none none £

**Caffola's** 75 Mespil Road, D4 (off Baggot Street upper)
Formica-clad caff best known by Dubs who call in for post-pubbing chips and bits. Trad and tasty.
☎ 660 3127 *12.15pm–midnight Mon–Fri (until 2.30pm Tue), 6.30pm–12.30am Sat.* 48 none £

**Harry Ramsden** Naas Road, D12 (around Parnell Street)
A branch of Britain's favourite name in cholesterol – battered everything and chunky chips.
☎ 460 0233 *12–9pm Mon–Sun (9.30pm Thur, 10pm Fri–Sat).* 300 all £

## cool med

**Cooke's Café** 14 William St South, D2 (around William St South)

Johnny Cooke was in at the start of the Dublin culinary revolution when he opened this Cal-Ital inspired restaurant in 92. His Caesar salad is still the best in Ireland, and other memorable dishes include deep-fried squid with hot tomato sauce, anything with pasta, and the unctuous pecan pie. Make sure to order plenty of Johnny's delicious bread and pesto dip.

£££ (£14–£23)
12.30–3pm & 6–10pm daily.
679 0536
40 all

**Morel's Bistro** 18 Glasthule Road, Sandycove (Co Dublin)

Good food and wine at down-to-earth prices. Tomato and basil tart, hot timbale of crab meat with a sharp *sabayon*, guinea fowl with lime and rösti potatoes – these are typical dishes on an ever-changing menu. Puds are luscious, service superb, atmosphere anything between calm and hectic, but always pleasant. There's also a big selection of very decent wines.

££ (£11.95–£15.75)
12.30–2.30pm Thu & Fri, 5.30–10pm daily.
230 0210
to Glasthule
110 all

**QV2** 14–15 St Andrew Street, D2 (around William Street South)

QV2 always seems to be busy which is a sure sign that the comfortable, easy-on-the-eye-and-wallet cooking is a winner with Dublin diners. What QV2 and chef Eoin McDonnell offer may not look difficult (no-frills international dishes with an Irish touch), but the subtle nuances in tastes will convince you to return. Brilliant service, a very good wine list and excellent ambience.

££ (£9.50–£15.50)
12–3pm & 6pm–midnight Mon–Sat.
677 3363
130 all (Sat)

## café culture

**Il Baccaro** Meeting House Square, Eustace St, D2 (Temple Bar)

Dublin's smart young Italian things gather here to sip espressos and wine until well into the small hours. At times, it's like hanging out in a rocking café in Milan with all the football talk; at other times, it's like chilling at Miuccia Prada's after-show party.

£–££ (£6.50–£12)
6–11pm Mon–Thu, 5–11pm Fri & Sat.
671 4597

**Bewley's Oriental Café** 78 Grafton Street, D2 (off Grafton St)

A place where the good, the bad and the hungry have supped tea, filled tummies and whiled away hours in the oriental rooms. Large and clattering, Bewley's [→51] is a favourite place for caffeine, cherry buns and hearty fried breakfasts. The front section sells the best array of edible goodies in Dublin.

£–££ (£5.25–£11.25)
7.30am–11.30pm Mon–Sat, 10am–midnight Sun.
677 6761

**Browns** Brown Thomas, Grafton Street, D2 (off Grafton Street)

This chic hang-out for the BT regulars serves coffee and dainty snacks to ladies who seem to always be on a diet. A good respite if the shopping gets too much, and you never know who will be sitting at the next table. Ideal spot to deposit partners who are groaning at the sight of another changing room.

£ (£3.45–£7.50)
9am–6pm daily.
677 6761

**Café Gertrude** 3 Bedford Row, D2 (Temple Bar)

Getting better all the time, Gertrude has a swell, best-kept-secret vibe to it, as the more sussed Temple Bar loungers call by for big bowls of soup, overloaded sandwiches and very good coffee. Great staff and a lovely room encourage lingering.

£ (£2.95–£3.75)
11am–7pm Mon–Wed, 11am–11pm Thu–Sun.
677 9043

**Prices quoted correspond to the cost of a main course in Irish pounds**

**Café Java** 5 Anne Street South, D2 (off Grafton Street)

Located a teaspoon's throw from Grafton Street, this is the best of the Café Java coffee houses. Great breakfasts, excellent lunch menu and very good coffee make this one to mark if you are planning a shopping spree.

£ (£2.75–£4.95)
7.45am–6.30pm daily (from 9am Sat, 10am Sun, to 9pm Thu).
☎ 670 7239

**The Dome** St Stephen's Green Centre (St Stephens Green)

Bird's-eye views tempt shoppers to rest their aching limbs. A good place for coffee – and the cakes will have you reaching for a plate too. If you want something more substantial, a selection of comfortable fare, with plenty for veggies, won't break the bank.

£ (£4.95–£5.95)
9.30am–5.30pm Mon–Sat.
☎ 677 6761

**Joy of Coffee** 25 Essex Street East, D2 (Temple Bar)

Looks like your living-room, filled with a dozen varieties of coffee, muffins, sweeter treats and a huge selection of board games. Very laid-back, and an ideal place to pick up the Temple Bar gossip.

£ (£2.95–£4.95)
7.45am–9pm daily (from 9.30am Sat–Sun 10pm Fri & 11pm Sat).
☎ 679 3393

**Kaffe Moka** 39 William St South, D2 (around William St South)

The best late-night spot in town, this three-storey coffee house gives you the bean any way you want it. You see the strangest people here at two in the morning playing chess, writing poetry or arguing about Miles Davis records.

£ (£3.50–£5)
10am–4am daily.
☎ 679 8475

**Panem** 20 Ormond Quay Lower, D1 (around the north quays)

Smashing new-skool Italian café on the quays that also manages to fit a funky deli, dinky sandwich bar and little bakery into the same space. Small and intimate, it's the perfect spot for 11am liaisons, but gets darn crowded at lunch.

£ (£1.65–£3.50)
9am–5pm Mon–Fri, 10am–5pm Sat.
☎ 873 3293

**Shelbourne Hotel** Lord Mayor's Lounge, St Stephen's Green North, D2 (St Stephens Green)

A visit to Dublin would not be complete without afternoon tea in the hotel's plush drawing rooms. Tables groan under plates of scones, fancy sandwiches and much more. Big armchairs are ideal for a post-tea snooze. Advance booking recommended.

££ (£13.50 set tea)
3.30–5.30pm daily.
☎ 676 6471

**Simon's Place** Sth Grt George's St, D2 (around Sth Gt George's St)

An old Dublin culinary hand, Simon McWilliams offers champion sandwiches, salads and soups, and the coffee here tastes superb – hence the legendary lunchtime queues.

£ (£2–£3)
8.30am–6pm Mon–Sat.
☎ 679 4698

**The Winding Stair** 40 Ormond Quay Lwr, D1 (around north quays)

A bookshop café, but don't go thinking Borders. This is the most idiosyncratic of Dublin's bookstores, and its café has been a winner for years. The soup and Irish fiction sections are recommended.

£ (£1.25–£4)
10am–6pm Mon–Sat, 1–6pm Sun.
☎ 873 3292

## ↓ late-night eats

**Blue Room** Lloyd's Brasserie, 20 Merrion Street Upper, D2 (off Baggot Street lower)
A popular late-night piano bar serving good wine and delicious eats. Officially members only.
☎ 662 7240 *12.30–2.30pm daily (1–4pm Sat–Sun), 6–late daily.* 220 all ££–£££

**Eddie Rockets** 7 South Anne Street, D2 (off Grafton Street)
American diner fare accompanied by a 50's jukebox soundtrack. Many branches open until 4am.
☎ 679 7381 *8am–1am daily (4am Thu–Sat).* 69 MC/V £

**Juice** 9 Castle House, South Grt George's St, D2 (around South Grt George's Street)
Credible, creative veggie hang-out. Modern, bright decor and an aversion to lentils keeps it busy.
☎ 475 7856 *9am–4pm & 5.30–11pm daily (from 12.30pm Sat–Sun).* 70 MC/V ££

**Trocadero** 2 St Andrew's Street, D2 (around William Street South)
Hang-out for luvvies and theatricals who fancy people-watching and eating lots, late.
☎ 679 9772 *6pm–12.15am daily (11.15pm Sun).* 100 all ££

# the inn crowd

Dublin is changing fast, but the pub remains the heart of its social life. Many are now mock-traditional rebuilds, but enough genuine articles survive to satisfy any purist – and more exotic superpubs ensure variety. So, enjoy the wait while the barman lets your Guinness 'stand'.

## ↓ the perfect pint

### Conway's

Slaking thirsts for over 250 years, this is a Dublin institution. Showcased in *The Commitments*, the yellowed interior is homely rather than spectacular, but the Guinness is as superb and seductive as the atmosphere of easy-going familiarity.

70 Parnell Street, D1 (around Parnell Street)
☎ 873 2687

### Dockers

Dublin's dock workers may be a dwindling breed but you'll still find a few drinking here, alongside music moguls, journalists and – if your luck's in – stars and supermodels. All rub shoulders in this simple and welcoming tribute to the time before pubs were 'designed'.

5 Sir John Rogerson's Quay, D2 (east of city centre) ☎ 677 1692

### Doheny & Nesbitt

Close to Ireland's parliament, the Dail, this may be a haven for sundry politicians, spin-doctors and flunkies, but the authentic setting and good pints easily makes up for the nods and winks of domestic VIPs.

5 Baggot Street Lower, D2 (off Baggot Street Lower) ☎ 676 2945

### Fitzsimons

Popular with students and academics, and often busiest in the early evening, this delightfully unfussy wooden affair is a great place to conclude a tour of Trinity College. A laid-back, relaxing drink is the reward in store for those who head a little off the beaten track.

32 Westland Row, D2 (east of city centre)
☎ 671 0179 ◑ *until 2am Thu–Sat.* (Thu–Sat)

### Grave Diggers

Hugging the wall of Glasnevin Cemetery [→55], this is the pub that time forgot. Once a country boozer, it has miraculously retained its rural charm despite being swallowed by suburbia. Settle into a snug and let the evening drift by as you sip the incredibly cheap, creamy Guinness. Well worth the bus or taxi ride.

1 De Courcey Square, D9 (Glasnevin)
13, 19, 19a, 134

### International Bar

A haunt of musicians and writers – including many of Ireland's new-wave comedians – this intimate and lively venue yields friendly staff, good Guinness, live music, and Wednesday's comedy club [→104] which remains an important showcase for up-coming talent.

23 Wicklow Street, D2 (around William Street South) ☎ 677 9250 (Tue, Fri–Sun)

### Mulligan's

An eclectic mix gathers in this crowded low-ceilinged, rough-hewn bar to pay their respects to what is often cited as the font of Dublin's finest Guinness.

8 Poolbeg Street, D2 (east of city centre)
☎ 677 5582

### O'Dwyer's

An accomplished all-rounder, this elegant Victorian-style establishment has it all. The food is renowned and the staff are helpful. Later on, as the twenty-somethings gather to dance and romance in the three-tier nightclub, it gets pleasantly hectic.

8 Mount Street Lower, D2 (aound Merrion Square) ☎ 676 1718 ◑ *1am–11.30pm Mon–Wed, 11am–1.30am Thu–Sat, 11am–6pm Sun.* (Fri–Sat) (Wed, Thu, Sat)

**Ryan's**

Dominated by a majestic horseshoe bar, this beautiful old-style establishment retains a sense of Victorian propriety. Blaring music is unheard of and rowdy carousing unthinkable. The food's superb, the pints peerless, and the elegant setting is ideal for an intimate chat or a solitary read.

28 Parkgate Street, D8 (near Phoenix Park) ☎ 677 6097 25, 25a, 26, 68, 69

**Toner's**

A connoisseur's delight, this place just oozes character. The Guinness here is famous, as are some of the creative and media types who clearly enjoy the ambience. Generations of devoted drinkers have enjoyed the pokey but charming timbered interior.

139 Baggot Street Lower, D2 (off Baggot Street Lower) ☎ 676 3090

## ↓ music on tap

**Devitt's**

While many of its neighbours have succumbed to extensive cosmetic surgery, Devitt's still presents the lived-in face of the old style Dublin pub. This is a no frills, hospitable boozer which remains the local of choice for many of the area's street traders. Gaelic Games paraphenalia line the walls and there's trad music six nights a week.

78 Lower Camden Street, D2 (around Camden St) ☎ 475 3414 16, 16a, 19, 19a ◑ *10.30am–midnight daily (from 12pm Sun).* (Fri–Wed) (Thu)

**Ferryman**

The recent shift from pub to hotel has left the attractive interior intact. The sponged orange walls and wood-with-everything decor create ideal conditions for enjoying real music played in an authentic setting.

35 Sir John Rogerson's Quay, D2 (east of city centre) ☎ 671 7053 (Wed & Sat)

**Keating's**

This pub has attracted a hipper, younger crowd since relocating to impressively swish new premises. Its reputation for good folk and traditional music sessions remains undiminished, however, and the more mature won't feel out of place. Good food is served all day.

9–10 Jervis Street, D1 (around the north quays) ☎ 872 4031 (Sat–Tue & Thu)

**O'Donoghue's**

During the 60's this was home to the legendary folk group, the Dubliners, and it trades successfully on its hallowed reputation. The prototype Irish theme pub, it's hugely popular. Not really for the purist, but it's alive with the sound of traditional music seven nights a week.

15 Merrion Row, D2 (off Baggot Street Lower) ☎ 676 2807 ◑ *until midnight daily.* (nightly)

**O'Shea's Merchant**

In this brazenly stage-Oirish setting, there's barely a square foot of wall-space that isn't colonized with rustic remnants from bygone times. Traditional sessions happen nightly, and whooping-it-up is mandatory. Rarely a dull moment.

12 Bridge Street Lower, D2 (west of city centre) ☎ 679 3797 (nightly)

**Renard's**

The images lining the walls of this pub/club [→99] recall its former pre-eminence as the Camelot of Ireland's burgeoning rock scene. The pace is slower these days, but the jazz sessions early in the week still swing till late.

35 Frederick Street South, D2 (around Dawson Street) ☎ 677 5876 ◑ *until 1.30am daily.* (Mon–Wed) (nightly)

**Whelan's**

Narrow, intimate and conducive to good conversation, the front bar attracts drinkers of all ages and backgrounds. The music venue [→101] out back holds about 300, and the excellent acoustics draw varied acts ranging from rock to traditional Irish.

25 Wexford Street, D2 (around Camden Street) ☎ 478 0766 ◑ *until 2am Thu–Fri.* 16a, 19, 19a, 122 (nightly) (Thu–Sat)

→ more pubs & bars

**Unless specified, opening hours are as standard: 10.30am–11.30pm Mon–Sat; 12.30–11pm Sun (legislation is due to change allowing pubs to stay open until 1am)**

## ↓ hip hangouts

**Café en Seine**

A continental-style café bar built on the scale of an aircraft hangar, this is where the upwardly mobile and painfully hip meet. A monument to aspiration, this is one for fans of cathedrals, good cocktails and people-watching.

40 Dawson Street, D2 (around Dawson Street) ☎ 677 4369 *until midnight Thu–Sun.*

**Chocolate Bar**

Possibly Dublin's most flamboyant drinking hole, the sunken bar – part of the PoD [→98] complex – looks like an art project come to life. Theatrical drapes, irregular angles, memorable toilets, a pool table and large couches for the cool crowd to lounge on, add to the laid-back feel. Sunday's late night *Loose* is a legendery recovery session for Dublin's clubbing mafia.

Old Train Station, Harcourt Street, D2 (Harcourt Street) ☎ 478 0166 *5–11.30pm Mon–Wed, 5pm–3am Thu–Sun.* 14, 14a, 15a, 15b, 48a (Thu–Sun)

**Drumm's Emporium**

More mature patrons shouldn't be fooled by the innocent-looking front bar – the pounding noise seeping in from the main lounge betrays Drumm's real nature. Expect instead a heady cocktail of pierced bellybuttons, first-time drinkers and low-flying pheromones.

1–5 Exchequer Street, D2 (around South Great George's Street) ☎ 679 1776 *until 1am Fri–Sat, until midnight Sun.* (Fri–Sat)

**The Globe**

The simple timber bar displays rotating exhibitions by local artists and is popular with cappuccino sippers and Dublin's clubbing clique (the acclaimed Ri-Ra club [→99] is part of the complex). All aim to be part of the beautiful set, many succeed, but the real catwalk is behind the bar.

11 South Great George's Street, D2 (around South Great George's Street) ☎ 671 1220 lunch Mon–Fri (jazz 5–8pm Sun) (nightly)

**Hairy Lemon**

An endearing maze of nooks and crannies scattered over two storeys, the Hairy Lemon deserves its reputation as one of Dublin's premier party pubs. Young, loud and brash, it fills up early at weekends, so sauntering in for a last pint is usually out of the question.

41 Stephen Street Lower, D2 (around William Street South) ☎ 671 8949

**Jute**

Jute's minimal decor provides a refreshing alternative to most Dublin bars. It enjoys a steady trade but never gets too full for comfort and the comfy couches are perfect for chilling out.

2 Aungier Street, D2 (around South Great George's Street) ☎ 475 5895 16, 16a, 19, 19a, 83, 155 *11.30am–11.30pm Mon–Sat, 6.30–11pm Sun.* (jazz Sunday night) (Fri)

**Life**

An unlikely fusion of Scandinavian interior design and *Voyage to the Bottom of the Sea* ensures this visually stunning venue draws a varied and youthful crowd. Angled surfaces, split-levels, lounge music and marine motifs lend it a unique spacey, clubby feel and justify its current status as one of Dublin's most 'in' hangouts. Weekend nights swing, particularly Saturdays when soul and jazz set the mood.

Irish Life Mall, Abbey Street Lower, D1 (around the north quays) ☎ 878 1032 *12–11.30pm Mon–Wed, 12pm–1am Thu–Sat, 12.30–11pm Sun.* (Thu–Sat)

**Odeon**

This palatial structure houses an incredibly long bar, some low-slung seating and an expanse of open space. By day it's an elegant setting for scribbling postcards, by night it hosts a lively throng of young professionals and clubbers.

57 Harcourt Street, D2 (Harcourt Street) ☎ 478 2088 *12pm–midnight Mon–Tue, 12pm–1.30am Wed–Sat, 12.30pm–midnight Sun.*

**Pravda**

First of the city's superpubs to go the full monty on a theme – and what a theme. A former lost-property office now looks like a vast Russian drinking factory. On weekend nights, laid-back music draws a stylish crowd keen to taste exotic beers and vodkas while staring at Soviet murals.

2–3 Liffey St Lower, D1 (around the north quays) ☎ 874 0090 *until 1.30am Thu–Sat.* (until 7pm) (Sun afternoons) (Wed–Sat)

### The Stag's Head

Elegantly oakey, this enduring gem amongst Dublin's pubs has finally been spruced up to look the part. Superb Guinness and top-class food (bacon and cabbage is the speciality dish) draw a lively mix of tourists, students and young professionals.

1 Dame Court, D2 (around South Great George's Street) ☎ 679 3701 ◑ *until 12.30am Thu–Fri (closed Sun).* ℘ (Mon–Fri) ◗

### Thing Mote

In essence Thing Mote is an unexceptional mock-authentic pub. However, its prime location delivers a nightly throng of students, ex-students and people with interesting piercings that brings the fixtures to vibrant life.

15 Suffolk Street, D2 (off Grafton Street) ☎ 677 8030 ◗

### Thomas Read

Sparse and roomy during the day, but packed with the articulate and creative by night. Huge windows make this big corner pub feel a bit like a goldfish bowl; but the cool crowd generates a warm sophisticated atmosphere and attentive staff keep the booze flowing freely.

1 Parliament Street, D2 (Temple Bar) ☎ 670 7220 ◑ *11am–11pm Mon–Wed, 11am–1am Thu–Sun.* ℘ ● (Thu–Sat)

### Vicar Street

An unusually comfortable live music venue [→101] – possibly due to its thirty-something feel. Vicar Street is a purpose built venue for gigs and a popular bar-cum-restaurant/café. High ceilings, plenty of space and a seated auditorium go hand in hand with civil security staff and enough pint-pullers behind the bar.

99 Vicar Street, off Thomas Street, D8 (west of city centre) ☎ 454 5720 ◑ *9.45am–11pm Mon–Sat, 5–11pm Sun.* ℘ (Mon–Fri) (Mon–Fri)

### Zanzibar

A mecca for Dublin's beautiful youth, not to mention an eye-opening homage to the sultry otherworld of the Arabian Nights. The scale is monumental, with lofty balconies overlooking an exotic indoor courtyard. Spectacular, and sheer bedlam at peak times. The door policy can be erratic and the weekend jostle can be energy sapping, so the spendid interior is best appreciated over an off-peak pint.

37–38 Ormond Quay Lower, D1 (around the north quays) ☎ 878 7212 ◑ *4.30pm–1.30am Mon–Fri, 3.30pm–1.30am Sat, 12.30pm–1am Sun.* ℘ (until 8pm) ● (nightly) ◗

## ↓ late licences

### Bleeding Horse

The agricultural bric-a-brac is laid on with a shovel, but the Bleeding Horse is one of the city's better traditional theme pubs. The good food, and split-level maze of twists and turns, draws a lively après-office mix; students and hipsters arrive later.

24 Camden Street Upper, D2 (around Camden Street) ☎ 475 2705 ◑ *until 1.30am Thu & Fri, midnight Sun.* 16, 16a, 19, 19a, 83, 155 ℘ (Sun afternoons) ● (Thu–Sat) ◗

### Foggy Dew

Smart and wood-furnished, there's no better place to discover a vibrant crowd determined to defy the Irish climate. Miniskirts, T-shirts and suntans are in fashion all year round and the music levels ward off middle-aged interlopers.

1 Fownes Street Upper, D2 (Temple Bar) ☎ 677 9328 ◑ *until 1am Thu–Sat.* ℘ (lunch only) ● (nightly) ◗

### Hogan's

Centred on a big oval bar, this roomy and high-ceilinged establishment is invariably packed as the night wears on, but the service never noticeably slacks. Its best attribute is its hip, young-ish, gay and straight clientele. Probably best to avoid the charmless cellar though.

35 South Great George's Street, D2 (around South Great George's Street) ☎ 677 5904 ◑ *until 1.30am Thu–Fri.* ℘ ● (nightly) ◗

### Messrs Maguire

A recent addition to Dublin's slew of superpubs, this Edwardian-style hostelry incorporates several elegant bars, each with a range of distinctive ales and lagers 'handmade' on the premises. DJs spin some cool beats and add to the party buzz on late nights. Door security can be tough.

1–2 Burgh Quay, D2 (east of city centre) ☎ 670 5777 ◑ *until 1am Thu–Sun.* ℘ ● (Wed–Sat) ◗

→ more pubs & bars

**Unless specified, opening hours are as standard: 10.30am–11.30pm Mon–Sat; 12.30–11pm Sun (legislation is due to change allowing pubs to stay open until 1am)**

**Porterhouse**

Foreign visitors regularly outnumber the natives in this multi-storey micro-brewery which stocks a range of customized brews on draught, each of them worth a try. There's live music and decent food, from burgers to seafood, but getting served at peak times can take an age.

16 Parliament Street, D2 (Temple Bar)
☎ 679 847 ◑ *until 1.30am Thu–Fri, midnight Sat.* ♿ ✎ (Sat–Wed)

**Turk's Head**

A mix of swish, luxurious café-lounge and dim no-frills bar, Turk's is a favourite haunt of the style-conscious. Sharp-dressed creatives congregate, many moving on to the Chop House nightclub attached (free entry). There's also belly dancing on Tuesdays.

27–30 Parliament Street, D2 (Temple Bar)
☎ 679 9701 ◑ *10.30–2am Mon–Sat, 12.30pm–2am Sun.* ♿ ● (nightly)

## ↓ sup with the lark

**Delaney's**

Bordering the cobblestoned Smithfield Market, you'll encounter a mix of traders, truck-drivers and homeward-bound night workers. A tranquil venue where Gaelic Games memorabilia proliferates, the mood is mellow, the prices rock-bottom, and there's something wonderfully wicked about being there at the crack of dawn.

83 King Street North, D7 (King Street North)
☎ 873 0824 ◑ *7am–11pm daily.* ✎ (Sat–Sun)

**Slattery's**

This famous Early House strikes the ideal balance between the trad and modern, accommodating folk sessions and gay nights while retaining its local custom. Dark, smoky and welcoming, it always does a roaring breakfast trade.

129 Capel Street, D1 (around Parnell Street)
☎ 872 7971 ◑ *7am–11.30pm Mon–Sat, 12.30–11pm Sun.* ♿ ✎ (Thu–Sun)

## ↓ talking heads

**Dawson Lounge**

One for the non-claustrophobics, this discreet cubby-hole is small but perfectly formed. The Guinness is good and the clientele mixed. Shoe-horn your way in, and you'll find it gives fresh meaning to the concept of an intimate drink.

25 Dawson Street, D2 (around Dawson Street)
☎ 677 5909 ✎ (Thu)

**Kehoe's**

Here, all-singin', all-dancin' mobile phones haven't displaced the dog-eared

paperback classic as the accessory of choice. The time-worn main bar may seem to be held together with tar and nicotine, and seating is a little scarce, but music never threatens to drown the priceless banter.

9 Anne Street South, D2 (off Grafton Street)
☎ 677 8312

**The Long Hall**

An extremely colourful, long-standing haunt of artists, musicians and a variety of chancers. The long, long bar is outstanding, and the whole venue rises to the challenge of matching its exotic clientele. A real treat.

51 South Great George's Street, D2 (around South Great George's Street) ☎ 475 1590

**McDaid's** ▲

Brendan Behan used to brawl here, so bookish pilgrims compete for limited seating with a youthful cosmopolitan crowd. Irrespective of its violent literary pedigree, the stained-glass windows and authentic wooden interior make it well worth a visit.

3 Harry Street, D2 (off Grafton Street)
☎ 679 4395 ✎ (Wed & Sat)

**O'Brien's**

This rambling, comfortable old pub is a popular retreat from the surrounding expanse of office-block purgatory. Full of inviting nooks and crannies, it provides welcome R & R for battle-weary yuppies and any others who should happen by.

8 Sussex Terrace, D4 (around Leeson Street Upper) ☎ 668 2594 🚌 11, 11a, 13b, 46a, 46b

**O'Neill's**

An authentic old-style frontage conceals a bewildering warren of lounges – some gems, some less impressive – with an equally varied crowd. Easy to see why it was once called 'eight fine pubs in one'. Night and day this place buzzes.

2 Suffolk Street, D2 (off Grafton Street)
☎ 855 6606

**The Pembroke**

This once-modest pub with an adjoining restaurant [→88] has been lavishly dolled up to cater for the well heeled of all ages. Now the opulent decor is impressive, and provides the perfect back-drop for those who like to chat in their Sunday best.

31 Pembroke Street Lower, D2 (off Baggot Street Lower) ☎ 662 2534

### Smyth's

These non-identical twin bars wouldn't win any beauty contests, which is fine with the punters who wouldn't approve anyway. Regulars dress for comfort, not style, and the friendly informality attracts all sorts, from media execs to country nurses.

10 Haddington Rd, D4 (off Baggot Street Upper) ☎ 660 6305 🚌 7, 7a, 8, 45

## ↓ gay thirst

### Front Lounge

This elegant piece of retro hotel-lobby chic attracts a hip, substantially gay, cosmopolitan crowd. The pub food here is amongst the best in Dublin, with well-priced Mediterranean dishes. Sink into the low-level seating and let the attentive staff fetch and carry for you.

33 Parliament Street,D2 (Temple Bar) ☎ 670 4112 ◑ *until midnight daily.*

### The George

Dublin's first and foremost gay bar, with mature drinkers occupying the more sedate front section while youngsters window-shop from the balcony or let rip in the back saloon. Madcap bingo nights are a regular treat and karaoke is all the rage. Live music on Wednesdays and late opening four days of the week are an added bonus.

89 South Great George's Street, D2 (around South Great George's Street) ☎ 478 2983 ◑ *until 1.45am Wed–Sun.* (Wed) (Wed–Sun)

### Out on the Liffey

Sophisticated it ain't, but this cluttered mock-traditional pub has an undeniable buzz, and the mainly gay crowd has a good male/female mix. Refreshingly unpretentious, it's generally liveliest on drag-show nights (Fri–Sun).

27 Ormond Quay Upper, D1 (around the north quays) ☎ 872 2480 ◑ *until 1.30am Fri.*

## ↓ the great outdoors

### Addison Lodge

With the enchanting Botanical Gardens [→55] opposite, this neighbourhood local makes an ideal stop-over on a warm afternoon. Relax on the well-tended lawn, enjoy some good food, and raise a cooling glass to the beauty of nature.

Glasnevin, D9 (Glasnevin) ☎ 837 3534 🚌 13, 19, 134

### The Barge

There's no beer garden, just a hotch-potch of seats and ledges, but on balmy summer evenings people swarm to laze and imbibe by the Grand Canal. A grassy knoll, lapping waters and sunny disposition complete the package.

42 Charlemont Street, D2 (around Camden St) ☎ 475 1869 🚌 44, 48a, 62 ◑ *10.30am–2am Mon–Sat (until 1.30am Mon–Wed) 12.30pm–1.30am Sun.* (nightly)

### Dicey Reilly's

This traditional hotel bar can often be clogged with stuffed shirts, but high summer brings out the butterflies in the city centre's best beer garden. Sunken split-level patios, good sun-exposure, barbecues and plenty of glam are among the delights in store.

Russell Court Hotel, 21 Harcourt St, D2 (Harcourt Street) ☎ 478 4066 🚌 14, 14a, 15a, 15b, 48a (Thu–Sat)

### Gibney's

On long evenings and sunny weekends, this is the social hub of a delightful fishing village turned moneypot. There's no real greenery, but the big courtyard is always buzzing with life. A stone's throw from the beach and harbour, Gibney's was made for boozy sunny afternoons.

New Street, Malahide (Malahide) ☎ 845 0242 to Malahide (until 8pm) (Fri–Sun) (Tue & Sun)

### Queens

The pick of the pubs in this affluent former fishing village, Queens is good for star-spotting and sun-lounging. The elegantly landscaped beer garden attracts families, day-trippers and celebs, and the back patio catches the pleasant evening rays.

12 Castle Street, Dalkey (Dalkey) ☎ 285 4569 to Dalkey (12–5pm)

### Schoolhouse

This designer conversion may not be too comfortable inside, but the beer garden is a treat. Sultry evenings and lazy Sundays see Dublin's smart young things mingling happily amid silver fittings, old-style street lamps and the finest shrubs.

2–8 Northumberland Road, D4 (Northumberland Road) ☎ 667 5014 🚌 7, 7a, 8, 45

### Summit Inn

This friendly local sits at the top of Howth Head and gets a lively passing trade from hill-walkers and sightseers. The sloping beer garden unfortunately faces away from the impressive cliff-top views out back, so take your scenic ramble first. Mainstream club nights Thursday to Saturday.

Howth (Howth) ☎ 832 4615 to Howth. ◑ *until 1.30am Thu–Sun.* (summer only) (Thu–Sat)

**Unless specified, opening hours are as standard: 10.30am–11.30pm Mon–Sat; 12.30–11pm Sun (legislation is due to change allowing pubs to stay open until 1am)**

# night fever

The early 90's saw a vibrant club culture emerge and there are now a myriad of one-nighters on Dublin's cool dance scene. A typical night on the tiles begins in one of the many pre-club hip hangouts [→94] and ends in a late night caff or even an Early House [→96] – in between the choice is impressive. Where techno and house once ruled, now hip hop, reggae, soul, drum & bass and garage are growing in popularity. If that's not enough, there is also old-style chart-hit smooching. Check listings magazines [→100], scour billboards and hang on to flyers handed out in shops and pubs.

### Annabelle's

Annabelle's is not to be taken seriously. A hit with students, trainee solicitors, rugby players and Dublin's affluent southside suburban set, it's a great place to let your hair down. There is one massive central bar and another smaller one serving Mexican food. The music is wonderfully predictable and even has two slow sets a night. Members get first preference at the door.

Burlington Hotel, Leeson St Upper, D4 (around Leeson St Upper) ☎ 660 5222 £6–£8 ◑ *11pm–2.30am Wed–Sat.* neat, no trainers, no baseball caps

### Club M

A Dublin institution, this harks back to the days when clubbing was about getting paralytically drunk and copping off. Blooms Hotel may be popular with visiting bands and DJs, but they wouldn't be seen dead in here – leave your pretensions at the door.

Blooms Hotel, Anglesea Street, D2 (Temple Bar) ☎ 671 5485 £8 ◑ *11pm–2.30am Tue–Sun.* all smart, no trainers

### The Funnel

In the downstairs bar sleek minimalism rules, while the murky main room has an excellent sound system used by some of the city's top promoters. Very friendly, it attracts an unpretentious crowd.

24 City Quay, D2 (east of city centre) ☎ 677 5304 £5–£12 ◑ *9pm–3am Wed–Sat.* A/MC/V cool'n'funky

### Gaiety Theatre

This Victorian theatre is now home to Latin, salsa and world beats at the weekend. As the auditorium is fully seated, the action mostly takes place in the venue's various bars and connecting corridors and stairs. Downstairs, John B's Bar showcases live bands, while in the Skylounge up top, the DJs take you on a global trip.

King Street South, D2 (off Grafton Street) ☎ 677 2956 £8 ◑ *11pm–2.30am Fri–Sat.* all clean'n'tidy

### The Kitchen

The vibe at this U2 owned pad is strictly underground – there's even a stream running around the small dancefloor. The music ranges from techno to house with drum & bass, and the crowd is a mix of tourists and stylish locals. The dancefloor can become a heaving sweat box.

Clarence, Essex Street East, D2 (Temple Bar) ☎ 677 6635 £4–£12 ◑ *11am–11.30pm daily.* AE/MC/V

### Lillie's Bordello

Decadent and exclusive, Lillie's is something of a legend – a haunt of supermodels, big-name bands and international footballers. The door policy is extremely selective, but more relaxed early in the week. Once in, if you want to seek out the beautiful people, head for the Library where you'll face another layer of security. The whole venue has over-the-top furnishings and couches to suit the bordello tag.

Adam Court, Grafton Street, D2 (off Grafton Street) ☎ 677 4208 £6–£10 ◑ *11pm–3am daily.* all no tracksuits, no trainers

### PoD

The tunnel-like Place of Dance (PoD) has won numerous international awards for its funky design. It's the original Dublin dance club and, in many people's eyes, still the best. Security can be moody.

The Old Railway Station, Harcourt Street, D2 (Harcourt Street) ☎ 478 0225 **w** www.pod.ie 14, 14a, 15a, 15b, 48a £8–£12 ◑ *11pm–3am Thu–Sun.* MC/V dress up

### Red Box

PoD's superclub features regular visits from the likes of Cream, Ministry of Sound, Renaissance and the other top UK clubs. The warehouse-like space is low on trimmings (plastic glasses) but on a Saturday night the atmosphere can be unbeatable. Powderbubble's sell-out monthly events are truly multimedia, featuring performance art, DJs, gay weddings and a host of other flamboyant attractions.

Old Railway Station, Harcourt Street, D2 (Harcourt Street) ☎ 478 0166 **w** www.pod.ie 14, 14a, 15a, 15b, 48a £6–£15 ◑ *11pm–3am Wed–Sat.* MC/V casual

## pick of the week

**monday**
*Strictly Handbag @ Ri-Ra*
A retro feast of tunes featuring lyrics.

**tuesday**
*Genius @ The Kitchen*
Hugely popular night of no-frills techno beats.

**wednesday**
*Blue @ The Kitchen*
The best in house and techno.
*Tongue 'n' Groove @ Ri-Ra*
Two floors of eclectic beats and grooves.

**thursday**
*Charged @ The Kitchen*
The Influx boys drop electro and nu-house.
*Funk off* @ Ri-Ra
A clubland institution of soul, funk and more.

**friday**
*Phunk City @ The Funnel*
Techno & electronica fest with international guests.
*Quadraphonic @ the Kitchen*
Premier league drum & bass (alternate Fri).
*Love Train @ the Red Box*
The last days of disco.
*Home Action Movies @ PoD*
Trashy gender-bending house for the mostly gay hedonists.
*JPD @ The Kitchen*
Top techno with UK and US guests (alternate Fri).

**saturday**
*Fever @ The Kitchen*
Wide range of heavy house.
*Deep Fried Disco @ Columbia*
Ten years of funky house.
*Honey @ Velvet*
Big house tunes.
*Influx @ Temple Bar Music Centre*
Techno to big beat.

**sunday**
*2 Damn Funky @ Ri-Ra*
Serious R&B and hip hop.
*Lost in Music @ Lillie's Bordello*
Live bands and DJ's playing everything from jazz to 70's soundtracks.
*Loose @ PoD*
Top daytime recovery session with eclectic house.

### Renard's

This is one for the older set and runs the gamut from trendies to saddos to in-town film folk. Despite the tackiness of the venue itself (the ubiquitous mirrors are disorientating after a few too many), it is extremely popular as a late-night drinking den. The sounds on offer may be retrospective of the last couple of decades but Renards is also building a solid reputation for live jazz. When busy, it's regulars only, but if you're polite and firm you should get in.

35–37 Frederick Street South, D2 (around Dawson Street) ☎ 677 5876 £5–£8 *11pm–3.30am Tue–Sat.* all neat casual, no trainers, no jeans

### Republica

Despite a recent high profile makeover, Republica hasn't really changed since the days of Club Nassau (when it was affectionately known as Club Nausea). Its sleek, curved walls and built-in aquarium are home to an accessible mainstream vibe – and occasional exotic gay nights.

Earl of Kildare Hotel, Kildare Street, D2 (around Dawson St) ☎ 679 4388 £6–£8 *11pm–3am Tue & Thu–Sun.* none smart casual

### Ri-Ra

Ri-Ra is pretty much a house-free zone, but does a fine job of covering all the other bases. The dance floor doesn't dominate proceedings, and there are plenty of nooks and crannies to hide away in. Bank holiday weekenders with the best of Dublin's DJ talent are a real treat.

Dame Court, D2 (around Sth Grt George's St) ☎ 671 1220 £4–£8 *11pm–3am daily.* none casual

### Temple Bar Music Centre

The austere Music Centre is guaranteed an up-for-it crowd. Independent promoters like Influx provide big beats and funky breaks, while Mau Mau delivers straight-up hip-hop jams with the occasional foray into reggae. Other nights vary from techno to drum & bass, and without regular tenants it can be a little hit and miss – but it enjoys many more successes than failures.

Curved Street, D2 (Temple Bar) ☎ 670 9292 £6–£12 *9pm–2.30am Thu–Sat.* DC/MC/V casual

### Velvet

This basement venue promises glam house, and isn't afraid to take risks – it was the first Dublin venue to promote a regular speed garage night.

Harcourt Street, D2 (Harcourt Street) ☎ 478 3677 14, 14a, 15a, 15b, 48a £6–£10 *11pm–3am Wed–Sat.* all smart, no trainers

## *post club hangouts*

*As licensing laws require clubs to close by 3am, cafés have sprung up to serve homeless clubbers who want to stay up till dawn – fuelled by strong coffee and chill-out tunes. The longest running is* ***Déjà Vu****, which rocks with clubland's die-hards who take a breather before the Early Houses [→91] open. The* ***Coffee Dock*** *– open 23 hours a day – is the place for hefty fry-ups, bowls of porridge and an endless flow of tea served by homely waitresses who've seen it all before. The bohemian style* ***@ Home****, meanwhile, has some cool sounds and easy chairs in which to mellow.*

**@ Home**
Creation Arcade, Duke St, D4 ☎ 672 9010

**Coffee Dock**
Jury's Hotel, Ballsbridge, D4 ☎ 660 5000

**Déjà Vu**
Dame Street, D2 ☎ 296 1230

A good night out in Dublin once involved a pint of Guinness and lots of prosaic chat. This still exists in hearty quantities, but there's plenty more to do besides.

# good craic

## the word is out



### *the papers*

There are two clear rival broadsheets. The *Irish Times* proudly errs on the side of objective reporting, intellectual columns, comprehensive world news and serious arts coverage. The less highbrow *Irish Independent*, baby of home-grown media guru Tony O'Reilly, is more gossipy, sensationalist and right-of-centre. The Cork-published *Examiner* is still struggling to shake off its image as a regional paper and get up there with the leaders of the pack.

Ireland's favourite tabloid, the *Star*, is less raunchy than the *Irish Sun*, which doesn't differ a lot from its hyper-salacious British counterpart. The *Irish Mirror*, for its part, tries hard to find a couple of native stories. The *Evening Herald*, the *Indo*'s sibling, won't overburden the brain cells but is good for sport, property, event listings and for the later news it sometimes catches.

Sundays are fairly lightweight in terms of indigenous newspapers. The *Sunday Independent* and *Sunday Tribune*, filled with lifestyle pieces and celeb writers, compete with the sports-laden new-kid-on-the-block *Ireland on Sunday* and the tabloid *Sunday World*. The *Sunday Business Post* offers more than economic analysis and has, on occasion, broken significant stories. For sheer bulk, there's nothing to compete with the Irish edition of *The Sunday Times*.

Most small Irish newsagents sell the chief English papers but, for the pick of the international crop, head to Eason's [→75], and Tower Records [→76].

### listings mags

*Sassy and opinionated,* In Dublin *(fortnightly) – one of the chief listings mags – flies in the face of political correctness by routinely adorning the cover with scantily-clad females. More overtly music-based,* Hot Press *(fortnightly) is sharp and eager to quibble with the status quo. The free* Event Guide *can be picked up from cafés, pubs and venues around the city; out every second Wednesday, it's full of reliable info about what's on. For the latest on clubs, film and fashion, the hip, glossy* dSide *(monthly) will let you know what's what, while the generally bland* RTE Guide *(weekly) tells you what's coming up on the box. For daily listings, try* The Irish Times.

### *television*

The floodgates have opened on Irish telly which was, until recently, dominated by RTE – the staid, conservative national broadcasting service. Viewers can now choose from a whopping four terrestrial channels. RTE1, though good for current affairs, remains true to form and rarely deviates from its traditional style. Network 2 makes an effort to be young and happening, but is by no means cutting edge. TnaG, an Irish-language station, displays sporadic flashes of excellence while TV3 is unashamedly commercial with a steady output of sitcoms and white-toothed smiles from trendy presenters. The British channels BBC1, BBC2, UTV and Channel 4 are almost always available and satellite channels like Sky pop up everywhere.

### *radio*

A repetitive diet of chart hits, call-ins and late-night chat shows are the mainstay of most Irish radio stations. 2FM (90.4–92.2), 98FM and FM104 are popular choices with some redeeming features. Radio 1 (88.2– 90 FM) is best for current affairs, media and arts analysis and for John Kelly's discerning melange of tunes at 8pm every weeknight. It's worth tuning in to Today FM (100–102) for Eamon Dunphy's unabashed subjectivity on 'The Last Word'. Other options include FM3 (90.4– 92.2) for classical music, BBC 1–5 and a host of community and independent stations.

### *websites*

For the low-down on the latest Dublin highlights, try:

**WOW** (What's on Where) at
**w** *www.wow.ie*
**Event Guide**
**w** *www.dkm.ie/events/*

# ↓ ceol like that

From trad lads in peaked caps to the rock upstarts of today, Ireland has had more than its fair share of influential and commercially successful musical stars. Nowadays, Dublin is one of Europe's major music cities, a venue for thoroughbreds, and very much the equal of London.

We can thank U2 for this. The 80's was their decade: they graduated from dodgy pub-punk to stadium demi-god status, becoming the biggest rock band in the world and spawning a thousand wannabes in the process. Indeed, the Dublin of the 80's crawled with bad taste as bands sought to emulate the fab four's formula – with little success but many ponytails. What they failed to realize was that U2 were übermasters of reinvention. When the going got tough for Bono and chums, a clever makeover kept them entertaining the planet while their imitators languished down the pub.

In the early 90's, Dublin looked to the provinces for inspiration. Culchies with attitude, such as the Cranberries (Limerick), Frank & Walters (Cork), Therapy (Belfast), Ash (Downpatrick) and the Divine Comedy (Enniskillen), swaggered centre-stage with originality, modern pop sensibilities and cliché-free zest. But their rise was paralleled by the boom in Dublin's clubland. International DJs and artists rapidly became major sources of entertainment and home-grown talent flourished as a result, with jocks such as Johnny Moy, Billy Scurry and Mark Kavanagh establishing healthy reputations.

Thankfully, the futile search for the next U2 has now been suspended and the live music circuit is a buzzing, eclectic miscellany of rock, jazz, trad, folk, world and electronic music. The most active venues [→108] are the **Olympia Theatre, Red Box, Temple Bar Music Centre, Whelan's, The Mean Fiddler, The Mean Fiddler, Da Club, The Funnel**, and **Vicar Street** – the latest addition to the city's gigscape. Mega indoor gigs take place at **The Point**, a multi-functional concert hall/theatre/conference centre, or the **RDS Concert Hall**. During the summer, outdoor shebangs go off at the **RDS Showgrounds** or at football stadiums such as **Lansdowne Road** and **Croke Park**.

## *good bets*

Currently, Ireland is most renowned for the European success of chart-topping pop acts like Boyzone and B*witched (both from Dublin), or the Corrs (from Dundalk). The future sound of Dublin is buried deep within the city's artistic underbelly, with the rise of independent labels such as Blunt, Dead Elvis, Hi-Tone and Lakota encouraging fresh new innovators, from the lo-fi to the no-fi and from the sublimely pop to the outrightly noisy.

The Ultramack label is a crazy-house of boffins based north of the Liffey, specializing in all forms of electronic sounds. They regularly test out their creations on a Friday night at Phunk City at **The Funnel**. Club promoters such as Influx and Quadraphonic have developed their own labels, with the success of Belfast producer/DJ David Holmes acting as a beacon for their efforts.

Take a trip down to **Whelan's, Da Club** or **The Funnel** to check out the current crop of guitar bands. Here, you may find the Great Western Squares whooping up a barn-storming brew of country and melancholic rock or the awesome Pet Lamb with their snarling, 70's fused punk-rock. If it's during the school hols, you may also come across teenage punka girls, Chicks, who were recently signed to Steven Spielberg's Dreamworks label. Others to watch for include Ireland's finest downbeat rock 'n' roll band Jubilee Allstars, new wave pop tarts the Ultra Montanes, the jangles and harmonies of Revelino, or Saville's brew of Moog boogies and righteous soul. All of the above bands have released material on indie labels so check records shops such as Freebird, Road Records or Comet [→76].

The arrival of tribute acts is a recent but somewhat avalanching addition to Dublin's music calendar. If you fancy some nostalgia, then Irish and international doppelgangers of everyone from the Stone Roses to the many Abba copycats will have you rolling in the aisles. All venues are liable to feature these acts but the infamous Midnight at the Olympia sessions are their spiritual home.

## *folk, trad & jazz*

The singer/songwriter has always played an important role in Irish music and, naturally, a new generation is following in the footsteps of Sinead O'Connor, Hothouse Flowers and Christy Moore. Dublin nurtures such artists with care, many beginning by busking on Grafton Street before graduating to singer-songwriter nights upstairs at the **International Bar** or at the **Temple Bar Music Centre**. Three of the most prominent starlets to emerge of late are Dubliner Paddy Casey, now signed to Sony Music, Tipperary girl Gemma Hayes, and Mundy from Co Offaly.

Trad music in Dublin is mainly oriented towards tourism and sessions can be found in numerous pubs and hotel bars.

→**venue directory 108**



more music | cinema

Normally free of charge, a session can evolve into the most uproarious night of entertainment in town. Two of the city's hottest haunts are **Slattery's** [→96] and the **Cobblestones**, but regular gigs are also held at the **Harcourt Hotel**, **Temple Bar Music Centre** [→99], **McDaid's** [→96], the **Porterhouse** [→96] and **Devitt's**. Good music and craic are guaranteed. If you're really in luck, your visit will coincide with the arrival from Kerry of Steve Cooney and Seamus Begley for one of their infamous **Whelan's** shows. How two men can raise such merry hell powered by mere Guinness remains one of life's great mysteries.

In the past, Cork has always been Ireland's big jazz town but, more recently, the Dublin Jazz Society and the Improvised Music Company have begun to promote one-off events. A huge breakthrough in 98 was the establishment of Dublin Jazz Week. Major jazz shows are staged at the **National Concert Hall** or **Olympia Theatre**, while smaller club nights are held at **Renard's** [→99], **J J Smyth's** and the **Norseman**.

## festivals

Despite the twin obstacles of Ireland's bizarre licensing laws and planning regulations, there are more festivals than ever to enjoy. Many have been scaled down from huge, open-air events and are now spread over a number of smaller venues. Sponsorship from the country's brewers has also increased the number of musical events.

The Heineken Green Energy Festival ☎ *284 1747* in May has become a significant landmark in the capital's calendar, incorporating major outdoor shows at Dublin Castle [→48] and numerous smaller indoor events scattered around the city.

The annual Guinness Blues Festival ☎ *497 0381* in late July is a weekend of international and Irish artists performing at the Red Box venue and other smaller locations. Previous line-ups have included legends such as B B King, Robert Cray and Taj Mahal.

The Dublin Jazz Week ☎ *670 3885* was established in 98 as a showcase for live jazz, film and workshops. Occurring in October and staged at various city centre venues including the Temple Bar Music Centre and the Irish Film Centre, its successful debut has ensured an encore in 99.

Heineken Weekenders ☎ *284 1747* brings the very best DJs and live acts to Dublin as well as to Cork, Galway and Limerick. With previous visitors of such calibre as the Chemical Brothers, Primal Scream and Carl Cox, it goes without saying that there will be plenty to look forward to in October.

## tickets & reviews

Many of the smaller clubs and venues have pay-at-the-door events, but tickets for bigger events are sold through Ticketmaster, either by credit card over the phone (24 hours) or in person at outlets such as HMV. Ticketmaster charges a booking fee which can be avoided by buying direct from the venue [→108]. Record shops such as Road Records [→76] sell tickets for smaller events. If all else fails, there are always the ticket touts who convene outside large venues: don't be afraid to haggle, but don't expect a bargain. One-day tickets and weekend tickets for large festivals are normally on sale up to the day before the event.

**Ticketmaster** ☎ *456 9569*
**HMV**, *Grafton Street & Henry Street, D2*
☎ *679 5334 & 873 2899*

£ Pay-at-the-door events are normally £4–£6. Prices for bigger, ticket-only affairs range from £7–£15, while mega-gigs and festivals cost from £18–£25.

Gigs usually kick off at 8.30pm with the main act taking the stage at around 10pm. Some venues, such as the Olympia Theatre, have late-night concerts, which means the earlier evening gig kicks off as early as 7pm.

Most venues are standing, with a smaller designated area for seating.

In addition to the listings mags [→100], national newspapers sometimes include music listings. *The Irish Times* has a good, if selective, guide on Saturdays. Anyone with internet access should consult Ireland's only weekly music digest *Muse* at *www.muse.ie* for a list of recommended gigs and clubs.

# movie magic

It's official! The Irish are Europe's premier cinema junkies! A recent EU study showed that cinema attendance in the Republic rose by 55% between 1990–96, while 6.2 million tickets were sold in the first half of 97 alone. Now, you can blame such fanaticism on the bad weather or dire telly, but it's no accident that this rise has coincided with a slew of acclaimed films and a mini-renaissance within the Irish film industry. Directors like Neil Jordan, Pat O'Connor and Jim Sheridan have won worldwide kudos, while Irish actors like Gabriel Byrne and Pierce Brosnan are seen as both household names and sex symbols. The reconvening of the Irish Film Board, plus tax incentives by successive governments, have ensured that more films are being made, and the country has become a prime film location for everything from sci-fi to period drama.

## tickets & reviews

Cinema-goers come out in force at weekends and 'sold out' signs are common. Most cinemas accept credit card bookings.

Tickets average £3 before 5pm, £5 afterwards. Certain cinemas have concessions if tickets are bought before 6pm.

Screenings take place from 1.30pm until around 8.30pm. There are usually three per day, with the feature beginning 15–20 minutes after the specified time.

In many Dublin cinemas, advance booking doesn't guarantee a specific seat, so turn up early and take your pick.

The *Evening Herald* and the *Irish Independent* review films on Thursdays, the *Irish Times* on Fridays. All nationals have listings every day. See also listings mags [→100].

While the multiplexes have taken much of the mainstream action into the suburbs, the city centre remains *the* place for movie buffs of all persuasions. Dublin has got it all sewn up: on any given day, you can check out 20-plus films – from high-octane blockbusters to low-budget gems. American releases usually hit town a few months after they're shown in the US, and British films are screened almost simultaneously with the UK.

If you're the arthouse type, then your first stop must be the **Irish Film Centre (IFC)**. Its two screens cover all bases from indie American numbers to Latin documentaries, career retrospectives to public interviews. There's also a swish café and bar in the complex where Dublin's cinema aficionados shoot the breeze. Staying with all things arthouse, **The Screen** specializes in the more commercial end of the market. Although its decor hasn't changed in years, the selection of films is always the right side of happening. Cross to the northside and you're in more familiar, Hollywood-formula territory. **The Savoy** boasts the largest screen in Dublin and covers every biggie from the US; similarly the spanking new **Virgin Multiplex** is where you can OD on all things American. If you're feeling more cerebrally inclined, right next door is the **Sheridan IMAX** theatre, with monster 3D screens showing factual/educational stuff.

A sedate way to spend a summer evening is at one of the free Saturday night movies in Meeting House Square. They're usually oldies picked and introduced by celebs. Contact the IFC for the lowdown.

## *festivals*

The daddy of them all is the Dublin Film Festival ☎ *679 2937* in March/April. Now in its 14th year, the festival covers the canon of cinema from forthcoming major releases to classics and shoestring-budget treasures. There's a real sense of community, thanks largely to the festival bar, viewers' forums and public interviews. The Independent Film Festival ☎ *868 1466* is a welcome companion to the mainstream festival, featuring up-and-coming Irish actors and film-makers. For Francophiles, the French Film Festival ☎ *676 1732* runs in late November/early December, and offers new features, shorts and retrospectives. Junior movie buffs have their own annual festival in November ☎ *671 4095*. The Gay and Lesbian Film Festival ☎ *492 0597* runs in early August.

## *film locations*

Over the last 10 years, Dublin's streets and suburbs have become fair game for movie-makers. One of the first big-budget features to set up in the city centre was Ron Howard's *Far and Away*. Over the course of summer 92 Tom Cruise and Nicole Kidman frolicked around a pre-restoration Temple Bar, trod in artificial snow around Leeson Street and hung out at the CIE building on Amiens Street. The film didn't really do the business at the box office, but the same can't be said for the Roddy Doyle trilogy of *The Commitments*, *The Snapper* and *The Van*. The first of these movies was ground-breaking in introducing international audiences to parts of Dublin that didn't involve Georgian fanlights and acres of green fields.

Dyed-in-the-wool Dublin director Jim Sheridan has a

→venue directory 108



more cinema | comedy | theatre

penchant for using his home turf for locations, and chose Sheriff Street for the opening scenes of *In the Name of the Father*, along with Kilmainham Gaol [→53]. Dublin was also the base for *My Left Foot*, but the most famous recent film shot entirely in the capital was Neil Jordan's *Michael Collins*. Filmed in the summer of 95, over 6,000 Dubs helped make movie history. Though things have settled down, 98 was busy down Ringsend way as John Boorman shot *The General*, only yards away from Angelica Houston's colourful comedy *The Mammy*. As production units make future plans, look out for location wagons and clapperboards – this could be your big opportunity.

# divine comedy





Although Dublin has long enjoyed the reputation of being a city full of characters brimming with both wit and wisdom (not to mention Guinness), successful, professional stand-up comedy is a relatively recent phenomenon. Throughout the 70's and 80's, while the rest of the British Isles embraced the notion of a bloke on stage telling mother-in-law gags, Dubliners had a very standoffish attitude to anyone foolhardy enough to expect payment for telling jokes.

Thankfully, though, attitudes have changed. The success of Irish comedy writers and comics abroad has had great consequence for those gigging on home soil. Over the last few years, two Irish comedians (Tommy Tiernan and Dylan Moran) have won the much-coveted Perrier award at the Edinburgh Festival. The domestic scene was also given a much-needed shot in the arm by sponsorship from a major brewery that resulted in a new dedicated comedy venue in the city – **Murphy's Laughter Lounge**.

At the bigger venues, the weekend comedy scene starts with a bang on Thursdays. Ranging from the genuinely surreal at the **Ha'penny Bridge Inn** to mainstream at Murphy's Laughter Lounge, the International Comedy Club night at the **International Bar** and the Corduroy Comedy Club at the **Norseman**, comedy evenings promise – and yes, it's a cliché – something for everyone. The rest of the weekend is dominated by gigs at Murphy's Laughter Lounge. On Sundays, comedy dining at the **Milano** restaurant takes centre stage, while on Mondays the International Bar, holds its infamous Comedy Improv. Some of the country's finest comics got their first break here (Ardal O'Hanlon, Barry Murphy, The Nualas *et al*), and this is a good place to see the stars and, occasionally, the no-hopers of tomorrow.

It seems that the weirdest and silliest comics emerge from their lairs midweek. Every Tuesday, the Ha'penny Bridge Inn sees all manner of performers, but mostly comics vying for the honour of a small plastic ornament called, ahem, the Lucky Duck Award. On Wednesdays, the longest-running comedy club in the city, the Comedy Cellar night at the International Bar, has amassed quite a reputation as a breeding ground for new talent (Kevin Gildea, Mark Doherty and Jason Byrne), and the odd high-profile act, like that Dylan Moran bloke, has been known to drop in.

## tickets & reviews

As comedy is centred round pubs, tickets for many performances can be purchased on the night. For big name acts at Murphy's Laughter Lounge and the Dublin festivals, advance booking is advised.

Seats at Murphy's Laughter Lounge range from £10–£15. Entry for pub shows is between £2.50–£5.

Performances at Murphy's Laughter Lounge start at 9pm (doors open an hour earlier). At smaller venues, the gigs begin around the same time but are more flexible.

Arrive early if you're going to one of the smaller venues as seating is limited. When booking for Murphy's Laughter Lounge, ask for seats a couple of rows back, unless you fancy yourself as a match for any japester.

Comedy doesn't get much coverage in the local papers but *The Irish Times* is the best place to look for reviews on a regular basis. See also listings mags [→100].

## *festivals*

Now cruising into its fifth year, the Kilkenny Cat Laughs Comedy Festival in early June has become something of a comics' festival of choice and one of this island's premier gatherings. Since over 30,000 people descend on Kilkenny for the festival, early reservations for gigs and accommodation are recommended ☎ *056 63837*. Due to its overwhelming success, other festivals have been established over the last couple of years. The highlight of the Dublin comedy calendar is the Ungagged Festival held in both April and November ☎ *456 9569*. Both festivals are usually based around international acts at theatre venues, with scores of other comics performing in pubs and venues. Coinciding with the Dublin Theatre Festival each autumn, Comedy at the Fringe ☎ *872 9016* boasts an impressive line-up over the two-week theatrical love-in.

# ↓ acting on impulse

With Irish writing currently on the crest of a wave, where better to experience it than in Dublin with its rich literary heritage? Enthusiastic audiences support a vibrant theatre community led by the two main producing houses – the Abbey Theatre and the smaller Gate Theatre.

In its glorious past, the **Abbey Theatre** was home to giants such as W B Yeats, J M Synge and Sean O'Casey. Today, artistic director Patrick Mason has rekindled the energy of the National Theatre, bringing on board a dynamic team of young directors and designers. On the main stage, you'll find large-scale productions embracing both Irish (O'Casey, Brian Friel, Tom Murphy, Frank McGuinness) and international theatre; its smaller sister, the **Peacock Theatre**, produces new Irish writing of a more experimental nature. Look out for Tom MacIntyre (*Good Evening Mr Collins*) and, in a more serious vein, Gary Mitchell (*In a Little World of Our Own*). Directors to watch are Conall Morrison *(Tarry Flynn)*, Mason himself (*Dancing at Lughansa*), and Lynne Parker (*Rough Magic*) in the independent sector.

The **Gate Theatre**, another institution, is extremely successful both here and abroad, regularly selling out entire runs of shows. It thrives on a clever mix of the relatively adventurous (Beckett, Pinter) and the ever-popular (Oscar Wilde). Whatever the show, expect great productions with plenty of style.

The **Gaiety Theatre**, a gem of Victorian architecture with its gilt and red velvet, is on a touring circuit and so has a good turnover of mainstream commercial theatre, some home-produced and some from the UK. The **Andrew's Lane Theatre** and the **Tivoli Theatre** do the same thing, but on a smaller scale.

## tickets & reviews

Advance booking (directly with the venue) is advisable, especially for opening nights. Larger venues offer credit card facilities.

You can see a show for as little as £5, but tickets are generally £8–£15, with musicals more expensive at around £12–£30. Previews are always cheaper, as are matinées. Some theatres offer lower prices at the start of the week.

Most shows start at 8pm. Saturday matinées at the Abbey and Peacock start at 2.30/2.45pm. There are occasional matinées elsewhere. Opening nights never start on time!

Smaller venues have unreserved seating, so make sure you get there early.

Other than the main listings mags [→100], the best sources for information/weekly listings are Saturday's *Irish Times*, *The Sunday Times* and Tuesday's *Irish Independent*. The *Evening Herald* has daily listings. Most shows run for at least two weeks, so it's also worth checking out the Sundays (*Tribune* and *Independent*).

Often, the most interesting productions are to be found at the smaller venues. Many established companies started life in the cramped confines of the **International Bar**. Other nurturers of theatrical potential include the **City** and **Crypt Arts Centres**.

**Project Arts Centre** (temporarily housed in Project @ the Mint, but relocating to Temple Bar before the end of 99) is where you'll find the best of the smaller companies. An adventurous artistic policy of commissions and co-productions makes for a lively mix of all kinds of theatre, from wildly experimental to the relatively straight.

Chief among the independent companies is Rough Magic, which champions new Irish writing (Declan Hughes, Gina Moxley) as well as adaptations of classics. Also worth checking out are Barrabas (fast-paced physical theatre), Bedrock (modern European theatre), Loose Canon (reworkings of Jacobean and Elizabethan drama), Passion Machine (contemporary Dublin subculture) and the Corn Xchange for *commedia dell'arte* humour. And don't miss Galway-based Druid, Sligo's Blue Raincoat or Waterford's Red Kettle if they're in town.

Musicals, usually West End imports from London, make an appearance from time to time. The main venues are the **Olympia Theatre** and the very large venue, **The Point**.

### *festivals*

The Dublin Theatre Festival ☎ *677 8439* in October is a two-week celebration of Irish and world theatre, with important new Irish writing rubbing shoulders with cutting-edge international shows. It's accompanied by an action-packed three-week Fringe Festival ☎ *872 9016* which takes over all kinds of unlikely venues and comes up with some high-quality material.

The International Theatre Symposium at the **Samuel Beckett Centre** ☎ *280 0544* in January (every other year) brings together avant- garde theatre practitioners from around Europe, while, in September, Monkstown's International Puppet Festival ☎ *280 0974* is well worth the short ride on the DART.

→venue directory 108

→ dance | poetry & literature | classical music & opera

# best foot forward

The dance scene in Dublin is definitely more geared to contemporary dance than classical ballet. A number of venues, notably the **Samuel Beckett Centre**, the **Tivoli Theatre** and **Project @ the Mint**, have the necessary wide open spaces, but dance is only part of their wider theatre programme. Among the leading companies are Footsteps, whose playful cultural explorations, fusing dance and theatre, have a broad appeal. The more esoteric Dance Theatre of Ireland, celebrating their 10th anniversary in 99, frequently work with top European choreographers – most recently with Munich-based Rui Horta.

The Irish Modern Dance Theatre also works extensively with international choreographers. Watch out too for the Limerick-based Daghda Dance Company and Cork's Fabulous Beast.

Indigenous classical ballet has been largely neglected over the years, but the recent emergence of Ballet Ireland looks set to change things. Led by principals of the Weiner Ballet Theatre, this company of young Irish dancers, currently working all over Europe, produces two shows annually in spring and autumn. Otherwise, ballet is in the hands of visiting companies, mostly from Russia – the Perm State Ballet is a particular favourite.

The best dance venue is the **Olympia Theatre**, with its large stage and ornate decor. Ballet is also performed at the **National Concert Hall** (although it lacks proper staging facilities) with occasional extravaganzas at **The Point**.

## *festivals*

There is a strong dance presence in the three-week Fringe Festival ☎ *872 9016* in late September/early October, while the International Theatre Symposium at the Samuel Beckett Centre ☎ *280 0544* in January also contains an element of dance.

### tickets & reviews

Dance isn't programmed on a regular basis, so check the press for details. Well-reviewed shows often sell out, so book in advance, directly with the venue. Larger venues offer credit card booking facilities.

Shows begin at 8pm, with occasional Saturday matinées.

Tickets range from around £8 in smaller venues (unreserved seating) to £20 for visiting companies.

Search the listings mags for details [→100]. Saturday's *Irish Times*, *The Sunday Times* and Tuesday's *Irish Independent* publish relevant information and weekly listings. Check *The Irish Times* and *Evening Herald* for next-day reviews.

# wilde thing

Poetry has recently acquired a certain sexiness, thanks to Poet Laureate Seamus Heaney. His success has encouraged many a fledgling poet, including Grafton Street buskers who, for a small fee, will recite from their own work or from a selection of favourites.

For poetry in a slightly more formal setting, Poetry Ireland runs a series of Thursday evening readings at the atmospheric **Winding Stair** bookshop [→75]. The monthly Speakeasy evening (Friday at the **Irish Writers Centre**) is a lively combination of poetry, fiction and drama, and the same venue also runs regular poetry readings and interviews, many of which are free. There are also occasional readings in the **Goethe Institute** and **Waterstone's** [→76] bookshop. Watch out for the subtle realism of Paula Meehan, the exuberance of Brendan Kennelly and the careful craft of Paul Durcan.

## *festivals*

A short trip on the DART brings you to Dun Laoghaire where the Poetry Now Festival ☎ *205 4749* takes place at the end of March. Local, national and international poets are celebrated in this very popular event. The annual Joyce celebrations ☎ *878 8547* on Bloomsday (June 16th) links in with the week-long Dublin Writers' Festival ☎ *872 1302*, when leading American, European, British and Irish writers feature at various venues around the city in a mix of poetry and literature, including the light-hearted Poetry Slam open-mic session.

### tickets & reviews

Pre-booking is advisable for festival events.

Many readings are free, particularly book launches. Otherwise tickets (available at the door) are around £3–£5.

Times of readings vary, but they usually start between 7–8pm, with book launches at 6 or 6.30pm.

Book launches are generally non seated and can get pretty crowded, so get there early.

Check the *Event Guide* and other listings mags for details of events [→100], alternatively find out from Saturday's *Irish Times*.

# orchestral manoeuvres

Given Dublin's vibrant cultural life and strong musical pedigree, it's not surprising that there's a lively classical music scene, which is becoming increasingly accessible to mainstream audiences.

The **National Concert Hall (NCH)** is the principal venue, and home to the National Symphony Orchestra (NSO), which plays there every Friday from November to May. The NSO is flourishing under two new conductors, the dramatic Russian maestro Alexander Annisimov and the cool German Gerhard Markson, with guest conductors and soloists from around the world adding an extra dynamic.

Programming follows the overture/concerto/symphony pattern, and sometimes features works by contemporary Irish composers – watch out for Raymond Deane, Gerald Barry and John Buckley. Popular performers include pianist John O'Conor and the excellent Vanbrugh String Quartet.

The NCH's annual Celebrity Concert Series features internationally acclaimed artists such as twinkling flautist James Galway and the Royal Philharmonic conducted by Sir Peter Maxwell Davies.

While there's not a strong tradition of church music in Ireland, there's usually some Mozart or Palestrina at the 11am Sunday mass in the **Pro-Cathedral**. **St Patrick's Cathedral** and **Christ Church Cathedral** both have choral evensong and Sunday services, and the **Christ Church Cathedral** choirs give a number of concerts throughout the year.

July and August are patchy, with most of the musical fare being decidedly lightweight, but check out recitals promoted by the Limerick Music Association, which usually manages to bring in some interesting musicians.

Outdoor music is mainly of the brass band variety, but the RTE Concert Orchestra gives free concerts in Meeting House Square during June and July.

Art galleries have been getting in on the music scene for some time; the **Irish Museum of Modern Art**'s [→56] spring and autumn seasons, which focus on a single musician or ensemble, are well established and very popular. The National Chamber Choir regularly sings from its broad repertoire at the **National Gallery** [→57] and the **Hugh Lane Gallery** [→56] is the place to be on a Sunday morning for the free Sundays at Noon concerts (get there early).

Spanish, German and Italian cultural institutes frequently sponsor visiting performers. They are also among the few venues to regularly programme contemporary music.

Other contemporary opportunities include the Mostly Modern series at the **Bank of Ireland Arts Centre** and the lively Crash Ensemble, whose electronic multi-media explorations are well worth catching.

Apart from a number of recitals and semi-staged operas at the NCH, opera in Dublin is largely confined to the spring and autumn seasons given by Opera Ireland at the **Gaiety Theatre**, and to smaller touring productions by the innovative Opera Theatre Company (OTC). Opera Ireland tends to concentrate on better-known Italian operas (Verdi is a favourite), with productions featuring a cross-section of international and Irish soloists.

## *festivals*

Festivals are generally held outside the capital but the upmarket AIB Music Festival in Great Irish Houses ☎ *278 1528* in June takes in some classy Dublin venues. Dublin Guitar Week ☎ *475 1572* in February is a celebration of the Spanish guitar, with performers from Europe and Latin America. If you enjoy classical, trad and a sprinkling of jazz, then check out Feis Ceoil at the RDS in March ☎ *676 7365*. For organ buffs, there's the International Organ Festival ☎ *677 3066* in May, and Beethoven fans can enjoy a mini-festival of his complete piano concertos at the National Concert Hall.

## tickets & reviews

Major international performers often sell out well in advance, but for lesser-known artists it's usually possible to get tickets on the night. Booking is directly from the venue. Larger venues offer credit card booking facilities.

Top prices at the NCH hover around £12–£15, but expect to pay more for high-profile events. Big gigs at mega venues like The Point are generally over-priced, ranging from about £22–£30.

Evening concerts start at 8pm (opera 7.30pm), NSO summer concerts at 6.30pm. Lunchtime concerts usually start around 1pm.

The NCH choir stalls are particularly good value, but their location above the percussion/brass sections can result in some sound distortion during orchestral works.

Check listings mags [→100] or Saturday's *Irish Times* and *The Sunday Times*. Look at the *Evening Herald* for daily information. Monthly NCH brochures are available from hotels etc.

→venue directory 108

# venue directory

**Abbey Theatre**
Abbey Street Lower, D1
☎ 878 7222

**Andrew's Lane Theatre**
95 St Andrew's Lane, D2
☎ 679 5720

**Bank of Ireland Arts Centre**
Foster Place, D2
☎ 671 1488

**Christ Church Cathedral**
Christ Church Place, D8
☎ 677 8099

**City Arts Centre**
23–25 Moss Street, D2
☎ 677 0643

**Cobblestones**
77 King Street North, D2
☎ 872-1799

**Croke Park**
Jones Road, D3
☎ 836 3222
🚌 51a

**Crypt Arts Centre**
Dublin Castle, Dame Street, D2
☎ 671 3387

**Da Club**
3 Clarendon Market, D2
☎ 670 3426

**Devitt's**
78 Camden Street Lower, D2
☎ 475 3414
🚌 16, 16a, 19, 19a, 83, 155

**The Funnel**
24 City Quay, D2
☎ 677 5304

**Gaiety Theatre**
King Street South, D2
☎ 677 1717

**Gate Theatre**
1 Cavendish Row, Parnell Square,D2
☎ 874 4045

**Goethe Institute**
37 Merrion Square East, D2
☎ 661 1155

**Ha'penny Bridge Inn**
42 Wellington Quay, D2
☎ 677 0616

**Harcourt Hotel**
60 Harcourt Street, D2
☎ 478 3677

**Hugh Lane Gallery**
Parnell Square North, D1
☎ 874 1903

**International Bar**
23 Wicklow Street, D2
☎ 677 9250

**Irish Film Centre (IFC)**
6 Eustace Street, D2
☎ 677 8788

**Irish Museum of Modern Art**
Royal Hospital, Military Road, Kilmainham, D8
☎ 612 9900
🚌 51b, 78a

**Irish Writers Centre**
19 Parnell Square, D1
☎ 872 1302

**J J Smyth's**
12 Aungier Street, D2
☎ 475 2565

**Lansdowne Road**
Lansdowne Road, D4
☎ 668 9300
Ⓓ to Lansdowne Road
🚌 5, 7, 7a, 8

**McDaid's**
3 Harry Street, D2
☎ 679 4395

**The Mean Fiddler**
26 Wexford Street, D2
☎ 475 8555

**Milano**
38 Dawson Street, D2
☎ 670 7744

**Murphy's Laughter Lounge**
Eden Quay, D2
☎ 1800 266339

**National Concert Hall (NCH)**
Earlsfort Terrace, D2
☎ 475 1572

**National Gallery**
Merrion Square West, D2
☎ 661 5133

**The Norseman**
29 Sussex Street East, D2
☎ 660 2096

**Olympia Theatre**
72 Dame Street, D2
☎ 677 7744

**Peacock Theatre**
Abbey Street Lower, D1
☎ 878 7222

**The Point**
East Link Bridge, North Wall Quay, D1
☎ 836 3633
🚌 53a

**Porterhouse**
16–18 Parliament Street, D2
☎ 679 8847

**Pro-Cathedral**
Marlborough Street, D1
☎ 874 5441

**Project @ the Mint**
Henry Place, D1
☎ 1850 260 027

**Project Arts Centre**
39 Essex Street East, D2
☎ 671 2321

**RDS (Royal Dublin Society) Concert Hall & Showgrounds**
Ballsbridge, D4
☎ 668 0866
🚌 5, 7, 7a, 8, 45

**Red Box**
Old Railway Station, Harcourt Street, D2
☎ 478 0166
🚌 14, 14a, 15a, 15b, 48a

**Renard's**
35–37 Frederick Street South, D2
☎ 677 5876

**St Patrick's Cathedral**
St Patrick's Close, D8
☎ 475 4817

**Samuel Beckett Centre**
Trinity College, D2
☎ 608 2461

**The Savoy**
O'Connell Street Upper, D1
☎ 874 6000

**The Screen**
D'Olier Street, D2
☎ 671 4988

**Sheridan IMAX**
Parnell Centre, Parnell Street, D1
☎ 817 4200

**Slattery's**
Capel Street, D1
☎ 872 7971

**Tallaght's Civic Theatre**
Greenhills Road, D12
☎ 451 8384
🚌 50, 77

**Temple Bar Music Centre**
Curved Street, D2
☎ 670 9202

**Tivoli Theatre**
135–138 Francis Street, D8
☎ 454 4472

**Vicar Street**
99 Vicar Street, D8
☎ 454 6656
🚌 51b, 78a

**Virgin Multiplex**
Parnell Centre, Parnell Street, D1
☎ 872 8400

**Waterstone's**
7 Dawson Street, D2
☎ 679 1415

**Whelan's**
25 Wexford Street, D2
☎ 478 0766

**Winding Stair**
40 Ormond Quay Lower, D1
☎ 873 3292

# dublin dates

An eventful guide to what's going on in the capital...

## summer

### Glen Dimplex Artist's Award

Similar in status to Britain's Turner Prize; shortlisted artists exhibit their works in the old Royal Hospital.

◑ *May–August*
Irish Museum of Modern Art, Military Road, Kilmainham, D8
☎ 612 9900 🚌 51b, 78a ▣ free

### Summer Sales

They say you have to spend in order to save and no better place for it. Summer sales are a cue to start shopping again.

◑ *June–July*

### AIB Music Festival in Great Irish Houses

Soothing chamber music in the plush surrounds of Georgian Dublin's great houses.

◑ *2 weeks in June*
Various venues around Dublin
☎ 278 1528 ▣ phone for details

### Women's Mini Marathon

A refreshing charity event for the spectators, and a calf-swelling 10 km for competitors.

◑ *2nd or 3rd Sunday in June*
City centre ☎ 294 0666 ▣ free

### Bloomsday

◑ *16 June* [→poetry & literature 106]

### Dublin Writers' Festival

◑ *1 week in mid June*
[→poetry & literature 106]

### Liberties Festival

So-called because this area was outside the tax-lines of the old city, the Liberties is a charismatic city quarter in danger of extinction. The festival celebrates the area's heritage with an annual kids' parade and a variety of competitions, bands and art displays.

◑ *4 days at end June or end July*
Liberties, D8 ☎ 453 6098
▣ parade free; bands £6–£7.50

### James Joyce Summer School

Ireland's favourite exile is the subject of this stimulating – if specialist – literary entrée of seminars and lectures.

◑ *2 weeks mid–end July*
University College Dublin, Earlsford Terrace, D2
☎ 706 8480
▣ £3.25 (book in advance)

### Guinness Blues Festival

◑ *3rd weekend in July*
[→music 102]

### Temple Bar Summer Season

Meeting House Square hosts music on Fridays, and outdoor cinema on Saturdays.

◑ *July & August*
Meeting House Square, Temple Bar, D2 ☎ 677 2255 ▣ free

### Dublin Horse Show

A real equine treat, with all the show-jumping, style and post-show synopses horse-lovers could wish for.

◑ *1st week in August*
RDS, Ballsbridge, D4 ☎ 668 0866
🚌 7, 7a, 8, 45 ▣ £7 admission, plus £5–£12 for individual events

### Gay & Lesbian Film Festival

◑ *early August* [→cinema 103]

### Dublin Regatta

A myriad of sails take to the wind in Dublin Bay, braving elements and amateur photographers alike.

◑ *August*
Dublin Bay ☎ 677 3066
Ⓓ to Seapoint or Dun Laoghaire
▣ free

### Dublin Flower Show

Satisfaction is guaranteed they say, for the itchiest of green fingers. Don't expect too many lawn-sprinklers though.

◑ *4 days at end of August*
Phone for venue ☎ 490 0600
▣ approx £5

## autumn

### The Liffey Descent

Up to 1,000 international canoeists career down the River Liffey. For the best vantage points, follow the race by car.

◑ *1st or 2nd Saturday in September*
Straffan, Co Kildare to Trinity Rowing Club, Co Dublin.
☎ 450 9838 ▣ free

### The Liffey Swim

Given the Liffey's impressive stock of traffic cones and shopping trolleys, this 22.5 km race is an obstacle course for hundreds of slightly insane participants.

◑ *one Saturday in September*
Watling Street to Custom House ▣ free

### All Ireland Hurling Final

Hear the ash clash in the fastest game in the world – as demonstrated by the world's best players.

◑ *2nd Sunday in September*
Croke Park, Jones Road, D3
☎ 836 3222 🚌 51a ▣ £30

### Dublin Toy & Train Fair

Ireland's most celebrated gathering of its kind. The original Trainspotters!

◑ *one day in September*
Rochestown Lodge Hotel, Dun Laoghaire ☎ 285 3555
Ⓓ to Dun Laoghaire ▣ £3

### All Ireland Football Final

After the final whistle a flood of people descends on O'Connell Street, defying every noise-pollution law ever made. If you must know who won – ask someone who's not wearing county colours.

◑ *4th Sunday in September*
Croke Park, Jones Road, D3
☎ 836 3222 🚌 51a ▣ £30

### Dublin Fringe Theatre Festival

◑ *3 weeks end Sep–Oct*
[→theatre 105]

### Dublin Theatre Festival

◑ *2 weeks early October*
[→theatre 105]

### Comedy at the Fringe

◑ *October*
[→comedy 104]

### Dublin Jazz Week

◑ *2nd week in October*
[→music 102]

### Octagon

Annual science-fiction convention, including stalls, lectures, signings and sci-fi screenings.

◑ *October*
Royal Marine Hotel, Dun Laoghaire ☎ 679 5099
Ⓓ to Dun Laoghaire ▣ free

### Rugby World Cup

Blood, guts, broken noses. If it happened anywhere but in Lansdowne Road you'd be in jail – but hey, that's rugby. Bring a hip flask.

◑ *October every four years*
Lansdowne Road, D4
☎ 668 4601 (IRFU)
Ⓓ to Lansdowne Rd ▣ £13–£32

### Heineken Weekender

◑ *October bank holiday weekend*
[→music 102]

### Wicklow Mountains Autumn Walking Festival

On a clear day – and contrary to popular myth, Dublin can have them – some of the best views are those of the city you've just left behind.

◑ *October bank holiday weekend (also May Day bank holiday)*
Glenmalure, Co Wicklow
☎ 0404 66058 ▣ £5



→ more events

### Mind Body Spirit Festival

A festival of all things healthy, holistic and occasionally, hokum.

◑ *3 days at end of October*
RDS, Ballsbridge, D4 ☎ 285 9294
🚌 7, 7a, 8, 45 🎫 £3–£5

### Dublin City Marathon

From giant hamburgers to the human credit card, the annual marathon welcomes every kind of lunatic. Do not drive!

◑ *last Monday in October*
City centre ☎ 676 4647 🎫 free

### Oscar Wilde School

'Either that wallpaper goes or I do!' A crash course in the writings of Ireland's wittiest poet and playwright.

◑ *4–5 days at end October*
Esplanade Hotel, Bray
☎ 286 5245 Ⓓ to Bray
🎫 £3–£8 per lecture

### Samhain

No outfit, no entry. The costumes are to-die-for during Dublin's Halloween parade and fireworks.

◑ *last Saturday in October*
City centre ☎ 855 7154 🎫 free

### Murphy's Ungagged Comedy Festival

◑ *November (also April)*
[→comedy 104]

### Dublin Antiques and Fine Arts Fair

Magpie heaven. Poking around the RDS (Royal Dublin Society), you're guaranteed an income-related bargain.

◑ *last weekend in November*
Serpentine Hall, RDS, Ballsbridge, D4 ☎ 285 9294
🚌 7, 7a, 8, 45 🎫 £4

### French Film Festival

◑ *2 weeks in November or December* [→cinema 103]

## winter

### January Sales

The days of queuing overnight may be gone, but the pushy-shovey spirit survives.

◑ *January*

### The Turner Watercolours

J W M Turner's superb water-colours, dating from 1807, can only be exhibited in the sensitive light conditions of January.

◑ *January*
National Gallery, Merrion Square West, D2
☎ 661 5133 🎫 free

### East Telecom Young Scientists' Exhibition

An entertaining mix of genius and downright arm-chancing, laid on by Ireland's secondary-school scientists.

◑ *2nd weekend in January*
RDS, Ballsbridge, D4
☎ 602 6182 🚌 7, 7a, 8, 45
🎫 £3–£5

### Dublin Guitar Week

◑ *1 week in early February*
[→classical music 107]

### Five Nations Rugby Tournament

Ireland hasn't won in living memory, nevertheless what really matters is that they knock the socks off England. Home matches are best viewed in pubs within earshot of Lansdowne Road.

◑ *February/March*
Lansdowne Road, D4
☎ 668 4601 (IRFU) Ⓓ to Lansdowne Road 🎫 £13–£32

## spring

### St Patrick's Day Festival

Whether it's your pint the evening before, or your face the morning after, green is very definitely the colour – at the parade to end all parades.

◑ *17 March*
Christ Church Cathedral to O'Connell Street ☎ 676 3205
🎫 free

### Alternative Miss Ireland

Male and female competitors don day, swim and evening wear for this glam charity bash with cult appeal. A real hoot.

◑ *St Patrick's week*
Red Box, Harcourt Street, D2
☎ 873 0006 🎫 £15

### Dublin Film Festival

◑ *10 days in March/April*
[→cinema 103]

### Irish Grand National

Good odds are usually available in any of Dublin's pubs – but that's not to say they're reliable.

◑ *Easter Monday*
Fairyhouse Racecourse, Ratoath
☎ 825 6151 🚌 40a, 120
🎫 phone for details

### The Trinity Ball

As famous for creative gate-crashing as any music on offer, since its recent 400th anniversary the Trinity Ball has become a firm fixture on the international social calendar.

◑ *May Rag Week*
Trinity College, City Centre, D2
☎ 677 6545 🎫 students/graduates of Trinity College only

### Heineken Green Energy Music Festival

◑ *May Day bank holiday weekend* [→music 102]

### FAI Harp Lager Cup Final

The Irish equivalent of the FA Cup. Not exactly Wembley, but that doesn't mean passions won't be aroused.

◑ *2nd weekend in May*
Dalymount Park ☎ 676 6864 (FAI) 🚌 10, 19, 19a 🎫 £18–£35

### Kilkenny Cat Laughs Festival

◑ *early June* [→comedy 104]

### Mardi Gras Weekend

A huge parade, top-notch costumes and general debauchery make this a firm festival favourite.

◑ *end May*
Temple Bar, D2 ☎ 454 0516
🎫 free

## public holidays

Most companies and shops are closed on public holidays. Public transport runs less frequently and not at all on 25 December:

**New Year's Day** – 1 January
**St Patrick's Day** – 17 March
**Easter** – March/April
**May Day Holiday** – first Monday in May
**June Holiday** – first Monday in June
**August Holiday** – first Monday in August
**October Holiday** – last Monday in October
**Christmas Day** – 25 December
**St Stephen's Day** – 26 December
**Millennium Holiday** – 31 December

## millennium events & information

A millennium committee (which includes Boyzone's Ronan Keating and U2 manager Paul McGuinness) has been charged with entertaining the nation on New Year's Eve, 1999. Early plans include the Kaleidescope Arts Exhibition, starting September 99. Millennium eve sees the official launch of the new monument, nicknamed The Stiletto in the Ghetto, to be erected in O'Connell Street and the creation of a millennium zone on the banks of the Liffey – bridges will be floodlit at midnight in Mexican wave format. Individual hotels and venues are also issuing their own millennium event packages – phone well in advance for information and bookings.

Dublin Tourism Information line ☎ 1850 230 330

Millennium Festivals **w** www.millennium-ireland.com

# the big sleep

Whether you want to wallow in the luxury of a top-notch hotel, or just need somewhere to dump your bag and grab some zzz's, Dublin offers plenty of choice. With an extra 76 hotels registered in 98 and a further 40 opening in 99, the city now has the variety and quantity of hotels befitting a bustling capital of Dublin's stature. Offering everything from designer elegance to homely guest houses and clean budget beds, most places are just a stroll away from the action. Rooms are generous, welcomes are big and breakfasts are bigger. With Dublin's current popularity as a party city, advance booking is advisable.

## ↓ what's where

↓ off baggot street lower

**Longfield's Hotel** [→115] £91

**The Merrion** [→112] £210

↓ off baggot street upper

**Hibernian Hotel** [→114] £150

**Number Eighty Eight** [→115] £99

**Schoolhouse** [→115] £139

↓ near christ church

**George Frederic Handel Hotel** [→116] £130

**Harding Hotel** [→117] £60

**Jury's Christchurch Inn** [→117] £62

↓ off grafton street

**Avalon House** [→117] beds from £7.50

**Brooks Hotel** [→116] £160

**Buswells Hotel** [→114] £150

**Mercer Hotel** [→116] £132

**Trinity Lodge** [→115] £95

↓ on the grand canal

**Mespil Hotel** [→113] £75

**Stakis Dublin** [→113] £165

↓ harcourt street

**Albany House** [→114] £90

**Harcourt Inn** [→117] £80

**Harrington Hall** [→115] £100

↓ herbert park

**Herbert Park Hotel** [→112] £185

↓ lansdowne road

**Butler's Townhouse** [→114] £143

**The Tower** [→113] £220

↓ around leeson street

**The Burlington** [→113] £120

**Clarion Stephen's Hall** [→116] £160

**Conrad International** [→113] £210

**The Grey Door** [→114] £100

**Number 31** [→115] £84

↓ north quays

**Jury's Custom House Inn** [→117] £62

**The Morrison** [→113] £155

↓ o'connell street

**The Gresham** [→114] £160

↓ rathmines

**Charleville Hotel** [→116] £120

↓ st stephen's green

**The Fitzwilliam** [→112] £210

**The Shelbourne** [→114] £215

↓ temple bar

**Aston Hotel** [→116] £96

**Barnacle's Temple Bar House** [→117] £18

**The Clarence** [→112] £180

**The Morgan** [→112] £127

**River House Hotel** [→117] £90

→ more hotels

**prices in Irish pounds – lowest quoted for double room in peak season 99 (unless otherwise stated)**

## the lap of luxury

**The Clarence** 6–8 Wellington Quay | D2 (Temple Bar)

Bought by Bono and the Edge of U2, the Clarence closed for 18 months, re-emerging in 96 – £5 million later. Contrary to cynical expectation there's great sensitivity to period. Fine original elements have been restored, while incorporating modern design and the latest technology – the result is sophisticated, understated and cosmopolitan. Bedrooms, though small, are brilliant in rich purples, blues and golds, with oak and leather furniture, and candles. Downstairs the residents' lounge is an oasis of calm in contrast to the Octagon Bar which hums with the chatter of well-heeled Dubliners. For lunch and dinner, the Tea Rooms [→87] is one of the city's most talked-about restaurants.

singles from £180
doubles from £180

☎ 670 9000
F 670 7800
e clarence@indigo.ie

50 all

**The Merrion** 21–24 Merrion St Upper | D2 (around Merrion Square)

No expense has been spared in converting these four Georgian houses into an intimate, luxurious hotel. The fine proportions of the interconnecting drawing rooms, the smell of wood smoke, comfy sofas and a magnificent collection of paintings give it a calm feel. Bedrooms in the main house and around the 18th-century garden are of the highest standard – period decor with cutting-edge technology – and bathrooms to-die-for. There's an original work of art or sculpture at every turn. The Tethra Spa [→62], with its sapphire pool and soothing treatment rooms, is another enticement, but the ultimate coup is Restaurant Patrick Guilbaud [→87] – Ireland's most famous multi-rosetted dining spot – which shares the jasmine- and lilac-drenched terrace.

singles from £190
doubles from £210

☎ 603 0600
F 603 0700
e info@merrionhotel.com

145 all

## designer label

**The Fitzwilliam** St Stephen's Green West | D2 (St Stephen's Green)

One of the flashiest additions to the Dublin scene – Sir Terence Conran's design delivers all in top style. The minimalist interiors are achieved with Conran's familiar cool lines, marble, parquet, steel, leather and contemporary Irish art. Conrad Gallagher – one of Europe's most adventurous young chefs – runs all the food outlets including Christopher's and the Michelin-starred Restaurant Peacock Alley [→87]. The height of contemporary chic, a fab location and the largest roof garden in Ireland, it's an obvious haunt of the Dublin in-crowd.

singles from £190
doubles from £210

☎ 478 7000
F 478 7878
e enq@fitzwilliamh.com

132 all

**Herbert Park Hotel** Ballsbridge | D4 (Ballsbridge)

From a wonderfully peaceful location overlooking Herbert Park, it's still only a 10-minute bus or taxi ride to the city centre. Loved by the movie industry, this hotel often becomes a base for film crews; it is spacious, comfortable, airy and relaxed, with good-sized rooms. Everything, from the sculptures to the table lamps, is made or designed in Ireland.

singles from £150
doubles from £185

5, 7, 7a, 8, 45

☎ 667 2200
F 667 2595
e reservations@herbertparkhotel.ie

153 all

**The Morgan** 10 Fleet Street | D2 (Temple Bar)

A deeply chic, modern boutique hotel – stark, uncluttered elegance with serious comfort. Decor is cream throughout. There's a cool roof garden, and big spenders can opt for the duplex monochrome suite. The busy, noisy All Sports Café and XS Bar/Restaurant do not detract from the hotel's peace and privacy. Venture out and try the area's many hostelries, or opt for room service on designer tableware. Great value: five-star facilities at three-star prices.

singles from £99
doubles from £127

☎ 679 3939
F 679 3946
e morganht@iol.ie

61 all

**The Morrison** Ormond Quay Lower | D1 (north quays)

The wrappings have just come off the newest style-orientated hotel to open – daringly enough on Dublin's northside. This one, however, can boast the input of über-designer John Rocha, who's brought a zen-like vibe to the place, with dark wood, pale upholstery and his ubiquitous crystal in precious places. Facilities in phase one of the hotel include two restaurants – up-market fusion and accessible Asian [→27] – and three bars, some of which go to make up the subterranean club level – a mecca for social Dubliners as well as hotel guests. Rooms are equally stylish, the best of which have views of the river Liffey.

room rates from £155

☎ 878 2999
F 878 3185
e info@morrisonhotel.ie

95 (pool & gym from autumn only) (limited) all

## ↓ big business

**The Burlington** Leeson St Upper | D2 (around Leeson Street)

Though this hotel will never win any design awards, it functions excellently for the huge volume of people who pass through its doors. A recent revamp has introduced the executive sixth floor dedicated to meeting rooms, secretarial service and exclusive access to the hotel gym. Bedrooms include fax, ISDN and modem. Downstairs the huge lobby and bar seem to buzz around the clock, while party animals shake their *thang* in Annabelle's nightclub [→98] – one of Dublin's most popular mega-venues.

singles from £100
doubles from £120

11, 11a, 13b, 46a, 46b

☎ 660 5222
F 660 5064
e burlington@doyle-hotel.ie

531 all

**Conrad International** Earlsfort Terr | D2 (around Leeson Street)

For reliability, comfort and efficiency, this airy, glass-fronted Conrad chain hotel is spot-on. In addition to a fairly central location and an impressive array of business and conference facilities, extra perks include an excellent hair salon, and a 24-hour gym for fitness freaks. Impressive quantities of Guinness are consumed in Alfie Byrne's pub downstairs, and there are two in-house restaurants.

singles from £185
doubles from £210

14, 14a, 15a, 15b, 44, 48a

☎ 676 5555
F 767 5424
e sales@conrad-international.ie

191 all

**Mespil Hotel** 40–50 Mespil Road | D4 (on the Grand Canal)

An unpretentious, good-value modern hotel with a glass-fronted reception, sitting area and brasserie all overlooking the Grand Canal [→54]. A bright, light and relaxed atmosphere is helped by the capable and friendly young staff. The decor throughout is simple and neat, and the bedrooms are a reasonable size. The bar at the back is a popular lunch venue for the locals.

singles from £75
doubles from £75

7, 7a, 8, 45

☎ 667 1222
F 667 1244
e mespil@leehotels.ie

153 all

**Stakis Dublin** Charlemont Place | D2 (on the Grand Canal)

Everything you'd expect from a Stakis, with wide-open spaces, marble floors and loads of light. Surroundings are sparklingly clean, with functional furnishings and welcoming, businesslike service. Every floor has an ice machine and chilled bar. Overlooking the Grand Canal [→54], are a themed sports bar (Champions) and the Waterfront Restaurant.

singles from £145
doubles from £165

44, 48a, 62

☎ 402 9988
F 402 9966
e reservations@stakis.co.uk

189 all

more hotels

**The Tower** Lansdowne Road | D4 (Lansdowne Road)

Set within the Jury's Hotel, The Towers is geared towards business travellers, with decor taking second place to facilities. Key to the concept is a ground floor lounge which provides plenty of peaceful space to relax or conduct business; it offers continental breakfast at cock crow and aperitifs at sun set (all included in the room rate). Photocopier, modems, private meeting rooms and a library are at guests' disposal, as is valet parking. Rooms are generous and bonuses include a walk-in wardrobe, plenty of desk space and a rocking chair. Suites include a kitchen, two bathrooms (ensuite with jacuzzi and TV) and a vast living room with facilities for meetings.

singles from £190
doubles from £220

5, 7, 7a, 8
D to Lansdowne Road

☎ 667 0033
F 660 5540
e jury@dubres.com

500 all

## ↓ old-fashioned charm

**Buswells Hotel** 25–29 Molesworth St | D2 (off Grafton Street)

Still considered one of Dublin's institutions, Buswells is a Georgian townhouse a few minutes from Grafton Street. Its hospitality is faultless with a uniformed doorman and a porter taking charge as visitors step through the door. Pristine decor and an old-fashioned atmosphere continue to lure Ireland's politicians and hacks, who regularly fill the bar and public rooms.

singles from £97
doubles from £150

☎ 614 6500
F 676 2090
e quinn-hotels@sqgroup.com

69 all

**The Gresham** 23 O'Connell Street Upper | D1 (O'Connell Street)

*The* hotel on the north side, a city landmark and a popular rendezvous. This is the place the Beatles held an impromptu jamming session – their only Dublin gig. Nothing is too much trouble: cars are parked for you and bags carried by a liveried porter. Period-style decor is immaculate. The new Lavery wing offers bigger, better-appointed rooms, business facilities and a health spa. A 12.5 % service charge is added to the bill.

singles from £140
doubles from £160

☎ 874 6881
F 878 7175
e ryans@indigo.ie

288 all

**Hibernian Hotel** Eastmoreland Place | D4 (off Baggot Street Upper)

In this splendid, lavishly restored Victorian building, smart and spacious bedrooms are decorated to make the most of architectural features, such as sloping ceilings and porthole windows. Superb decor, antiques and fine paintings create an oasis of calm and cosiness, enhanced by the clubby bar and classy restaurant.

singles from £120
doubles from £150

5, 7, 7a, 8, 10

☎ 668 7666
F 660 2655
e info@hibernianhotel.com

40 all

**The Shelbourne** 27 St Stephen's Green N | D2 (St Stephen's Gr)

Featured in the novels of Henry James and Elizabeth Bowen, this is one of Dublin's great traditional meeting places. Rooms at the top are quieter. Discreet modern perks include an 18m swimming pool and a fitness and health club. The timber-floored Shelbourne Bar is an obvious oyster-and-Guinness stop. For celeb-spotting, try the Horseshoe Bar or Lord Mayor's Room and for top nosh head for The Side Door [→82].

singles from £180
doubles from £215

☎ 676 6471
F 661 6006
e rooms@shelbourne.ie

190 all

## ↓ home from home

**Albany House** 84 Harcourt Street | D2 (Harcourt Street)

Albany House has three unusual details. Firstly, the plentiful Georgian features have been well preserved, and enhanced further with antique furnishings. Secondly, breakfast is a phenomenal affair – even the breads are home-baked. Thirdly, this is one of Dublin's few completely non-smoking establishments. If you favour size over light, opt for rooms 10, 11, 12, or 14.

singles from £60
doubles from £90

14, 14a, 15a, 15b, 48a

☎ 475 1092
F 475 1093
e albany@indigo.ie

32 all

**Butler's Townhouse** 44 Lansdowne Road | D4 (Lansdowne Road)

The epitome of style and restrained good taste, this small town house has an atmosphere of peace, indulgence and pure pampering. Individually designed rooms make the most of space and include elegant furnishings, bed canopies and clever storage. Breakfast is reputedly one of the city's best, while a delicious room-service menu comes complete with cheese board and wine list. An honesty bar operates in the plush, comfy drawing room.

singles from £96
doubles from £143

5, 7, 7a, 8 D to Lansdowne Road

☎ 667 4022
F 667 3960
e info@butlers-hotel.com

20 all

**The Grey Door** 22 Pembroke Street Upper | D2 (around Leeson St)

An interesting mix of modern and traditional, this guest house offers foodie heaven. The Grey Door restaurant opened first and the owners then carefully converted the upstairs floors to offer generously-sized rooms with original features such as marble fireplaces and window seats. The restaurant serves superlative modern and trad Irish food while Pier 32 is simpler in style serving fresh seafood and hearty pints of Guinness.

singles from £80
doubles from £100

10, 11, 11a, 13b, 46a, 46b

☎ 676 3286
F 676 3287
e info@greydoor.ie

7 all

**Harrington Hall** 70 Harcourt Street | D2 (Harcourt Street)

Beautifully refurbished, this pair of Georgian houses is geared for maximum comfort. Rooms are large, some massive, and two have mezzanine sleeping areas separate from a big lounge. Public spaces include a comfortable drawing room where a blazing turf fire glows on colder days and piles of newspapers rest on the sideboards. Twinkling chandeliers and period furniture provide the backdrop while modern touches such as fax/modem facilities, secondary glazing, secure car parking and an elevator complete the picture.

singles from £75
doubles from £100

14, 14a, 15a, 15b, 48a

475 3497
F 475 4544
e harringtonhall@tinet.ie

30
AE/MC/V



**Longfield's Hotel** Fitzwilliam St Lower | D2 (around Merrion Sq)

Traditional hospitality in Georgian splendour, just around the corner from the National Gallery [→57]. Swagged curtains and warm colours in the sitting room create a welcoming, relaxed atmosphere conducive to unwinding. The bedrooms, in impeccable condition, are similarly cosy. The Number 10 restaurant in the basement doubles up as a breakfast room.

singles from £78
doubles from £91

11, 11a, 13b, 46a

676 1367
F 676 1542
e lfields@indigo.ie

26
all

**Number Eighty Eight** 88 Pembroke Rd | D4 (off Baggot St Upper)

A smoothly-run, popular b&b which in spite of its large size does not compromise in standards. The split-level mezzanine rooms, exploit huge Georgian windows which bathe the room in light. Furnishings throughout are functional and flawless, as is the bright spacious breakfast room which serves until 11am on weekends. Hotel facilities include plenty of off-road parking, access to a nearby gym and a fully equipped boardroom.

singles from £79
doubles from £99

5, 7, 7a, 8, 10

660 0277
F 660 0291

50
all

**Number 31** 31 Leeson Close | D2 (around Leeson Street)

Small, unusual, discreet and excellent value, this place is a real find. It was designed by architect Sam Stephenson in the early 60's and bedrooms are now divided between No. 31 and a Georgian house across the garden. Those in 31 are more interesting, featuring sunken baths and original 70's design. The laid-back sitting room, with a sunken seating area, is packed with pictures and collectors' pieces. A silver-mosaic courtesy bar in an alcove adds to the casual, vaguely bohemian feel.

singles from £60
doubles from £84

11, 11a, 13b, 46a, 46b

676 5011
F 676 2929
e number31@ iol.ie

19
AE/MC/V

**Schoolhouse** 2–8 Northumberland Rd | D4 (off Baggot St Upper)

Expert restoration accentuates this restful hotel's origins as St Stephen's Parochial School – beams, polished staircases and galleried areas abound. Breakfast or dine in Satchel's Restaurant, and have a drink in the Inkwell Bar – a popular meeting place which spills out onto the terrace in summer. Bedrooms are smart and comfortable and the all-mod-con communications are a bonus.

singles from £109
doubles from £139

7, 7a, 8, 45

667 5014
F 667 5015
e school@schoolhousehotel.iol.ie

30
all

more hotels

**Trinity Lodge** 12 South Frederick Street | D2 (off Grafton Street)

This smart combination of guest room and adjacent apartments is an interesting mix of Georgian features with colourful modern decor. Rooms are spacious and light, with the added touch of candles and excellent art. Ensuites are shower only, but in some rooms, the stone-flagged floors more than compensate. Air conditioning is standard throughout, and the crisp white bedlinen compliments the red, green and yellow palate. Breakfast is informal and caters for all appetites. Very centrally located, the hotel is situated a short walk away from Trinity College [→49].

singles from £60
doubles from £95

679 5044
F 679 5223
e trinitylodge@tinet.ie

13
all

## ↓ D.I.Y

**Charleville Hotel** Rathmines Road Lower | D6 (Rathmines)

This spanking new hotel opened at the end of 98. All rooms are suites, with sliding doors to separate the bedroom from the sitting room-cum-kitchenette. King-sized beds have orthopaedic mattresses and the interior design features strong colours. The pub on one side may be noisy at weekends. On the other, the Italian hotel restaurant is decorated with photos of an array of stars from Fellini films. It serves reasonably priced lunches and dinners and doubles up as a breakfast room.

singles from £95
doubles from £120

14, 14a

406 6100
F 406 6200
e prembuss@iol.ie

52
all

**Clarion Stephen's Hall** 17–14 Leeson Street Lower | D2 (around Leeson Street)

Behind a Georgian façade and trad, welcoming reception area, lurks ultra-modern design. The apartments, suites and townhouses, situated in different buildings, are chic and simple in design, with galley kitchens and dining areas providing a self-catering option. Highly recommended for the standard of its business facilities (including PCs, modems and fax machines), convenience and value. The exceptional Mediterranean-flavoured Morel's Restaurant is popular with residents and local regulars alike.

singles from £130
doubles from £160

11, 11a, 13b, 46a, 46b

638 1111
F 638 1122
e stephens@premgroup.com

37
all

## ↓ shoppers paradise

**Aston Hotel** 7–9 Aston Quay | D2 (Temple Bar)

Great value for such a central location, this excellent small, modern hotel on the quays is seconds from the mayhem of Temple Bar, but manages to remain quiet and unobtrusive. Decor is simple and appealing in the reception area, bar and breakfast room. Spotless and neat with excellent staff and a relaxed atmosphere.

singles from £63
doubles from £96

677 9300
F 677 9007
e aston@indigo.ie

27 all

**Brooks Hotel** 59–62 Drury Street | D2 (off Grafton Street)

Don't be put off by external appearances, this efficient yet comfortingly clubby hotel offers individual sound systems (with pre-selected CDs for regulars) and VCRs, which sit happily alongside good-quality antiques and old-style Roberts radios. The oak-panelled residents' sitting room, complete with a fire and soporifically comfortable sofas, combines with a smart, up-to-the-minute bar and brasserie. Rooms are snug, service is friendly, and location is super-convenient.

singles from £120
doubles from £160

670 4000
F 670 4455
e sinnott@iol.ie

75
all

**Mercer Hotel** Mercer Street Lower | D2 (off Grafton Street)

This small, modern hotel may not have the most idyllic location, but it is extremely handy for Grafton Street. High-tech connections include CD and video to all of the bedrooms, which are mahogany and chintz with smart ensuite bathrooms. The compact bar and neat, traditional-style sitting room are restful places for aperitifs, and there's a light, bright restaurant. Cheap and secure daily parking is a huge perk for car users.

singles from £100
doubles from £132

478 2179
F 478 0328
e mercsi@iol.ie

21
all

## ↓ close to the action

**George Frederic Handel Hotel** 16–18 Fishamble Street | D2 (near Christ Church)

The hotel is on the site of the former Musik Hall where Handel's *Messiah* was first performed in 1742. The original, crisp and stylish interiors were masterminded by the Grafton Street store, Brown Thomas [→72]. Cream fabrics, unusual lamps and sleek, wooden furniture give the bedrooms a calm, uncluttered feel. Handel's Café Bar is a trendy venue for trad Irish and contemporary music, with space and acoustics enhanced by multi-level design.

singles from £90
doubles from £130

670 9400
F 670 9410
e gfhhotel@aol.com

40
all

**prices quoted in Irish pounds for rooms in peak season 99**

**Harding Hotel** Copper Alley | Fishamble St | D2 (near Christ Church)

This new, lively hotel is full of character. Its clever design makes great use of the natural features: Dublin's oldest medieval street, Copper Alley, runs through the reception area. Brilliant views of Christ Church Cathedral [→48] can be had from the simple, pine-furnished bedrooms. The hotel pub, Darkey Kelly's, shares its terrace with the youth hostel and puts on lots of live entertainment. No-fuss decor and facilities, but good value.

singles from £45
doubles from £60

☎ 679 6500
F 679 6504
e harding@usit.ie

53 MC/V

**River House Hotel** 23–24 Eustace Street | D2 (Temple Bar)

Slap in the centre of Temple Bar this is an ideal base if you can cope with the most boisterous part of the city. The style is simple and modern giving good, clean comfort, with basic rooms decorated in plain, pale colours – those overlooking the street can be noisy. Any flourishes of originality have been saved for the Danger Doyle's hotel pub [→14], where a young raucous crowd mingle against a backdrop of space-age design and surreal sculpture and art.

singles from £60
doubles from £90

☎ 670 7655
F 670 7650
e 101473.1007@compuserve.com

29
all

## ↓ crash pads

**Avalon House** 55 Aungier Street | D2 (off Grafton Street)

Starting life as a Victorian medical school, this listed building offers excellent budget accommodation for singles, couples, families and groups in a variety of dorms and rooms all neat and freshly decorated. Opening onto the street, the café has a high ceiling, a pine floor and a huge fire. The food is good, though it's just as popular for a quiet cappuccino with the newspapers. Tables are painted with original designs and the walls hung with kilims and posters. Internet facilities available.

beds from £7.50

☎ 475 0001
F 475 0303
e info@avalon-house.ie

242 (beds)
MC/V

**Barnacle's Temple Bar House** 1 Cecilia Street | D2 (Temple Bar)

If budget is what you're after, this is hard to beat. Rooms are simple, basic and clean, with space at a premium, and all have ensuite showers. A large Swedish-style TV/sitting room with an open fire and wooden armchairs is light and spotless in bright primary colours. Self-catering facilities include a communal kitchen with a cheerful breakfast room. Populated by young backpackers, and close to the Temple Bar action, this is a good place to meet people.

beds £10–14
doubles £18

☎ 671 6277
F 671 6591
e templeba@barnacles.iol.ie

20 MC/V

**Harcourt Inn** 27 Harcourt Street | D2 (Harcourt Street)

A newcomer to Harcourt Street, this non-smoking house offers airy rooms furnished with natural wood and decorated in fresh blues and greens. Those on the upper floors are slightly smaller. The bright breakfast room has a choice of full Irish or continental breakfast, and there is an ample sitting area with stripey sofas to lounge on. Great value .

singles from £55
doubles from £80

14, 14a, 15a, 15b, 48a

☎ 478 3927
F 478 2550

15 MC/V

**Jury's Christchurch Inn** Christchurch Pl | D8 (near Christ Church)

Centrally located opposite the cathedral, this is at the cheap end of the chain, known as Jury's Inns. It is a straightforward and effective formula: rates are for the room only – singles, doubles or families can stay for the one price. Both design and facilities are unaffected and practical. If you arrive by car, check in before 12pm to ensure a parking space at a reduced rate.

room rate £62

☎ 454 0000
F 454 0012
e enquiry@jurys.com

182 all

**Jury's Custom House Inn** Custom Hse Quay | D1 (north quays)

Another Jury's Inn on the north side of the Liffey close to O'Connell Street. Rooms – plenty of which are large enough for two adults and two kids – are immaculate, if rather uniform, with colour schemes varying from floor to floor. Ask for one at the front for a view down river to the sea. The hotel has its own pub and eaterie.

room rate £62

☎ 607 5000
F 829 0400
e enquiry@jurys.com

239
all

# bare necessities ↓





## admission charges

Quite a number of Dublin's sights [→44–57] are free. Others make a reasonable charge or ask for a voluntary contribution. It's worth asking if there are concessions for children, full-time students and over 60's.

## banks

Banks usually offer a better exchange rate than bureaux de change. The main banks are Allied Irish Bank, Bank of Ireland and Ulster Bank (affiliated with NatWest UK). Opening hours are 10am–4pm Mon–Fri (to 5pm Thu). The Bank of Ireland bureau de change at Dublin airport is open from 5.30am–9pm daily. Banks are closed on public holidays [→110].
Most banks have cashpoint machines where you can obtain cash [→credit & debit cards].

Euro currencies can be changed into Irish pounds free of charge at the Central Bank. Rapid international transfers can be carried out at the Western Union office.

**Central Bank**, *Dame Street, D2* ☎ *671 6666*
**Western Union**, *Clery's, O'Connell Street, D1* ☎ *878 8291*

## bureaux de change

Check commission and minimum charges before exchanging money and cashing travellers' cheques [→travellers' cheques] as rates vary. Beware of places advertizing no commission as their rates can be very poor. Sometimes it is possible to negotiate the rate.
There are bureaux de change at the airport, Heuston and Connolly stations, Busaras coach station and Dun Laoghaire ferry port. For changing money out of banking hours try the following city-centre bureaux:

**American Express** has branches at:
*41 Nassau Street, D2* ☎ *679 9000*
◑ *9am–5pm Mon–Sat.*
*Dublin Tourism Centre, Suffolk Street, D2* ☎ *605 7709* ◑ *9am–5pm Mon–Sat.*

**Fexco**:
*Arnotts, Henry Street, D2* ☎ *872 1663*
◑ *9am–6.30pm Mon–Sat (until 9pm Thu), 12–6pm Sun.*

**Thomas Cook**:
*118 Grafton Street, D2* ☎ *677 1307*
◑ *9am–5.30pm Mon–Sat (10am–5.30pm Wed).*

## children

**Transport:** under-16's travel half-price on trains and buses [→6].

**Restaurants**: mid-price restaurants usually offer an inexpensive children's menu – phone in advance to check.

**Pubs and bars**: the attitude towards children is fairly relaxed but pubs in the centre are likely to restrict children's access after 7pm.

**Child minders**: many hotels offer a baby-sitting service. B&B and guest-house owners can usually arrange someone for you.

**Activities**: [→58–59] Check the Bulletin section in the *Irish Times* for a list of interesting things going on.

## conversions

**Women's Clothing**

| | | | | |
|---|---|---|---|---|
| British/Irish: | 8 | 12 | 16 | 18 |
| American: | 6 | 10 | 14 | 16 |
| Continental: | 36 | 40 | 44 | 46 |

**Men's Clothing**

| | | | | |
|---|---|---|---|---|
| British/Irish: | 36 | 40 | 44 | 46 |
| American: | 36 | 40 | 44 | 46 |
| Continental: | 46 | 50 | 54 | 56 |

## courier services

Larger post offices offer a reliable and competitive overnight special delivery service (SDS) for sending parcels and documents abroad:
*Naas Road, D22* ☎ *459 1133*

Services are also offered by:
**DHL** ☎ *1800 725 725*
**Federal Express Ireland** ☎ *862 2800*
**On-line Despatch** ☎ *492 2258*
**UPS** ☎ *830 4003*

## credit & debit cards

Credit cards are widely accepted. Visa is the most popular, followed by MasterCard, American Express and Diners Club. If you have an internationally-recognized credit card, cash advances can be obtained at any cashpoint machine displaying the appropriate card sign. Fees for this service range from 1.5–4%.

Often, a cheaper way to get your money is to use a debit (cashpoint) card (note that Switch is not accepted). To minimize charges, check with your bank which Irish banks are part of the same network.

To report lost or stolen credit cards call:
**American Express** ☎ *1800 282 728* (freephone)
**Diners Club** ☎ *1800 409 458* (freephone)
**MasterCard** ☎ *001 314 275 6690* (reverse charge call accepted)
**Visa** ☎ *1800 406 136* (freephone)

## currency

The Irish pound or punt (IR£) is made up of 100 pence and can be obtained from any bank in Ireland. Ireland joined the EMU on 1 January 1999 at the rate of 1 euro=IR£0.787564 (just under 79p). Euro notes and coins will come into circulation on 1 January 2002. Until then cash transactions continue in Irish pounds. Cashless transactions, such as cheques, can be carried out in either Irish pounds or euros.

## customs & quarantine

At airports, customs is divided into three routes: the blue lane is for anyone travelling from within the EU; the red and green lanes are for people travelling from outside the EU – red for those with goods to declare, green for those with nothing to declare. Animals are subject to six months' quarantine before they can enter Ireland unless travelling from the UK.

## dentists

Free dental treatment is not available, so keep receipts for insurance claims. For a list of dentists contact one of the following:

**Dental Hospital**, *20 Lincoln Place, D2* ☎ *662 0766*

**Irish Dental Association**, *10 Richview Office Park, Clonskeagh Road, D14* ☎ *283 0499*

## disabled visitors

Many hotels, restaurants and public places are adapted for people with disabilities, but older buildings may be restricted by conservation orders. Useful contacts include:

**Iarnród Éireann**, which publishes a *Guide for Mobility-Impaired Passengers*, with advice on planning journeys. ☎ *836 6222*

**National Rehabilitation Board of Ireland,** which provides a fact sheet on accessibility. *Access Dept, 25 Clyde Road, D4* ☎ *668 4181*

## driving

You can drive in the Republic with an overseas driving licence so long as it has been held for more than a year. Some car hire firms impose age restrictions [→7].

## duty free

Regulations vary and are subject to change. Check locally at the time of travel for details on allowances.

## electricity

Mains electricity is supplied at 220 volts (50 cycles). Plugs have three square pins. A transformer is needed to convert American appliances. Adaptors are available at the airport.

## email & internet

Internet cafés allow you to surf the net and send/receive emails (approx £3 for 30 minutes). They also offer word processing and faxing.

**Arthouse Internet Café**, *Arthouse, Curved St, D2* ☎ *605 6800* ◑ *10am–9pm Mon–Sat.*

**Cyberia Café**, *The Granary, Temple Lane South, D2* ☎ *679 7607* ◑ *10am–11pm daily.*

## embassies & consulates

**Australian Embassy**, *6th Floor, Fitzwilton House, Wilton Terrace, D2* ☎ *676 1517*
**British Embassy**, *31 Merrion Road, D4* ☎ *205 3700*
**Canadian Embassy**, *65–68 St Stephen's Green, D2* ☎ *478 1988*
**South African Embassy**, *Alexandra House, Earlsford Terrace, D2* ☎ *661 5553*
**US Embassy**, *42 Elgin Road, D4* ☎ *668 8777*

## emergencies

☎ **999 or 112** (24 hours – strictly emergencies only) covers fire, Gardai (police) and ambulance, as well as boat, coastal, mountain and cave rescue.

For emergency medical attention:
**Beaumont Hospital**, *Beaumont, D9* ☎ *837 7755*
**Mater Hospital**, *Eccles Street, D1* ☎ *453 7941*
**St James Hospital**, *James Street, D8* ☎ *830 1122*
**St Vincent's Hospital**, *Elm Park, D4* ☎ *209 4358*
**Tallaght Hospital**, *Tallaght, D24* ☎ *414 3500*

## help & advice lines

**AIDS Helpline Dublin** ☎ *872 4277*
**Drugs Advisory & Treatment Centre** ☎ *0677 1122*
**Gay Switchboard** ☎ *872 1055*
**Rape Crisis Centre** ☎ *1800 77 88 88* (freephone)
**Samaritans** ☎ *1850 60 90 90* (callsave)

## hotels

**Charges**: Most hotels give prices inclusive of all taxes, VAT, service charge, etc. Prices can double during peak periods. Some hotels offer reduced rates for off-peak periods, regular corporate customers and weekends. It is worth checking on these as even the plushest hotels can offer some affordable treats. Prices for smaller hotels, B&Bs and guest houses usually include a full Irish breakfast.

**Tipping** is not usually expected.

**Smoking**: there are a number of completely non-smoking hotels, and some of the larger hotels retain non-smoking rooms or floors.

**Checkout**: usually 11.30am on the day of departure – most places will store luggage.

**Reservations**: book in advance for weekends at any time of the year and in particular for peak times such as St Patrick's Day, Easter and Rugby Internationals. Advance booking is also advisable throughout the summer. Make independent bookings by fax or email – a 10% credit card deposit is usually required. Alternatively contact Dublin Tourism's reservation service [→tourist information].

**Alternative accommodation**: the Tourist Office's *Dublin Accommodation Guide* (£3) covers every kind of accommodation available. Trinity College and University College Dublin let out rooms in the summer (mid-Jun–Sep) and these can be booked through the Dublin Tourism Centre. Prices range from £28–£36 for a single room with access to a shared kitchen; excellent value four-bedded rooms are also available. Accommodation at UCD is in modern, self-catering apartments; Trinity College is more central and has more character.

**Trinity College**, *Trinity College Green, D2* ☎ *608 1177*
**UCD Village**, *Bellfield, D4* ☎ *269 7111*

## immigration

Control on entry to Ireland can be strict. Lanes are divided into EU nationals, who don't need visas, and other nationalities, who should check entry requirements before leaving their country [→visas & entry requirements]. No vaccinations are required.

## insurance

Comprehensive medical insurance is highly recommended for non-EU members [→medical matters].

## left luggage

Left luggage offices operate at the airport [→4] and main railway stations [→5]. Charges are from £2.25 per suitcase for 24 hours. The airport office is open from 6am–10pm daily; Connolly station has a left luggage office, open 9am–9pm daily; lockers at Heuston station are accessible at all times.

## lost property

Report all lost items to the police [→police] to validate insurance claims. Lost passports should also be reported to your embassy or consulate [→embassies & consulates]. For items lost in airports, taxis or on public transport, call the relevant number: **airport** ☎ *814 4483*; **ferry** ☎ *855 2296*; **taxi** ☎ *475 5888*; **train** ☎ *836 3333*; **bus** ☎ *703 3055*

## maps

Collins *Illustrated Dublin Map* (£4.70) is an attractive map with lots of useful information, while Bartholomew's *Handy Map of Dublin* is good if you are planning to travel around the suburbs. The tourist office and many hotels have free maps.

## measurements

The metric system is used officially but imperial measures are still common.

| imperial to metric | metric to imperial |
|---|---|
| 1 in = 2.5 cm | 1 mm = 0.04 in |
| 1 ft = 30 cm | 1 cm = 0.4 in |
| 1 mile = 1.6 km | 1 m =3.3 feet |
| 1 oz = 28 g | 1 km = 0.6 miles |
| 1 lb = 454 g | 1 g = 0.04 oz |
| 1 pint = 0.6 litres | 1 kg = 2.2 lb |
| 1 gal = 4.5 litres | |

## medical matters

**Hospital treatment**: accident and emergency treatment is available free to visitors at the hospital's discretion [→emergencies]. Treatment is also free to visitors attending clinics for the treatment of sexually-transmitted diseases.

For non-emergency treatment, visitors may be charged. However, anyone from within the European Economic Area (EEA), or from a country with which Ireland has a reciprocal agreement, is normally eligible for free hospital treatment if the need arises during a visit to Ireland. You must have an E111 form, validated in your own country.


➔ more practical information

**General Practitioners**: emergency treatment from a GP is available free of charge to all. For non-essential treatment it is up to GPs to decide on what basis they accept a patient. To find a GP, look in *Golden Pages* under 'Doctors–General Practitioners'. Or ask your hotel or a pharmacy for a list.

## medicine & chemists

Many medicines are available only on prescription; others can be purchased from chemists or supermarkets. Late-night chemists:

**Dame Street Pharmacy**, *16 Dame Street, D2* ☎ *670 4523* ◑ *8am–10pm daily.*
**Donnybrook Pharmacy**, *8 The Mall, Donnybrook, D4* ☎ *269 5236* ◑ *9am–10pm daily (including bank holidays).*
**Hamilton Long**, *5 O'Connell Street Lower, D1* ☎ *874 8456* ◑ *8.30am–7pm Mon–Wed & Fri, 8am–8pm Thu, 8.30am–6pm Sat.*

For information on complementary and holistic medicine contact:
**Complementary Healing Centre**, *91 Terenure Road North, D6* ☎ *492 9077*

## mobile phone hire

**Aircall** at Dublin airport hires mobile phones from £14.95 for one day to £99.99 for a month, plus the cost of calls. In all cases you must pay by credit card, which acts as a deposit. ☎ *844 8444*

## newspapers & listings magazines

[→100]

## office & business services

Most four- and five-star hotels offer business facilities for residents' use only.

**Reads Printing Shop** has copying, binding, and laminating facilities and a stationery/office supplies outlet.
*5 Nassau Street, D2* ☎ *679 9117* (printing shop)
*24 Nassau Street, D2* ☎ *679 6011* (stationery).
[→e mail & internet]

## opticians

**The Royal Victoria Eye and Ear Hospital** gives advice and treatment:
*Adelaide Road, D2* ☎ *678 5500*

**Specs Xpress** can make up glasses from an existing prescription in one hour. They carry out pre-bookable eye tests for £12:
*55 King Street South, D2* ☎ *677 5404*
*Liffey Street Upper, D1* ☎ *873 4256*

**Specsavers** offers a similar range and service, with eye tests from £11:
*112 Grafton Street, D2* ☎ *872 8155*
*GPO Arcade, Henry Street, D1* ☎ *677 6969*

## photography

**One-hour developing services:**
**Ilac Centre**, *Henry Street, D1* ☎ *872 8824*
**One Hour Photo**, *110 Grafton Street, D2* ☎ *677 4472*

**Equipment and supplies:**
**Camera Centre**, *56 Grafton Street, D2* ☎ *677 5594*
**Dublin Camera Exchange**, *63 South Great George's Street, D2* ☎ *478 4125*

## police

For local police stations look up Garda in the green-edged pages at the front of the Dublin *01 Area* directory or call Directory Enquiries ☎ *1190*. Dial ☎ *999* only in an emergency.
**Garda Síochána HQ**, *Harcourt Square, D2* ☎ *475 5555*

## postal services

**Post offices** are usually open 9am–5.30pm Mon–Fri, 9am–1pm Sat. Local offices have a green sign '*Oifig An Post*/Post Office'; collection times are displayed on green post boxes.

**The General Post Office**, *O'Connell Street, D1* ☎ *705 7000* ◑ *8am–8pm Mon–Sat (parcel post closes 7pm), 10am–6.30pm Sun & holidays.*

**Stamps** can be bought from post offices and newsagents. Postage for a letter or postcard within Ireland and the UK is 30p; 32p for the rest of Europe. Outside Europe, postage for postcards is 45p; letters and parcels vary according to weight.

**Poste restante**: the main post offices operate a free *Poste Restante* system. Mail must be addressed with the name on the first line (surname in block capitals), 'Poste Restante', then the name and address of the post office, including the post code. Letters are kept for three months, packets for two weeks.

## public holidays

[→events 110]

## pubs & bars

**Opening hours** vary but normal opening is 10.30am Mon–Sat, 12.30pm Sun. Doors close for 'holy hour' from 2–4pm on Sundays. Closing time is 11.30pm from May–Sep; 11pm in winter and on Sundays, but many bars have late licences. Half an hour drinking-up time is allowed.

**Age restrictions**: the legal age for drinking and buying alcohol is 18.

## religion

For details of church services check the Saturday edition of the *Irish Times*.

**Church of Ireland**: *Christ Church Cathedral, Christchurch Place, D8* ☎ *677 8099; St Patrick's Cathedral, Patrick Street, D8* ☎ *475 4817*
**Roman Catholic**: *Pro-Cathedral, Marlborough Street, D1* ☎ *874 5441; University Church, 87a St Stephen's Green, D2* ☎ *478 0616*
**Methodist**: *9c Abbey St Lower, D1* ☎ *874 2123*
**Muslim**: *163 Circular Rd South, D8* ☎ *453 3242*
**Jewish Synagogue**: *37 Adelaide Road, D4* ☎ *676 1734*
**Buddhist**: *56 Inchicore Road, D7* ☎ *453 724*

## restaurants

**Booking** is essential for popular restaurants, particularly at weekends.

**Credit cards** are accepted in most restaurants.

**Tipping**: some restaurants add a service charge, generally of around 12.5%; if it's left to the customer, 10% is the norm.

**Opening times**: restaurants are generally open from 12–2.30pm and then 6–11pm; some stay open throughout the afternoon until midnight.

**Prices** include VAT. Restaurants are generally more pricey than in other capital cities. Many restaurants do a set-priced lunchtime menu.

**Smoking**: most restaurants have designated no-smoking areas.

## safety

As in any major city, keep close hold of handbags and wallets. Don't carry passports or large amounts of cash and don't leave valuables on show in a car. Be careful in the northern part of O'Connell Street at night.

## shopping

**Opening times** are generally 9am–6pm Mon–Sat, with late-night shopping until 7 or 8pm on Thu. Food shops stay open much later, some 24 hours. Some department stores and bookshops in the centre are open on Sun from around 12–6pm.

**Payment** can be made in Irish pounds, Eurocheques or by credit card. Euros will be introduced in 2002. Some tourist shops accept pounds sterling.

**Export**: non-EU visitors can claim a rebate on the purchase price of any item carrying VAT [→VAT].

**Guarantees**: if buying equipment such as cameras, radios and electrical goods, make sure that guarantees are validated.

**Returns**: most high street shops will refund or exchange goods – keep your receipt and return the items within 10 days of purchase.

## smoking

Smoking is forbidden in all theatres, most cinemas and on the public transport system. Many restaurants have no-smoking sections.

## students

An International Student Identity Card (ISIC) entitles students to discounts on travel, goods and services and entrance to museums. The card costs £8, plus £8 for a Travelsave stamp, which allows discounts on travel within Ireland. To obtain a card, take a photo and proof of your full-time student status to:

**USIT**, *19 Aston Quay, D2* ☎ *677 8117*

## telephoning

**Telephone boxes**: accept coins, phonecards or credit cards. Phonecard boxes are most common, so it's worth getting a card.

**Phonecards**: come in units of 10 (£2), 20 (£3.50), 50 (£8) and 100 (£16). Local calls are 3 minutes per unit at all times.

**Private phone rates**: local calls cost 11.5p per unit, which lasts 3 min from 8am–6pm (standard rate), 15 min from 6pm–8am and all day Sat, Sun and bank holidays (reduced rate).

**Mobile phone rates**: calls cost 11.5p for 25 seconds standard rate (8am–8pm) and 11.5p for 37 seconds reduced rate.

**Freephone**: all numbers preceded with 1800 are free of charge.

**Premium rates**: calls with the 1550 prefix are charged at premium rate.

**Codes**: numbers for Dublin, Co Dublin and parts of Meath, Wicklow, and Kildare close to the Dublin county boundary are prefaced by *01*. Other areas have their own prefixes: see the back of the Dublin *01 Area* directory.

**International codes** are listed at the front of the telephone directories. Dial 00 followed by: USA & Canada ☎ *1*; Australia ☎ *61*; New Zealand ☎ *64*; South Africa ☎ *27*; UK ☎ *44*.

**International calls**: the cheapest way to make an international call from Ireland is to purchase a disposable card:
Swiftcall and Switch 2000 are two of the brands widely available (£5–£20).

**Operator**: Ireland/Northern Ireland/Great Britain & alarm/wake-up calls ☎ *10*

**International operator:** ☎ *114*

**Directory enquiries**: Ireland/Northern Ireland ☎ *1190*; Great Britain ☎ *1197*; International ☎ *1198*

**Directories**: are available in post offices and libraries. The directory for Dublin is *01 Area*. There is one volume of *Golden Pages* for Dublin and *The Independent Directory*; both list businesses by subject.

## television

[→100]

## time

Clocks are set to Greenwich Mean Time (GMT); they go forward by one hour at the end of March to start Summer Time, reverting to GMT at the end of October.

☎ *1191* to check the time on the 24-hour speaking clock.

## tipping

Porters expect 50p per bag, taxi drivers 10% and hairdressers a little more [→restaurants; →hotels]

## tourist information

**Dublin Tourism Centre** provides an excellent service. They offer plenty of free brochures and a reservation service for everything from city bus tours [→44–45] to theatre tickets and car hire. A £3 booking fee is charged, £1 for Dublin reservations made in person.
*Suffolk Street, D2*
☎ *1850 230 330 (for information)*
☎ *1800 668 668 66 (for reservations)*
**w** *www.visitdublin.com*
**e** *reservations@dublintourism.ie*

Information offices and touch-screen booking services are also located at the airport and Dun Laoghaire ferry port. The latter office is open only when the ferry arrives.

The **Irish Tourist Board**, *Bord Failte*, shares the same numbers as the Dublin Tourism Centre. For information and reservations from the UK contact: ☎ *0171 518 0800 (for information)*
☎ *0800 668 668 66 (for reservations)*
**w** *www.ireland.travel.ie*

## transport

Airports [→4]; ferries, trains & coaches [→4–5]; buses [→6]; the DART [→6], taxis [→7]; cars [→7].

## travel agents

Reliable agents for cheap flights:
**Trailfinders**, *4–5 Dawson St, D2* ☎ *677 7888*
**USIT**, *19–21 Aston Quay, D2* ☎ *679 8833*

General travel arrangements:
**Thomas Cook**, *118 Grafton Street, D2* ☎ *677 1721*

Specialist Irish tours:
**CIE Tours**, *35 Abbey St Lower, D1* ☎ *830 0777*

## travellers' cheques

Travellers' cheques are the safest way to carry money – pounds sterling and US dollars are the most widely accepted. The best places to cash travellers' cheques are bank-operated bureaux de change, American Express or Thomas Cook [→bureaux de change].

## VAT (Value Added Tax)

If you hold a non-EU passport, it is worth investigating the VAT Retail Export Scheme. In Ireland, VAT is charged on most goods, apart from food and children's clothing. The rate of 21% on items such as clothing, jewellery and cameras can be claimed back if purchases are taken out of Ireland within three months. Tax is paid at the point of purchase and claimed back later. When shopping, ask for VAT vouchers. When leaving the country, go to the VAT-back desk at the airport and they will assist you with your claim. You may be asked to present the goods and, if the vouchers equal more than £200, you might be asked to report to the nearby customs desk for authorization.

## visas & entry requirements

Check on travel document requirements before leaving home. Some visitors must obtain entry clearance before coming to Ireland. Passport, sufficient funds and proof of onward travel are required of Australian, Canadian and US citizens. British citizens are advised to bring a passport.

## weather

Dublin has a fairly mild but wet climate with few extremes of heat or cold. Spring is the driest time and May the sunniest month. Keep abreast of the weather by checking the national newspapers, TV weather reports or by contacting:
**Weather information** ☎ *1550 122 1121*
**w** *www.weather.com.*

more index

## where to shop





more index | acknowledgements

## where to eat

# ↓ acknowledgements



Conceived, edited & designed by
Virgin Publishing Ltd
London W6 9HT
Tel: 0171-386 3300

**Project Editor: Ella Milroy**
**Designer: Lisa Kosky**
Assistant Editor: Claire Fogg
DTP Designer: Ingrid Vienings
Researcher : Joanne Hayden
Design & editorial assistance: Cooling Brown, Niall Kennedy (Dublin Tourism Centre), Tony Limerick, Irene Lyford, Sally Prideaux, Annie Reid, Jane Simmonds, Clare Tomlinson, Fiona Wild, Trond Wilhelmsen, Simon Winstone
Series Editor: Georgina Matthews
Proof Reader: Stewart Wild
Index: Hilary Bird
Design concept: Paul Williams
Jacket concept: Debi Ani
Jacket: Button Design Co.

Maps:
Cartographic Editor: Dominic Beddow
Cartographers: Jethro Lennox, Simonetta Giori
Draughtsman Ltd, London
0181-960 1602
maps@atlas.co.uk

Photography:
Photographers: Anthony Coleman, Brendan Duffy

Additional photography:
Ella Milroy [2c, 29b, 47b, 74t, 76b, 113b]

Reproduced by Colourwise Ltd
Printed by Jarrold Book Printers

Features were written and researched by the following: Transport: Polly Phillimore | Getting Your Bearings (areas & shopping): Joanne Hayden | Area write-ups: Suzie Coen (shopping), Jim Carroll (introductions, cafés & Camden Street), Damian Corless (pubs & bars), Tom Doorley (restaurants) | Coastal Towns: Jim Carroll | Wicklow: Joanne Hayden | Boyne Valley: Joanne Hayden | Sights, Museums & Galleries: Pol O Conghaile, Harry Guerin, Joanne Hayden | Kids: Lucinda Thomson | Games & Activities: Alanna Gallagher | Body & Soul: Joanne Hayden | Spectator Sports: Harry Guerin | Shopping: Suzie Coen, Francis Powers, Lucinda Thompson | Restaurants & Cafés: Jim Carroll, Tom Doorley, Alanna Gallagher, Lucinda Thomson | Pubs & Bars: Damian Corless | Clubs: John Collins | Media: Joanne Hayden | Music: Jim Carroll Leagues | Cinema: Harry Guerin | Comedy: Gareth Murphy | Theatre, Dance, Poetry, Opera & Classical Music: Trish Murphy | Events: Pol O Conghaile | Hotels: Polly Phillimore | Practical Information: Polly Phillimore

Acknowledgements:
Virgin Publishing Ltd would like to thank all galleries, museums, shops, restaurants, bars and other establishments who provided photographs.

Virgin Publishing Ltd are grateful to the following for permission to reproduce their photographs.
(t=top, b=bottom, c=centre):
Douglas Hyde Gallery: Keith Edmer 1998 [56] | *dside* [3c, 69t, 70b] | Dublin Tourism: Christ Church Cathedral [44] | Dúchas, The Heritage Service: Newgrange [42]; Kilmainham Gaol [53]; Phoenix Park [55] | James Joyce Centre [50] | National Museum of Ireland: Lizmore Crozier [48] | The Slide File: County Wicklow [38]; Powerscourt Gardens [39] | The Board of Trinity College: Trinity College Library [49];

Great care has been taken with this guide to be as accurate and up-to-date as possible but details such as addresses, telephone numbers, opening hours, prices and travel information are liable to change. The publishers cannot accept responsiblility for any consequences arising from the use of this book. We would be delighted to receive any corrections and suggestions for inclusion in the next edition.

Please write to:
Virgin Travel Guides
Virgin Publishing Ltd
Thames Wharf Studios
Rainville Road
London w6 9ht
Fax: 0171-386 3360
Email: travel@virgin-pub.co.uk

# key to symbols

telephone number
fax
email
web
hot tips
good points
bad points
opening times
wheelchair access (phone to check details)
age group
sports & activities
shop
restaurant/café *or* food available
bar/pub
club
hotel
tourist information
price
times/frequency
picture arrow
map reference
credit cards
AE = American Express
DC = Diners Club
MC = MasterCard
V = Visa
all = AE/DC/MC/V are accepted
★ recommended (featured in listings section)

## *shopping*

£ cheap
££ moderate
£££ expensive

## *key to maps*

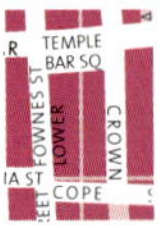

white roads = streets with lots of shops, restaurants, bars etc

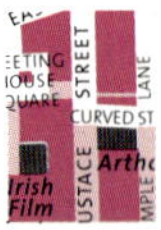

grey block = sight/venue

## *transport*

bus
coach
DART
train
taxi
airport
ferry port
parking

## *sights, museums & galleries*

don't miss
future exhibition
recorded information line
small collection/sight
medium collection/sight
large collection/sight
guided tours
audio guides

## *restaurants & cafés, pubs & bars*

£ cheap meal (main courses under £7.50)
££ moderate meal (main courses between £7.50–£15)
£££ expensive meal (main courses over £15)
capacity
set menu
separate bar
no alcohol served
no smoking section
air conditioning
outdoor area/garden
good vegetarian selection
live music
DJs
satellite/cable TV
children allowed
open late (after midnight)

## *clubs*

small venue
medium-sized venue
large venue
dress code

## *hotels*

number of beds
breakfast included
air-conditioning
24-hour room service
swimming pool
fitness facilities
business facilities
outdoor area/garden
separate bar